An Unprecedented Life

Denise Lunt

ISBN: 978-1-914933-00-4

Copyright 2021

All rights reserved. No part of this publication may be reproduced, stored in a retrieval system or transmitted in any form or by any means, electronic, mechanical, photocopy, recording or otherwise, without prior written consent of the copyright owner. Nor can it be circulated in any form of binding or cover other than that in which it is published and without similar condition including this condition being imposed on a subsequent purchaser.

The right of Denise Lunt to be identified as the author of this work has been asserted in accordance with the Copyright Designs and Patents Act 1988.
A copy of this book is deposited with the British Library

Published By: -

i2i
PUBLISHING

i2i Publishing. Manchester.
www.i2ipublishing.co.uk

Dedication

This book is Dedicated to the men and women who have served and continue to serve in the Royal Air Force. In particular, those who gave their lives without question defending this great Country.

Acknowledgements

I would like first, to thank my family for their deep love and constant support, allowing me the many hours it has taken to write this most amazing of stories.
Unlike writing a novel, every word in this book is accurate, all facts are true and are now part of English history.

Every book needs a brilliant editor, most certainly in my case being dyslexic. I would like therefore, to thank sincerely my wonderful friend and teacher, Ken Parker, who gave so much of his precious time reading through this manuscript and providing his professional advice.

Lastly, and most importantly. I would humbly like to say a huge and sincere thank you to Squadron Leader Harrington-Brown, for giving me the incredible opportunity to write a part of his stupendous and unique career in the RAF and civilian life.
As a fairly new author, I feel amazingly lucky to be entrusted with precious personal papers as well as his trust.

Both Squadron Leader Harrington-Brown and I, would like to take this opportunity, to sincerely thank Lionel Ross of i2i Publishing, for publishing this incredible book. His kindness and understanding have been exceptional, and we are deeply indebted to him.
Also, thanks are due to his editor Charley Sixsmith for completing the process.

An Unprecedented Life.

Hermes, so history informs us, was the Greek god of messengers. Throughout history, man has always loved to be informed of his world. Whether it be close to home, or from a distance. Not just to have the means of communicating, but the longing to conquer worlds beyond his own borders. Today in our modern world, man has achieved both...

Through war he has gained kingdoms. The hazardous journeys he has undertaken, sailing across fearsome Oceans to distant lands, going on to conquer and claim far off lands for his country. Man also found, to his amazement, that the world was round and not flat as he first believed. Man's ultimate achievement of course, was to conquer the skies. This, he has also done with great tenacity and courage.

The book you are about to read is the true story of one such very special and remarkable man. A man who not only learned at a very young age how to fly, but has in his lifetime, journeyed, and lived in ninety-two countries.

How indeed Alexander the Great, Julius Caesar, and many other such conquers throughout history who would love to have had the privilege of seeing so many distant lands, and to fly the array of aircraft, he has flown or flown in.

My name is Denise Lunt, and I would like to tell you how this exciting man and his story entered my life.

As I sat in my warm, comfortable sitting room, on a bitterly cold winter's day. A place where I am always happy to be writing, not expecting any further interruptions that afternoon, the phone rang out, loud and clear making me jump. I swear, Hermes himself must have had something to do with what turned out to be an incredible call.

The quiet cultured voice of the gentleman at the other end, asked most politely if he may speak to me. Accepting his call, he then went on to tell me who he was, and the reason he was phoning. After describing a little of himself, time itself suddenly felt it had stood still. I listened intently at what he had to say. Until eventually, the gentleman asked, would I be interested in helping him write his memoirs.

Would I be interested? Of course, I was interested. Not just interested but, totally intrigued would be nearer the mark. Maybe, only a half percent of mankind throughout history, has been as fortunate to have succeeded in achieving what this incredibly special man has accomplished.

The story you are about to read is that of Squadron Leader Roy Harrington-Brown, an Officer, a Diplomat, and a man who is so much more.

Squadron Leader Roy Harrington Brown.

Chapter 1

I entered the world on 12th of April one minute after midnight in 1930, weighing in at exactly eight pounds. I was to become the only child of Harold and Edna Kathleen Harrington-Brown. My parents had decided I was to be christened Roy at the local Church of England, which was close to my home. Many years later, my mother informed me she had chosen the name Roy for two reasons. Firstly, it could not be shortened. More importantly, she felt it was a strong name for her little boy, knowing she was unable to have further children.

At the time we lived in Saltaire, close to Bradford in the West Riding of Yorkshire. Sadly, my parents were divorced by the time I had reached the age of two and I never had the privilege of meeting my real father again. Strange how life turns out, as it was only after my father passed away, that I found out he had lived all his life in the same house which was just a short distance away. Even to the day my mother passed away, she never revealed any knowledge about my father's identity. Leaving me for many years to wonder why, and occasionally to feel rather sad.

I was four when my mother met and eventually re-married a man called Geoffrey Hoyle. While my mother was strict, she was also very possessive of me. I saw very little of my stepfather. Geoffrey had returned home some years previously, having served in the RAF during the 1920s. He had served from 1920 to 1923 with an RAF Armoured Car Squadron in Mesopotamia, now known as

Iraq.

We settled down to what I thought was a normal family life. I had grown very little and remained quite small until my teens. I was though, very wiry for such a little boy, and blessed with bags of energy. I had inherited my grandfather's deep, auburn coloured hair and huge ice blue eyes. I loved going to church which was just as well, as my mother was quite religious. I became a choir boy until my voice broke at the age of thirteen. Little did I realise by 1937, that my stepfather having rejoined the RAF, meant we had to move from where I had grown up, to RAF Martlesham Heath near Ipswich in Suffolk.

My early years, like those of my generation, were to be disrupted further by WW2.

Due to my stepfather's unit being so close to the East Coast, his unit was moved to RAF Boscombe Down in Hampshire. This meant my mother and I were evacuated back to Yorkshire.

Most service children often have the need to change schools and I was not the exception. My mother was a great believer in education, and not happy about mine being constantly disrupted in this way; leaving her once again with the need to move me to another school. Luckily for me, there was a local primary school close to where I had been born.

By September of 1939, England was at war. The Government of the day declared that women were to work in industry to help the war effort. My mother was no exception and went to work for an engineering company.

With the blackout strictly enforced, children did not play out after dark. To ease the boredom I now had to endure, my mother would return home with a great number of rubber grommets [washers] in various sizes. I was blessed with a vivid imagination, even at the age of nine. So, I now had army regiments, naval vessels and aircraft which were all arranged on the carpet performing imaginary operations. I spent many contented happy hours in this, my make-believe world.

Fortunately for me and by the time I was ten, my mother found out about a scholarship, which, should I win it, would go on to give me a stable education.

Several weeks later during a morning assembly, along with four other pupils, my name was called out. Being a reasonably behaved child, my first thoughts were: "Oh Lord what have I done."

Once the five of us had made our way up to the stage, the Headmistress then announced that we had won County Minor Scholarships, and that only I had been awarded a bursary to Giggleswick School.

Giggleswick School was a public school situated in North Yorkshire, which left me to feel very proud that I had gained such an honour.

I was not only proud, but so excited, that I ran all the way home to tell my mother the good news. Quite an effort when I look back for such a little chap, as it was a mile back to home.

My stepfather, as previously mentioned, served overseas most of the war years in the RAF, returning to England only at the end of the war. My family, though comfortable, were not wealthy. During my school years, I became aware of attitudes and thoughts of various social classes unfamiliar to those I had known. Had I not attended Public School, I am sure I would not normally have encountered such experiences during my formative years. I remain grateful for the superb education I received, which has served me well, in both my long life and career.

Fortunately for me, school was not a problem. I was academically capable of fulfilling the expectations of my tutors. I also excelled at sport, especially, in cricket and football, playing both sports for my school teams. Eventually, I was selected to represent Yorkshire Schoolboys in the English Schools Football Shield. My final game being against Glasgow School Boys, resulting in a 7-0 defeat.

By 1943, despite food rationing being in force, the British Isles were suffering very badly from many things including the shortage of food. The enemy blockade meant that home grown food was a necessity, even the Royal Gardens were turned into producing various foods. Males between 18 and 40 years of age were conscripted into the armed forces, thus leaving a significant shortage of farm workers.

Many senior pupils from schools throughout the Kingdom were expected to help out. Pupils from public schools were given no option, they found themselves sent for periods of up to a month at a time to many farms across the land

My school was no exception. A number of other boys and I found ourselves on a farm near the city of York, during part of the summer harvest. I had never worked on a farm before and it was a shock to my system. The work was backbreaking as we worked from sunrise to sunset. We basically became the unpaid slaves to a very unpleasant farmer and his wife. The work was very hard, as we relentlessly followed an ancient harvesting machine which spewed out tied bundles of wheat or barley. We then had to stack them into mini haystacks.

Our morale was low, due to the behaviour extended to us by the gruesome pair who ruled our life. Each lunchtime, the ugly farmer's wife fed us with inedible beetroot sandwiches and cold tea which she brought to us. I always thought her thinking being in case, *heaven forbid*, we may have taken a break.

During WW2, Great Britain operated under Double British Summer Time. This meant long daylight hours, and we worked late into the evening until we left the fields exhausted. Not just exhausted and extremely hungry, but very dirty. We retired to the local church hall, there unfortunately life did not improve. There were no showers, and we were made to sleep on a hard wooden floor with a straw filled mattress, and very threadbare bedding. After having been given a hot meal by members of the local church, the only thing provided allowing us to wash, were a few sinks with very limited hot water.

After a month and with great relief, we returned to school. Just before we left, we exacted our revenge as teenagers do. With great delight each of us peed in the fuel tank of the tractor belonging to the farmer. Hopefully, this caused him problems starting up the vehicle.

Generations of my family had served in either the Army, the RAF, or the Police Force.

All which obviously coloured my career ambitions. The end result being that after considerable thought, I turned down a place at Leeds University to study medicine.

By this time mother nature had done her work, I had grown to a good height for a young man, and like all young people, I changed my mind about becoming a doctor. This time cherishing hopes of joining the Merchant Navy as a

Deck Officer. Annoyingly, these hopes were quickly dashed. Learning to my dismay that cadetships in the major shipping lines required graduation from special public schools, such as Pangbourne in Berkshire. I therefore decided to follow my stepfather and enlisted in the Royal Air Force.

Chapter 2

My Wings and a Maltese Adventure

With the requisite academic qualifications, I had achieved at my public school, I was fortunate enough to be offered a 3-year RAF Radio Engineering Apprenticeship. Initially, I was required to report to RAF Halton for processing. Not knowing what to expect, and to my surprise, I found that a particularly interesting week, and one which proved to be exceedingly very busy. After several aptitude tests, plus a medical, I was fortunate to be selected to receive training at No 1 Radio School at RAF Cranwell.

On arriving at RAF Cranwell, the experience was to prove a shock to my system. Particularly the Apprentice Wing which was to become my home. A home I was to share with around 360 other young men, all drawn from different walks of life. 130 of the young men, who had entered the same time as I did, 3 became Sergeant Apprentices and 12 others, became Corporal Apprentices, similar to Senior prefects at a public school.

As a Corporal Apprentice, I had the luxury of servants. One to clean my kit, the other to clean my room. I will indeed hold my hands up and say, that was without doubt something I thoroughly enjoyed. Discipline was quite brutal and training hard. As the years progressed, sadly we lost 55 men. This in the end, resulted that only 75 graduated; myself included.

Towards the end of my Apprenticeship, I annoyingly managed to fall on the highly polished floor of the barrack room. I thought perhaps I had torn a muscle, as I was in some considerable pain. I said nothing, hoping by the morning the pain would have eased off. The following morning nothing had changed, in fact, the damn pain was excruciating. I decided to go on sick parade which was held at 6-30 am outside the barrack block.

How indeed things have changed, from my day to today when military personnel are injured. I can remember along with several other apprentices, being marched (painfully) to the medical centre.

After the RAF doctor had completed his examination, he sent for an ambulance, which then took me to RAF Nocton Hall Hospital. After having been X-Rayed, it turned out that I had a minor fracture of my hip bone. This ensured a stay of two weeks in the hospital, which in turn provided me with some amusement involving other patients.

One such tale, was the unfortunate young airman in the next bed who had suffered from peritonitis. A pretty rough operation to have sustained in those days.

The day came when a very pretty staff nurse arrived, (in RAF speak: All Bust and Knickers) at his bedside to remove his stiches. She decorously removed his pajama trousers, then placed a sterile towel over his private parts.

Carefully she then proceeded to remove the large quantity of stiches from the wound, placing each one on the towel. Turning to the young man she then said,

"My goodness that was a serious operation you have had; how many stiches do you think it required?"

The young airman then stated he had no idea, and then asked her,

"Can you tell me how many?"

The staff nurse replied with a smile,

"I can if you wish to know."

She then went into her pocket and proceeded to pull out the metal outer case containing her thermometer.

Carefully, she then commenced counting each of the stiches laid on the sterile towel, by tapping then with the metal case.

"One…Two…Three…"

Touching each stitch with the thermometer case, produced an upward movement in unison of the young airman's manhood. I had to turn away to stifle my laughter.

The three years of hard work and discipline had at last paid off when I gained a Diploma in Radio and Radar Engineering, coming fifth in my intake. I achieved a Distinction Pass in the final examinations, allowing me to enter the Real Air Force in the rank of Leading Aircraft Man. Not quite the lowest rank in the RAF, though pretty close.

Towards the end of the following twelve months, I decided to volunteer for air crew. This required me to attend a selection board at RAF Biggin Hill. After three days of aptitude tests, special leadership tests and a stringent medical test, I returned to my unit nervously awaiting the results.

A month dragged by, when at last I received the amazing news that I had been successful in obtaining a Commission. I was so excited; knowing this was the first step towards pilot training.

Annoyingly, I had to wait impatiently for another month, until at last I received orders to report to the Officer Cadet Training Unit at RAF Jurby on the Isle of Man.

There I would spend the next four months training with Blue Squadron. After the four months were completed, I graduated as a brand-new Pilot Officer. This though was just the beginning.

After Jurby, I completed initial and advanced flying

training at RAF South Cerney.

For the best part of twelve months, my initial training commenced in the Tiger Moth. Each flight would normally last around 30 to 40 minutes. Then on one particular day after landing, having already completed eight hours of instruction, the Flight Lieutenant who was my instructor, unexpectedly turned to me and said:

"Roy, everything is fine. Go ahead and carry out your first solo flight. Good Luck."

My thoughts during takeoff and the flight itself ranged from incredible excitement to extreme nervousness, until at last I made an acceptable landing. The feeling of relief and utter exhilaration consumed my emotions. All pilots understand how one feels after their first solo flight, it truly is amazing. Similar training was then to follow in the American Harvard, culminating in a similar flight.

On the morning I was due to receive my wings, I remember my emotions being all over the place. From being incredibly excited, to disbelief that I was now a fully-fledged pilot, to the point where I could not eat my breakfast. That day I made sure my Batman put an extra shine on my shoes and my uniform looked immaculate. The round of emotions grew, the thought that shortly I was to be presented with my wings seemed unbelievable. As I stepped out of the Officer's Mess, the excitement I was unnaturally feeling, continued as I joined my fellow graduates.

The wings ceremony was very impressive. I was so thankful to have reached this point in my career as a new pilot. Even though, at that moment I found it hard to believe I was one.

The parade was followed by a formal luncheon for

graduates and guests, with the celebrations continuing in the Officer's Mess until the early hours.

The adage in the RAF: "bottle to throttle requires a period of eight hours," did not apply that evening. Just as well, as none of us would have been fit to fly the following morning. Even to this day it is the proudest moment of my life...

The only thing that tinged my happiness that day, my parents were not there to see me graduate.

My next step was to receive further training at an Operational Conversion Unit. This was at RAF Church Fenton, which qualified me to fly the Meteor F8 and Meteor T7 aircraft.

Directly after completing that training, I received orders confirming I was to undergo an exchange visit with the 77 Squadron of the Royal Australian Airforce. The Squadron had recently been transferred from Japan to Korea.

The sickening war in Korea was entering into its final months. As a fully qualified Meteor pilot, I did as ordered. Preparations were made at RAF Transport Command at Lyneham to fly me out there. The journey seemed never ending, eventually taking twenty hours. We flew via Cyprus, the Maldives, Singapore, and Japan to Kimpo Airbase near Seoul.

On arrival, I had what one would describe as a real wakeup call, in a place that was less then primitive. The temperature in the late summer of that year, was hot and the place dusty.

When the rains fell, the ground would then become like a quagmire. There were very few permanent buildings, apart from a few Quonset huts for senior officers. All other personnel lived in tents. The showers, if that is what you could call them, had no hot water. When a newcomer arrived, enquiring,

"Where are the Latrines?"

The stock answer would be,

"Follow your nose."

The food unfortunately left a lot to be desired, and all personnel supplemented it with "C" Rations.

The Chinese having entered the war, flew the Russian built Mikoyan-Gurevich MiG-15 aircraft. This aircraft being superior in every way to the American F86 Sabre and the English Meteor F8. The Meteor therefore was restricted in air, to ground operations only. The introduction of the American F100 Super Sabre rectified the situation, restoring parity in the air, and the rest is history. Well not quite...

Many years later while on holiday, I visited the UN building in New York. On a wall in the building was a list of United Nations Operations Worldwide. I was amazed and somewhat upset that the Korean War did not appear on the list. When asking a guide why, he explained that only Peace Keeping Operations were recorded on the wall. Having served in Korea and remembering those who gave their lives during that war for their countries, I was disgusted. I was relieved to return to the UK after a tour of six months. Returning home, I reported to No 1 Air Navigation School at RAF Hullavington, there to await an assignment to an RAF Fighter Squadron.

Hullavington was situated near Chippenham in Wiltshire. Having a motorbike at that time, provided me nicely with a means of transport, rather than having to make my journey by train. I was so thankful, as it saved me the wretched wait for trains on various platforms, including waiting for necessary connections. Forty years later, I still hate train journeys when having to change trains.

On arriving at RAF Hullavington, firstly reporting to the Officers Mess, I was then shown to my room which would become my home for the following two years.

Duties commenced the following day, these consisted of flying with and instructing students of various ages for their initial navigation training. Students at that time, were flown in AVRO Anson Mk22 aircraft on relatively short flights. During the months to come, advanced training was given in vintage Vickers Wellington T10 aircraft. These relics of bombing operations in WW2, were capable of longer flights.

On the days I found myself free, there was nothing I enjoyed more than a game of football. My team, RAF Hullavington, eventually reached the RAF cup semifinal. Unfortunately, by the end of play, we had been beaten by RAF St Eval.

I had also joined the Cheltenham Motorcycle Club, frequently travelling to the Isle of Man, to watch the TT-Races.

The following two years passed pleasantly enough. The final phase of advanced training involved students in a flight to RAF Luqa, on the beautiful island of Malta.

This flight was called Operation Impair. As a member of the staff crew, I enjoyed the scenic route to the George Cross Island without incident using the old Wellington. This ancient piston-engined aircraft, required refueling in Sothern France. The journey taking eight hours ten minutes, in comparison with the two hours twenty minutes it would take a modern jet today.

On the first night in Malta, my colleagues decided that as I was the youngest of the crew, my social education required widening. This involved a visit down Straight Street, better known worldwide as Malta's ignominious 'The Gut'. This infamous street in Valetta, which is Malta's capital, housed many bars of questionable credentials, and our destination was to be the "Egyptian Queen."

We entered a smoky, dimly-lit, grubby basement, containing a neglected, cigarette marked, beer-stained dirty bar. The basement also provided its customers with tables and several rickety chairs to sit on.

The British Fleet had arrived in port, docking in Grand Harbour. Like all Navies, depositing ashore scores of young men on liberty. As the crew and I stepped into the Egyptian Queen, I was amazed to see a queue of sailors lining up against one wall, the queue ending at a curtain drawn across the corner. I was told that behind the dirty curtain, was a Maltese female, aptly named Pee Bucket Annie...

She stood astride an ELSAN chemical toilet ready to dispense social services to the impatient sailors. My social education increased no end.

As was usual in Malta, the night air during spring and summer is warm and balmy, allowing everyone who wished to, the pleasure of sitting outside. My crew and I were no exception, having returned to base from having had a very successful evening all round. After a while we noticed John, one of our crew and a Senior NCO, had still not returned. Not overly worried about him, we continued to sit and chatted enjoying the evening air. Our missing crew member eventually did return and to our astonishment, we realized he was in some discomfort.

Appearances, it seems, can occasionally be misleading. Questioning him as best as we could under the circumstances, he told us,

"I am in a lot of fucking pain, I picked up a smashing bit of stuff, with a brilliant pair up front. Thinking my luck was in when she said she would let me shag her for a certain sum of money.

"Like a bloody fool I handed over what she asked for. She then asked me to use some cream she had brought with her, telling me it would stop her getting pregnant, otherwise she was unable to cater to my needs. After putting the fucking stuff on, the bloody pain was awful."

A couple of the crew then took care of John, leaving me to wonder if, in reality, that was perhaps his first experience. Or due maybe to her anatomical structure, which one could have described as 'like a mouse's earhole.'

To this day, I look back on this tale with a great deal of merriment, often wondering if the symptoms John had exhibited, may well have indeed been due to the use of fiery jack.

Malta's capital, Valetta, is a city steeped in history and one that was nearly destroyed during WW2. The island actually suffered more than thirty air raids a day during the height of the Italian Air Force campaign. The campaign was meant to destroy the island as an important Allied base in the Mediterranean. They were not successful, and Germany also attacked in 1941 before the Luftwaffe was diverted to North Africa.

Before leaving Valetta, the crew and I decided to do a little shopping by buying an assortment of tinned goods. These goods were still not readily available in England, because England was still suffering from wartime rationing. The goodies we purchased were stowed in various apertures of the aircraft to avoid Customs inspection in the UK.

After a couple of enjoyable days in the sunshine, we prepared to depart RAF Luqa at three a.m. under the cover of early morning darkness.

Shortly after takeoff, we ran into one of the notorious Mediterranean storms which are characterised by Cumulus Nimbus. These are dense, towering, vertical, black clouds associated with thunder and lightning, causing atmospheric instability. Powerful upward air currents produce torrential rain within the clouds themselves. Not a safe environment for a vintage Vickers Wellington aircraft.

With storm clouds rising from sea level to at least 30,000 feet, we had a difficult decision to make. Descending to sea level did not sound too attractive, in fact quite dangerous. The vintage Wellington was incapable of reaching no more than 10 to 15,000 feet. The aircraft therefore was unable to climb above the storm.

The captain of the aircraft was an ex Polish military officer. His Co-Pilot turned to him and said,

"Skipper, perhaps we should return to Malta."

For reasons best known to himself, and in an unpleasant voice, he reminded his Co-Pilot who was the captain of the aircraft. He also chose to ignore our collective pleas and advice, deciding to fly through the storm…

The feeling of being terrified, was an understatement. The vintage aircraft was tossed around the sky like a lightweight plastic toy. The static electricity from the lightning, produced blue lights on the aircraft structure known as St Elmo's Fire. By the Grace of God, and good luck, we made it to Southern France, managing to land at the French base of Istres.

The Wellington aircraft was based upon a Geodetic structure, the fuselage being made of a metal grid, covered in fabric. This had been designed by Barnes Wallis, the inventor of the famous bouncing bomb. The bomb having been used in the attack and destruction of the Möhne Dam in Germany WW2.

As we disembarked, we saw that on one side of the aircraft, the fabric had been torn off completely by the storm and had disappeared.

After temporary repairs had been made, along with drinking some vile and gritty French coffee, we continued to RAF Hullavington without further incident.

Fortunately, soon after our arrival, my movement orders appeared. I was thankful to be spared further flights to Malta, though destiny in time, had other ideas planned for me.

Common practice during RAF service meant you would find yourself placed on the Special Duties List. This normally meant a period of loan service with a Foreign or Commonwealth Air Force for training purposes. To my delight, I received orders to proceed for duty with the Royal Pakistan Air Force.

Chapter 3

The Sind Desert

The Islamic Republic of Pakistan, due to political and religious issues, was born in 1947 following the partition of British India. Pakistan has a population of over 212 million, 10 million of those being Muslim refugees who fled from India. By doing so, they hoped to find a peaceful safer life as they settled into the newly created state of Pakistan.

Finally, my movement orders arrived, and I could now depart from RAF Hullavington for loan service with the Royal Pakistan Air Force, established during the same year as Partition.

During that time, it inherited a conglomerate of ex-RAF aircraft from India, some barely in flying condition.

Prior to my arrival, they had entered the jet age and under British pressure, they had bought a number of Supermarine Attacker fighter jets.

RAF personnel proceeding overseas, (draftees) were processed at a Personnel Deployment Centre at Lytham St Anne's, close to Blackpool in Lancashire. One felt you had literally entered a sausage machine. Draftees in various groups were inserted at one end of a line of wooden buildings, emerging eventually at the other end fully processed. Having been documented, medically examined, inoculated, including being in possession of tropical clothing, along with the equipment they may need.

Each group was assisted through this necessary process by a junior NCO (in this case, a Corporal).

Strange as it may seem, it is a phenomenon in all three services that such NCOs, given a modicum of power over personnel of superior rank to themselves, develop a power complex becoming thoroughly unpleasant and frequently rude. To say the least, our NCO was no exception. Due to his own stupidity, he got his comeuppance in an embarrassing fashion.

We filed through the final building to collect various items of different sizes of clothing, along with our kit bags. With everything we required, we made our way to leave the building. Before doing so, we were told somewhat brusquely to leave the 15 kitbags, which were now full to the brim, and ordered to proceed to the next stage.

Unfortunately, the NCO, missed the necessary stage of ensuring our name, etc., had been stippled on each kitbag! Never having experienced such a situation, he was at a loss on how to rectify his mistake and what to do with 15 nameless kit bags. So much for one nasty NCO.

The day of departure arrived, and our draft was bussed to the Lytham railway station. The station staff informed us that the express service to Euston London would be making an unscheduled stop. We were told to stand at a special position on the platform enabling us to load a sizeable number of kitbags and personal luggage.

On the train's arrival, the doors of the guard's van opened where we stood. Thus, allowing the 15 of us to hurl a veritable mountain of kit into the van. There was complete silence after boarding the train! As nothing moved, panic-stricken rail staff raced to the guard's van to find the unfortunate guard pinned against the far wall, submerged funnily enough under a large pile of our belongings. The guard was quickly rescued; we were then able to continue with our journey to London without further incident.

I had to smile on our arrival at the capital, as we managed to cause a further incident.

This time by commandeering what we presumed was a luggage truck, only to find we had appropriated a GPO mail truck. After being cursed at by a number of postmen, being officers and gentlemen, naturally, we apologized. An altercation, therefore, having been averted as we made our way to leave the station.

As was normal in those days, major airlines had check-in offices in central London. This avoided the need for their passengers to check-in at the airport. We presented ourselves at the desk of the Royal Dutch KLM airline, without causing further mayhem and checked in.

The men and I were then bussed to Gatwick. There we boarded a KLM Douglas Skymaster aircraft bound for Karachi. Although a large 4-engined airliner, the Skymaster required at least three transit stops en route. The first of those stops being Rome, the others were Damascus in Syria and Basra in Iraq.

Damascus was to be an overnight stop. On our arrival, my colleagues and I found we had been pre-booked into a hotel in central Damascus. The hotel and food as I remember it, were both clean and acceptable, if somewhat noisy. The following morning, having a few hours to spare, we decided to visit the huge Medina (Bazaar) in central Damascus. After an interesting haggle, I purchased a pair of multi-coloured socks. On my arrival in Karachi, I handed my laundry to the Dhobi Wallah (Laundry Boy).

As he washed my personal belongings, including what has now become the infamous socks, which to our joint amazement, melted and disappeared down the waste pipe! Obviously, they were neither wool nor cotton.

Our final destination was to be the Royal Pakistan Airforce base, Mauripur. The flight in total had taken over

21 hours.

Mauripur housed 11 Squadron, "The Arrows" of the PAF - no connection to the Red Arrows. This base had been previously built by the British, similar in design to the many bases in India.

We were allocated single rooms with high ceilings, each accommodating the welcoming fan. One can only describe the building as typical white and tropical in design. All the rooms of course had whitewashed plain walls and the necessary mosquito nets to sleep under.

One night, I can remember a colleague failed to tuck the edges of his mosquito net firmly under his mattress. The result of this error had left a foot exposed. He found the following morning, a visiting rat had nibbled away the hard skin on his big toe, giving him a free pedicure, and the rest of the crew a great deal of merriment.

During the time I was there, the Royal Pakistan Air Force decided to install a swimming pool. On completion, the pool was a magnificent piece of workmanship. It allowed us to thoroughly enjoy this most welcome of amenities. As pools constantly require the need for attention, sadly after just one week, the contents of this pool resembled pea green soup. On investigation, it revealed the construction company had forgotten to install a means of emptying the pool. To the amusement of all personnel, the local fire brigade had to be summoned to empty the disgusting water. After which, a new drainage and filtration system was then installed.

Being a Yorkshireman, as I previously mentioned, my love of sport, in particular cricket, has never left me. I thank my lucky stars I was pretty good, and besides cricket, I had been blessed with the ability to play football. This being the case, it became very useful during this time, as I was chosen to play alongside members of the Mauripur football team. While at Mauripur, I sustained a pretty awful injury to one of my legs. Unfortunately, in those days, various members of the Pakistani teams did not wear football boots. Their feet were like leather. So much so, that when one of the Pakistani players tackled me, he cut my leg open with his toenail. I still have the scar to this day, something of a souvenir to remind me of that game. I also had the privilege to be selected to play for the Royal Pakistani Airforce cricket team. An honour indeed, as I was the only Brit on the team.

Another amusing diversion for some of the RAF personnel involved the local traders. The main road to Karachi was close to Mauripur. This road over the centuries had been used by numerous camel-drawn carts. The carts were loaded with vegetables and other goods destined for the markets in Karachi. The drivers would make long journeys from the north, often falling asleep during that time.

The RAF had some jokers in the pack, who after dark would find it amusing when coming across one of these sleeping drivers. They would go and turn the cart around, knowing the strange phenomenon that camels knew their way home. Eventually, when the driver awoke, he would find himself halfway back from where he set out. Only heaven knows what he must have said, perhaps he increased the camel's knowledge of swear words in Urdu.

At that time, 11 Squadron was operating the Supermarine Attacker. This aircraft was a single-seat interceptor. The aircraft had been "Navalised" and used briefly by the British Fleet Air Arm. Unfortunately, it was an aircraft that required frequent maintenance and had a high attrition rate. This aircraft was a variant based upon the Supermarine Spitfire of WW2 fame. To facilitate its use on aircraft carriers, a heavy oversized undercarriage had been added, which produced a nose up, tail down attitude when on the ground. On take-off, its jet exhaust often burnt a furrow on the surface of the runway.

As a member of a Training Team, my role was to assist in the advanced flight training of relatively new Royal Pakistani Air Force pilots. Competent enough though they may have been in most respects, they did not seem to be fully confident in handling emergency situations or non-routine problems in the air. The Attacker aircraft being a single seater, meant I did not have to fly with one of them. To my eternal relief, I had my own aircraft...

Two tragic accidents exemplify this problem. During air-ground attack training, a flight of three aircraft would adopt a "V" formation with a leader and two wingmen.

The exercise required the flight to descend, and then dive at a target on the ground. Bombs or rockets would then be released, and the leader would immediately issue the order,

"Pull Up. Pull Up."

Those two words were vital, as they would ensure the aircraft returned to a safe altitude.

During this exercise, a colleague or myself was required to fly alongside the formation acting as safety observer. During one of my training flights, the leader had reported sick, his wingman, therefore, had taken over the lead. Unfortunately, after releasing the munitions with me flying alongside, it was obvious to me that the wingman had failed to give the necessary order.

I called over the radio, "Pull up, Pull up!" but to no

effect.

Regrettably, my call was ignored, and the three aircraft crashed into the Sind Desert killing all three pilots. I returned to Mauripur deeply upset at this avoidable accident.

On another occasion, a pilot flying back to Karachi in a southerly direction requested the air traffic control centre at Karachi, to confirm the required heading. As he was flying south, the correct compass bearing should have been180 degrees. Confused, or otherwise. The air traffic controller instructed the pilot to fly 360 degrees, or in a northerly direction. This unfortunately took the pilot away from Karachi. The aircraft finally ran out of fuel and crashed. The Sind Desert once again had claimed another victim.

The Royal Pakistan Air force base had been constructed in 1942 as an RAF Staging Post. At that time, it had been used for the movement of troops and supplies from the UK to Asia during WW2. Some of its buildings still had the original primitive toilets or latrines in military parlance.

These ancient facilities consisted of a pit that had been dug six-foot-wide, by six-foot-long, and six-foot-deep. To accommodate the human rear, a wooden plank had been placed across it. The plank had several apertures of various sizes cut into it, a necessity for this facility.

Pakistan, unlike India, did not have a caste system but had grades of employment. These ranged from wet sweepers, being the lowest grade, to dry sweepers. Personal servants known as bearers were regarded as a much higher grade.

The unfortunate wet sweepers' job would be to sit in

the bottom of the pit armed with a pot of tar and a long-handled brush. Once a person had evacuated his or her bowels. His role required him to apply the tar to the material deposited to deter flies.

I can remember on one occasion, the sweeper's brain probably due to the heat and boredom snapped. Instead of doing what he would normally have done, he applied the tar to the rear of the person protruding from the plank above him.

The white buttocks in view must have been like a red rag to a bull. Unfortunately, it belonged to a senior officer's wife!

I will not provide further detail except to say, the base was in hysterical laughter, and we did not see the lady for a number of weeks thereafter.

On weekdays the children of RAF personnel at Mauripur were bussed to school in Karachi.

An officer at all times travelled as an escort to the children. On one particular day, I drew the short straw and joined around twenty excited very noisy children en route into Karachi.

We entered the capital and drove down one of the many narrow streets. Suddenly, a rickshaw cyclist appeared from another side alleyway. Unfortunately, our bus driver could not avoid hitting him full-on. Although unhurt, the rickshaw owner proceeded to lie under the front wheel of the bus. He was obviously intent on obtaining compensation.

As was usual in such situations, a mob quickly gathered, and I knew a nasty situation was imminent.

The children loved the situation, jumping up and down and banging on the windows of the bus. I instructed the driver once I stepped down from the vehicle, to jam the doors closed, as the children's safety was naturally paramount...

My efforts to remove the cyclist annoyingly were in vain. The damn man was determined to stay exactly where he was comfortable, under the front wheel.

The mob by this time had become an ugly crowd, having increased dramatically in size. Mob behaviour in my experience is extremely unpredictable and violence can flare up without warning. I had no fellow officer or military backup, leaving me to become increasingly apprehensive for the sake of the children. The dilemma that faced me was: one, I had no direct communication with Mauripur. Second, I dare not leave the children to find a public telephone.

Fortunately, and to my great relief, an Inspector accompanied by a Constable of the Pakistan Police arrived.

Questioning the cyclist, the police discovered that he did not have the required rickshaw license. They then proceeded to drag him from under the wheel and once having done so, they went on to administer some heavy punishment with their lathi batons, which were long hollow bamboo canes filled with lead. A very nasty weapon!

The solution resolved, we continued into Karachi. My cold sweat finally disappeared and my blood pressure returned to normal. Just another day of my life as an RAF Officer in Karachi.

The Muslim community regarded each Friday as a Holy Day. Work, therefore, ceased, leaving my colleagues and me, free to travel into the city. Our destination was normally the Chinese restaurant in Elphinstone Street. The reason was twofold. The restaurant provided the equivalent of a full English Breakfast along with all the trimmings. Secondly, the restaurant had a unique facility… a Christian toilet. All enjoyed the use of this porcelain throne.

As is common in tropical countries, nasty bugs ruled the day. Once again, I was no exception to being attacked by one. This very unpleasant bug entered my system, ensuring I went down with an unspecified intestinal infection. Known colloquially for decades by British troops as Delhi Belly, Tanzania Trots, Malta Dog, or Singapore Shits. Depending of course where you were stationed. Sustaining a severe dose, I was hospitalised for a week and lost a significant amount of weight, enough to leave me too weak to write home. I was eventually discharged with my uniforms hanging off me, at least around a couple of sizes too big.

My tour of two years came to an end, and to my delight and amazement, I was offered the choice of repatriation home by either air or sea. This was something which was, indeed, very unusual. Attracted by the thought of a 3-week seaborne holiday, I opted for the sea trip. The ship, I hoped would take me safely home, was the MV (or MS) Batory. She was docked at that moment in Karachi.

The MV Batory was a passenger ship of some 14,000 tons. The vessel belonged to the Polish Ocean Lines. Having been named after a sixteenth-century Polish King Stephen Batory. She was also known as the LUCKY SHIP, due to her most remarkable history.

This very special ship had been built in 1936 and had been in service with the Polish Navy. One of her most vital operations was assisting in the evacuation of the British

Expeditionary Force at Dunkirk, in France in WW2.

There were many other more famous voyages for this amazing ship, including the transportation of British gold reserves to Canada. Another of her precious cargos were the children she took from the dangers in war-torn England to safety in Australia.

Little did I realise until boarding this special ship, this trip too was to prove eventful for me.

Given a cabin to myself, for which I was both thankful and delighted. Food on board proved excellent. One of the highlights as I remember, was a certain Polish barman who served the most incredible vodka cocktails. Amazingly, one could consume copious quantities of these drinks and still awake the following morning without a trace of a hangover.

Leaving Karachi, our first port of call was to be Bombay. On arrival waiting to join the ship were several Indian families. Like most Indian families, this one had a very attractive daughter, who I dare say may have been in her late teens.

Once the ship sailed gracefully out of Bombay, and to my daily embarrassment, which became very clear for all to see, his young lady constantly sought my company during the rest of the entire trip home.

I had the feeling she may well have been encouraged by her family, scenting the possibility of a marriage to a British RAF Officer, would indeed be perfect. Needless to say, despite my attempts to avoid her while onboard, the moment we docked at Southampton, prompted my rapid exit from the ship. I had though, a long way to go before making my escape, as our next port of call was to be Aden.

By the time we reached Aden, I decided to tread terra

firma by going ashore and do a little shopping. Making my way to the local market, as I love nothing more than the joy of haggling. I decided to take the opportunity to see if I could buy a new camera. While enjoying this pastime, I almost missed the last launch back. Had I have done so; the camera would have proved to have been a seriously expensive purchase. As it was, thanks to my Guardian Angel, I returned to the ship with a twin-lens Rolleiflex camera in hand.

Enjoying my regular evening drink, I smiled to myself briefly, giving a thought to what would have happened had I indeed missed the ship. One thing for sure, I would have been severely reprimanded. Maybe even worse, as the RAF would have had to repatriate me from RAF Khormaksar.

Our journey continued onto Port Said, and then onto Malta. Transiting through the Suez Canal was an unusual experience. Seeing a large ship travelling through the desert was indeed unique. Enabling it to do so, by using this fantastic engineering project. What would the ancient Egyptians, who loved to build monuments that we are still able to enjoy today, have thought of this amazing construction.

With having very little to do during this time at sea, except naturally relax, sleep, and eat. I found myself reminiscing about my time at Cranwell. The Senior Technical Officer back then was a chap called Wally Dunn. He was a keen radio amateur [HAM]. I remember him coming to me one day and suggesting I obtain a radio license. A Wing Commander's suggestion... is a euphemism for an order! One which I obeyed without question.

After taking the radio theory examination, along with a morse code test, I obtained my license along with a call sign. Even though I did not think about it at the time, this enabled me to enjoy a hobby for many years to come, and would prove to be more than useful in the future...

The ship eventually moored at the head of the canal at Port Said. There, we were surrounded by local entrepreneurs in bumboats. These small boats sold leather, wooden, and silver goods. Their method was to throw a rope over the rails to a prospective customer. The individual was expected to choose an item, place money in a basket and lower both money and goods back down to the bumboat. Unfortunately, a colleague let go of one of these ropes. Both basket and goods disappeared into the murky depths of the canal. This unfortunate accident provoked a torrent of abuse from the boatman below. Fortunately, none of us spoke Arabic. We did though assume that somewhere in the phrase, the words meant 'Filthy English,' maybe even worse.

Leaving the Suez Canal and entering the Mediterranean, we encountered rough seas, leaving many of the passengers to turn various shades of green, as they rapidly left the dining room.

This left me to enjoy my food and have the place to myself for several days, including not being harassed by a certain female.

My only claim to fame during the voyage was to become the Shuffleboard Champion. This game required one to push large wooden discs by using a long wooden pole. The discs had to be placed onto numbered squares painted on the deck. I loved my brief period as Champion on that very special Polish Ship.

On arriving safely back in England, my adventure with the Royal Pakistan Air Force ended on a grey cold winter's day as we docked at Southampton.

Chapter 4

Taxiway Kill

Arriving back in the UK, I found myself posted to 56 ("Punjab") Fighter Squadron, at RAF Waterbeach, near Cambridge. The Squadron was established in 1916, as part of the Royal Flying Corps. The merger of the Royal Flying Corps and the Royal Naval Air Service in 1918, had been the predecessor of the RAF.

The squadron was flying the Gloster Meteor F8 fighter aircraft. This became the UK's first jet fighter to fly in combat operations during WW2.

As I was still single and lived in the officer's mess, duties were pretty routine. I had now grown into a fairly presentable young man, in mess dress the ladies appeared to find me quite attractive. At this time, I met a sister of a colleague who had served with me in Pakistan. Her name was Dawn. She had the most wonderful long auburn hair, similar in colour to my own, and lovely green eyes. I found myself seriously attracted to her, in fact in a short time, quite in love. We dated on and off for many months until fate stepped in and made decisions that would stay with me and change the rest of my days.

Military aircraft on routine flights in the UK, with pre-approval, may use civil airways. On one occasion flying east from Waterbeach in a Meteor F8, my aircraft suffered a severe electrical failure, together with a possible hydraulic problem. At the time I was flying at an altitude of 20,000 feet. This resulted in a temporary loss of control, coupled with a loss of altitude. I thought for a few seconds, this could be it. However, my guardian Angel once again took control.

During those few precious seconds, the ramjet system deployed under the aircraft and restored the necessary basic flying instruments, enabling me to gain full control and to level off. Declaring an emergency, air traffic control cleared me to land at Birmingham International Airport. With some relief I landed, hoping as I did so, I had sufficient hydraulics to bring the aircraft to a standstill.

Luckily, and to my enormous relief, the aircraft eventually stopped, although a little too near to the end of the runway for my peace of mind. While waiting to be towed off the runway, white-faced and trembling, I noticed a large number of people on the balcony of the terminal building. They were waving enthusiastically, probably under the impression that my emergency landing was part of a military exercise. I had to smile, if only they knew how close they came to observing a fighter jet crash into the terminal building, maybe even killing some of them. My only reward was the standard green endorsement placed in my logbook.

On one particular morning. I remember very clearly an incident involving the ground crew personnel. They were preparing an aircraft on the flight line and caught a large rat. Sadistically, the crew doused the rodent in kerosene and set the creature alight. The Commanding Officer [Twinkle Storey] looking out of his office window, saw a ball of fire amongst the parked aircraft. Reaching for his telephone, he hysterically asked the Senior NCO,

"What the hell is that?"

"Just a rat on fire, Sir," the NCO replied, in a laconic voice.

A similar incident involved the same NCO while organizing the movement of an aircraft. The new, young pilot about to taxi, inadvertently became somewhat heavy on the throttle and the rudder. By doing so, caused the aircraft to move forward and swing rapidly to one side.

Unfortunately, a young airman was standing in front of the wing. His collision with the wing assisted by the jet engine influx forced the young airman's arm and shoulder into the engine intake. As there was a metal spar across the intake of the engine, this prevented him from sustaining further serious injury. The NCO climbed onto the wing, tapped on the cockpit canopy, and in his laconic tone of voice, informed the young pilot,

"Excuse me, Sir, you have an airman trapped in the port engine!"

The young pilot immediately fainted.

The daily routines were occasionally interrupted by annual visits to RAF Acklington in Northumberland, for air-to-air live firing practice.

Deployment of the squadron continued to various other RAF East Anglian bases, including Coltishall, Wattisham and Stradishall.

While at Acklington, there was an interesting diversion each afternoon, should members of the base feel they wished to take it up. This was at the Working Men's Club in the nearby village of Red Row. While the miners worked the swing shift as it was called, (afternoon), their wives were keen to enjoy our company.

RAF Acklington's claim to fame, strangely enough, was its perfect flying weather all year round. Quite a unique phenomenon, as mist and fog back then were non-existent.

At Waterbeach for entertainment, we would occasionally go into Cambridge. There we would have the opportunity of visiting various cinemas, coffee bars, also a live theatre.

During those far off days, nude females were allowed on stage providing they did not move. On one evening, a group of officers and myself decided it was time we enlivened up one of those shows. We reserved a box that overlooked an end of the stage. Having armed ourselves with tennis balls and other soft missiles, we chose a particular scene where the nudes appeared in statuesque poses. After a few moments, we then proceeded to throw our tennis balls and other missiles, scattering the nudes much to the delight of the audience. Unfortunately, not of course the theatre management. We found ourselves escorted from the theatre by several angry security personnel. The following morning, we were summoned to appear before our Commanding Officer, all receiving extra Orderly Officer duties as punishment. Well worth the enjoyment.

A year later in 1955, I was transferred to 253 (Hyderabad) Squadron. This squadron was newly formed at Waterbeach, flying the Venom NF2 night fighter. A rare variant of the original Vampire aircraft. This aircraft was equipped with vintage airborne interception equipment of American design. Several years previously, by some strange coincidence as an Aircraft Apprentice. I had been trained on this equipment at No 1 Radio School, Cranwell.

After completing the required familiarisation, I was cleared to fly the Venom. An unusual feature about this fighter aircraft meant that the pilot and navigator are required to sit side by side. Strangely, this aircraft was not equipped with ejection seats. The normal procedure in an emergency would be to jettison the cockpit canopy then turn the aircraft upside down. After releasing the safety harness, the crew would then literally fall out of the aircraft enabling them to open their parachutes.

Sadly, during the next couple of years, the squadron suffered two tragic accidents.

The first was during a night exercise known as QRA, Quick Reaction Alert. On an airfield at night there is a profusion of coloured lights. These include red, blue, green, yellow, and white. Aircraft also carry various coloured lights. Red and green on the port and starboard wingtips and white navigation lights.

On this night, QRA required two aircraft, all ground crew personnel and ground equipment to be readied then positioned at the end of the duty runway. Once having done so, it enabled the aircraft to be in direct communication with the control tower. Once this was done, it enabled the two aircraft to perform a rapid take-off eliminating a long taxi from a hard standing.

Unfortunately, the wind changed direction, this meant the two aircraft then had to be repositioned at the opposite end of the runway. This required the aircraft to use the perimeter taxiway. Before doing so, I needed permission from the control tower to carry out this manoeuvre.

"Tower this is Red One. Request permission to reposition QRA aircraft to Runway 09."

"Red One this is Tower. Affirmative. Proceed to Runway 09. Await further instructions," was the response I received.

"Tower this Red One. Wilco."

The two aircraft then entered the perimeter taxiway proceeding to a new position at Runway 09.

Taxying slowly behind my colleagues in Red 2. Suddenly there was a flash of light, followed by a loud screeching noise of tortured metal, which appeared as if the aircraft wing had been hit.

My navigator's immediate response was,

"Christ, what the hell was that?"

Stunned, I answered him, "My GOD!"

I saw a Land Rover had collided with my colleague's aircraft. Over the radio, Terry, the pilot of the aircraft said to me,

"Skipper I have been hit, not sure by what."

"Evacuate the aircraft immediately," I replied, deeply concerned about his safety

Should the wing had sustained damage as it was full fuel, then there would have been a serious risk of fire. I then contacted the tower, stating:

"Tower, this is Red One. Serious accident at the junction of perimeter taxiway and C1 Taxiway. Request emergency services."

The Tower responded,

"Red One, this is Tower. Emergency services alerted."

We closed the engines down and climbed out of the aircraft.

The scene which confronted us was one from hell, resembling that of a slaughterhouse. My stomach heaved to the extent of I could feel vomit rising in my throat, finding it difficult to control.

An open Land Rover carrying three members of the ground crew, for some unknown reason had collided with the taxying aircraft. The wing had indeed been hit going on to destroy the top of the Land Rover, decapitating all three of its passengers. The word horrific is an understatement and one I would not wish to witness again. Eventually, the incident was followed by military funerals.

A board of enquiry found in this case, that the Land Rover had entered the perimeter taxiway without obtaining permission from the tower. A secondary finding suggested, the Land Rover to avoid dazzling aircrew had been driving only on sidelights.

The second accident occurred when an aircraft on take-off at night, lost the use of its artificial horizon instrument. At night, a pilot has no natural horizon for reference and so requires this particular instrument. This will allow him to confirm height and position. The instrument on this occasion failed. Tragically, the aircraft flew into the ground, killing both members of the crew.

Ironically, the subsequent Court of Enquiry, discovered the cause of the accident was due to a small screw that had become loose on the face of the instrument.

The death of any member of a military unit causes a significant slump in morale. Sadly, this accident was no exception.

I have many such memories of various incidents. One that occurred involved another Venom aircraft. The Venom NF2 fighter aircraft were normally fitted with additional fuel tanks. The tanks were torpedo-shaped, (Tip Tanks) attached to the wingtips and secured by long bolts.

On the day of a routine mission, a problem occurred with the port tip tank...

After take-off, airflow forced the tank from its normal horizontal alignment into a vertical position at 90 degrees to the wing of the aircraft.

This resulted in the aircraft suffering a severe Yawing

motion which eventually rendered the aircraft uncontrollable.

The pilot and his navigator had no other option than to abandon the aircraft. Thankfully, both landed safely, with the aircraft crashing on uninhabited farmland in Norfolk.

A subsequent enquiry established that the bolt securing the port tip tank to the wing tip had fractured.

On another occasion, I was on a routine mission and managed to fly into a flock of large birds. Fortunately, many of the beasties did not manage to take up refuge in my engine intake. Such an ingestion would have caused me major problems. On returning to the airfield with a damaged radome, while alighting from the aircraft, one of the ground crew who came to meet me and said,

"Christ, Sir. With that damage, you are lucky to be here."

"Yes, but I made the buggers eyes water," I replied.

Another, and very strange incident that occurred while I was at RAF Waterbeach, involved an aircraft belonging to 253 squadron.

The aircraft while flying on a normal day exercise, hit a patch of bad weather by flying through a pretty awful thunderstorm. The aircraft safely returned to Waterbeach, even though it had suffered a terrific lightning strike. On landing the aircraft was found to be heavily charged by static electricity.

Conventional methods of degaussing [demagnetizing] failed completely. The only solution was to store the aircraft in a hanger hoping that the static charge would eventually decay naturally. No doubt the aircraft spent a great deal of time out of action.

RAF Waterbeach occasionally held a ladies' night in the Officers Mess. My friend Andrew and I who was another pilot decided to accompany me to one of these evenings. While circulating we spotted two young ladies, I guess chemistry was in the air. Andrew quite fancied the look of one of them, the other had her back towards us. As we reached their side to introduce ourselves, the other young lady turned around. The first thing I noticed was her large green eyes which reminded me of Dawn, though instead of auburn hair, both young ladies had dark brown hair.

The ladies happened to be sisters, they informed us their names were Debbie and Diane. The evening went pleasantly enough, as Diane and I seemed to get on quite well. At the end of the evening, Diane told me they lived in Ely. Being Officers and Gentlemen, we offered them a lift home. Andrew owned a two-seater sports car, which meant Diane had to sit on my knee. No complaints from me.

As was usual in those days, an Officer had to wait until he was 27 years old and obtain his Commanding Officers permission to marry. This meant Diane and I courted, became engaged, then married after two years.

We were married in some style in Ely Cathedral. On our exit, a guard of honour had been provided by fellow officers with drawn swords.

Even as I walked down the aisle, fate played her hand to the full and I knew I had made one hell of a mistake.

The love that I had for Dawn after dating for four months, had been denied me. She ended our affair by informing me, that she herself had fallen in love with an American airman and was having his child. The American airman had been shipped back to the USA, leaving Dawn to face the future and that of their baby on her own.

TB was quite rampant in those days, with many sanatoria in use across the kingdom. Dawn sadly succumbed to this illness and ended up in one at Mundesley on the Norfolk coast.

I went to visit her, first in Highgate Hospital in London, where the baby had been born and then adopted. Later I visited her again only this time in the Sanatorium in Norfolk. I never saw her after that.

On the eve of my engagement to my future wife, I received a letter from her, begging me to take her back. Had her letter come just a little earlier, then all would have been so different. I did not mind her having a child, even had she kept it. As it was, I was now committed to my future wife, and as stated our marriage took place shortly after.

Our union produced a child, and although Diane was an excellent mother. Unfortunately, she suffered bouts of extreme anxiety. She was though not on her own. Most wives in those days, suffered as she did during their husband's long absences on operational deployments. Diane had few friends, she also had a severe dislike of the formal social events, which were an essential part of Royal Air Force life. This resulted in our marriage slowly disintegrating. I felt very isolated, both emotionally and socially. We parted and eventually divorced, though it would not be for 27 years. Little did I realise back then, I would be facing a dreadful acrimonious divorce, but more of that later.

My tour at Waterbeach ended, and I awaited new movement orders. What would they bring?

Chapter 5

Escape from the Euphrates

I continued my normal duties for several months, waiting patiently until at last my new orders arrived. I must admit after reading them, they came as somewhat of a surprise. The orders clearly stated that I was to return to Special Duties. Duties which were to send me this time on loan to the Royal Iraqi Air Force. However unlikely this may have seemed; I had obviously impressed their Lordships with my service in Pakistan.

By coincidence, as I stated previously, my stepfather had served in Mesopotamia (Iraq) in 1922. He had served with an RAF Armoured Car Squadron at RAF Hinaidi, close to Baghdad. Those vehicles were based on a Rolls Royce Silver Ghost chassis, with a Vickers turret and armament, which were still in use at the outbreak of WW2.

I felt somewhat emotional, realising that now in 1957, I was to serve in almost the very same location as my stepfather previously had done all those years ago. With luck, I may even be fortunate enough in being able to experience some of the things he did.

At the time, although the Ba'athist Party was emerging. Saddam Hussain had not yet become Iraq's President.

I discovered that HM Government, was concerned at Russian interest and possible intervention in the Middle East. HM Government had offered the Iraqi Government a gift. The gift: was, six Hawker Hunter Mk 6 fighter aircraft for the Royal Iraqi Air Force assigned to 6 Squadron. Hence the reason I was sent to be a member of the RAF support and training team. Yes! I was excited at the thought of participating in this unusual project.

The original Personnel Deployment Centre situated in Lytham St Anne's, had closed. Draftees who were going overseas, were now processed at a new Trooping Centre at RAF Hendon in London. Luckily for me being stationed at Waterbeach, it took roughly an hour to reach London by train. After joining up with the rest of the group that had been chosen, going on through the usual processing. My group and I were then taken to Southend Airport. On our arrival we found a Bristol Britannia aircraft of British Eagle Airways, was being made ready to fly us to Iraq. British Eagle had been awarded the trooping contracts for the RAF. After a short wait we departed for RAF Nicosia in Cyprus.

I noticed among the passengers an ENSA Concert Party, who were due to entertain the troops in Cyprus.

One of its members was a small, pretty little blonde lady, who as it turned out was none other than Miss Barbara Windsor. Little did I think back then, she would become the landlady of the now, famous Queen Vic Public House in the TV Soap, EastEnders. Along with Miss Windsor, was a Welsh comedian by the name of Stan Stennett. I could not imagine back then that fate would ensure both Cyprus and Malta would figure in my future, with Cyprus nearly claiming my life.

On arrival in Cyprus, I found myself billeted in a most unpleasant tented transit centre. This damn place was situated on a dusty hillside site in RAF Nicosia. There I had to spend several uncomfortable days awaiting onward transport to Iraq. Living out of a suitcase in a tent with a sandy floor, was not to be recommended. Eventually, an RAF Hastings transport aircraft was made available, and we departed with some relief from Nicosia. However, the departure was aborted. On the climb out, one of the aircraft engines commenced smoking, the captain wisely returned to RAF Nicosia. Unfortunately, there we had to spend another foul night in the transit camp. Our destination was to the ex-RAF Base at Habbaniya, 55 miles west of Baghdad.

The base was situated in the desert on the bank of the River Euphrates, close to Lake Habbaniya, and occupied by the Royal Iraqi Air Force. Originally called RAF Dhinnan, having been built in 1936, and was a major airbase for the entire British Empire. The base was renamed RAF Habbaniya on May 1st, 1938, by the Iraqis.

The population of the base had grown fairly quickly due to the influx of men who worked there. They made it into a pleasant green oasis in the desert, including being fully self-contained by having its own power station and water purification plant.

One of the more amusing amenities at the base, was an open-air cinema. A relic of the British occupation. The cinema had four walls and no roof. Along most of the outside walls of the building, grew tall palm trees. With the trees being conveniently situated along those walls, besides giving shade, they enabled the locals to view the films free of charge. Films most frequently shown were westerns which the locals loved. Unfortunately for some, their excitement would reach fever pitch, to the extent that screams during the performance, indicated that one or more had fallen out of the trees.

The vintage projection equipment normally broke down two or three times during most performances. A one-hour film could require up to four hours to complete.

Water which flowed from the River Euphrates, enabled lawns, trees, flower gardens and even a botanical garden to be maintained by means of an ingenious irrigation system. A unique feature was the vast amount of eucalyptus trees that had been planted. As eucalyptus have a substance which repels mosquitoes, this ensured there were no cases of malaria at RAF Habbaniya. This system has since suffered from a lack of regular maintenance by the Iraqis. Allowing the desert once again to slowly reclaim the land.

The Iraqi pilots were competent, though very similar in attitude to the pilots in Pakistan. As Muslims, they exhibited a philosophical attitude to flying,

"Allah will take care of me."

This thought, or saying, provoked this response on several occasions. When one pilot on landing had his aircraft inspected, it revealed a severe and dangerous hydraulic leak. The Royal Iraqi Air Force approach to routine maintenance was problematic.

Spares were soon running low, despite the UK Government already having provided additional spares for the short term. The Iraqi's had made no provision for long term maintenance, to the point the situation became farcical. There was almost a complete lack of serviceable radio equipment available. The Iraqi solution to the problem during air operations, was to ensure when number of aircraft were involved, only the leader had the luxury of having radio communication. As the Hunter was a single seater aircraft, it was with enormous relief, I did not have to fly with them.

The Ba'ath Political Party in 1958, having risen to some supremacy, and sadly achieved their aim of abolishing the Iraqi Monarchy. Murdering King Faisal II, along with his family. They revoltingly went on to drag their bodies through the streets of Baghdad.

Shortly after this appalling event. The Iraqi Army arrived at Habbaniya and surrounded the British area of the base. Their message being,

"We have come to protect you," while promptly cutting off our water and other supplies. A strange message with their guns pointed towards us.

During that time, the senior officer of the British contingent was a Group Captain McDonald VC. Group Captain McDonald, having won his Victoria Cross in WW2. He was a strict disciplinarian, often very unpleasant and extremely unpopular with the troops.

One of his many foibles, was to insist on a parade every Friday in temperatures approaching 100 degrees. Demanding his men wear heavier dress khaki uniforms, on dazzling white concrete aircraft hard standings. These hard standings are where aircraft are normally parked.

Shortly after the arrival of the Iraqi Army, "Black Mac" as he was known, accompanied by his Adjutant, drove out to the perimeter of the British area. He then demanded that the Iraqi Army Commander restore our water supply immediately or face serious consequences. To our amazement, the Iraqis complied.

Before that incident, our troops would not have followed Black Mac to their dining hall. After Group Captain McDonald's intervention, they would have followed him anywhere.

Tensions were high, the Iraqis making it clear we were obviously no longer welcome in Iraq, and therefore shortly after we departed. Flying out from Baghdad International for the UK. The Russians arrived almost immediately, they too did not stay long, Iraq obviously not being to their liking.

As a matter of interest many years later, the Iraqis used Habbaniya as an air training station and believe it or not an aircraft parts depot. Sadly, this included a weapons development centre, and chemical training base for the Republican Guards units.

The airbase was attacked and bombed during operation Desert Storm in 1990-91 and again later in Desert Shield. The original British buildings were untouched. The old airbase buildings whose walls were riddled by the effect of the heat, stood defiantly like faithful sentinels in the sky.

Chapter 6

Boffin World

During one's career, an RAF Officer would normally be posted to a ground job between flying tours. This was usually a desk bound appointment with the Ministry of Defence. I was fortunate enough in that I was sent to the Central Servicing Development Establishment (CSDE) at RAF Swanton Morley, in Norfolk.

My family and I moved into a hiring which became home for the next couple of years. When personnel and their families arrive at new bases, they are sometimes moved into married quarters or a hiring. Hiring's are homes that the Forces rent from the general public. They are often more comfortable than normal quarters. The one I was fortunate enough to be offered was a lovely bungalow at Costessey, in a pleasant suburb of Norwich.

Nearing the end of my football career, or so I felt at the grand old age of 32. Although unable to play at a reasonable standard, this did not stop me from becoming a referee, of course first needing to qualify to do so.

After having attained a class one status, I went on to officiate in both Service and civilian football in the Norfolk and Suffolk League. I continued to play cricket in the Norwich and District League. Both experiences being most enjoyable. Sadly, it was not until middle age that I was forced to give up my beloved game of cricket. Settling down to be a compulsive TV viewer instead.

The history of this particular base is exceptionally interesting for RAF Personnel. Maybe even for the general public, as so little knowledge is known even today of the unique part it played during the Second World War.

The station was home to the Bomber Support Unit of No.100 Group RAF. On June 29th, 1942, American and British airmen took over the station as part of the first combined bombing raid of World War Two.

Both Sir Winston Churchill, and General Eisenhower were at RAF Swanton Morley for this mission. Six crews from 15th Bombardment Squadron, flew a raid with six crews from the RAF using Boston aircraft belonging to the RAF's No. 226 Squadron.

After the war, the base had various uses until CSDE became responsible for the research, writing and publication of documents. These were intended for use for the servicing and maintenance of electronic systems in aircraft. CSDE also had a satellite unit, this was known as the Radio Installation Unit - within the Royal Radar Establishment (RRE) at Malvern, in Worcestershire.

By 1958 it is exactly where I found myself on detachment. The RRE employed many eminent scientists and engineers, all engaged into research and the design of future electronic equipment for the Armed Services.

Malvern became another two-year posting, and I became a Project Manager.

The RAF provided my family and I, with a house situated in the pleasant suburb of St Johns in Worcester. This city turned out to be a most pleasant for a number of reasons. While there, my son was christened at the local parish church.

The house we occupied at that time, had been built close to the Worcestershire County Cricket ground. As a Yorkshireman who enjoyed cricket. One of the perks of living in that house, enabled me to watch my favourite sport for many happy hours, that was when the ground of course was not flooded!! Unfortunately, this occurrence happened frequently as the River Severn regularly burst its banks.

The work I was asked to undertake, one could say was highly interesting, more than interesting, it was unique.

I became responsible for overseeing the writing of servicing schedules for an advanced airborne interception system. This was to facilitate its introduction into the RAF, specifically for installation in the new English Electric Lightning fighter aircraft.

The Royal Radar Establishment was an amazing place. During 1942, the UKs Telecommunications Research Establishment was moved to Malvern College. By doing so, the work in developing the range and direction technology continued, enabling Robert Watson-Watt and others, to continue the development of airborne interception. Thus, allowing the RAF and its allies to detect incoming German aircraft.

RRE was staffed by an army of eminent scientists and research engineers. All housed in a collection of wooden buildings with a maze of corridors which contained small offices and workshops. When a technical query arose, I knew I could find the solution in a small dusty office, with documents spilling from a desk onto the floor.

Behind this desk would sit a person wearing corduroy trousers, an English gentleman's sports jacket, complete with the ubiquitous leather patches on the elbows. My technical queries, I am pleased to say, were always solved.

My duties consisted of regular meetings with the

manufacturer of the required project equipment. These necessitated several trips for consultation with Ferranti UK. Ferranti had chosen to have its main offices in Edinburgh, Scotland.

On one memorable visit, while talking to an employee of Ferranti, I stepped back into an elegant ornamental fishpond in the main foyer. The pond was not deep, and I am pleased to say. I avoided damaging any of the inhabitants, as they were large, expensive Koi Carp. While doing so, suffering the indignity of wetting my trousers, thankfully only to the knees. To my relief, I was kindly offered a pair of track suit bottoms, ending up having to wear them for the rest of the day.

My normal mode of travel from London to Edinburgh, would be by rail. Returning the same way on a noisy night sleeper train. On the train's arrival in London, normally around 6 am, a cup of tea was provided by a steward. Passengers at that time were allowed to stay in bed until 7 am. A very civilised affair, which I doubt very much is in service these days.

My ground tour was a great experience, as I found Malvern to be both a place of tranquil beauty and one full of interesting history. From Bronze Age man, to one of its famous sons, Sir Edward Elgar, his music of course being part of a great many military parades, including the annual Proms.

Just to finish, I would like to state being a Yorkshireman, cricket is not a matter of life and death, it is far more serious than that.

Chapter 7

Singapore Sojourn

After having spent two years at RRE, I returned to RAF Swanton Morley to await new orders. Once having received them, I was delighted. The new orders informed me that my next temporary duty was to be in the City-State of Singapore. The weather in England that year was poor, even in summer and the thought of going to warmer climes seemed perfect.

Singapore, better known as the Lion City. A name given by a Sumatran Prince called Sejarah Nila Untam, who had landed on Temasek, Singapore's old name. The fable tells us; he saw a lion which is called Singa in Malay. Thus, he gave the island the new name of Singapore. However, studies indicate that lions never lived there, and the animal seen by the Prince was most likely a Malayan tiger.

One of the resident squadrons was the RAF's 45 Squadron. This squadron was to replace its current English Electric Canberra B2 aircraft, with the newer Canberra Photo Reconnaissance aircraft. I was to be a member of a team, which had been assembled to provide familiarisation on the new PR9 aircraft, for both aircrew and maintenance personnel of 45 Squadron.

At RAF Wyton, a PR9 aircraft had been made ready and available. The flight plan was to fly the aircraft to Singapore with several transit stops en route. Unfortunately for me, the Canberra aircraft only carried a crew of 2.

As I drew the short straw, the majority of the team, including myself, found we had to travel by RAF Transport aircraft from RAF Lyneham. The aircraft we flew in was a

De Havilland Comet C2 of 216 Squadron, our destination was to be RAF Tengah. The route would take us via Nicosia in Cyprus, Karachi, and then on to the Maldives at RAF Gan. Thank heavens, this was only a transit stop, as there is literally nothing there unless of course, you like sun, sea, and sand. Fortunately, it was a place where RAF personnel only had to serve a twelve months' tour and families were not allowed to accompany the men.

Finally, after a flight of 17 hours, we landed at RAF Changi. We were then taken by bus to our final destination at RAF Tengah. This had been a Japanese WW2 airfield situated on the western side of the island of Singapore.

The quality of the tropical, pleasant, and comfortable accommodation we were provided with, was a delight. Here we were offered liberal quantities of food, which enabled us to eat both Asian and European meals.

Singapore is a vibrant city, with a reputation being well known by many generations of servicemen. I was not the exception, and therefore keen to explore its delights as soon as possible. During 1960, it still had numerous bars, a euphemism for brothels and many other amusements, including a site named The Brave New World.

The new Prime Minister, Lee Kuan Yew, who was appointed in 1959, had committed himself to turn what he had described as,

"A cesspool of squalor and degradation, into a prosperous, Asian nation." A task, which amazingly he eventually achieved.

He commenced his campaign with the closure of numerous interesting bars. Going on to include the banning of long hair and dropping litter in the streets. Maybe this process is something we should do here in England.

The British military authorities, in support of his aims, introduced a nightly Morality Patrol: a duty in which I was ordered to participate in.

To enable us to carry out our duty, we patrolled in a Jeep. We went in teams consisting of an officer, and three military police NCO's. All drawn from the three services.

During this time, several bars had been placed out of bounds to servicemen. Due to this fact, the team were tasked to visit certain of these establishments to ensure that troops were not enjoying "social-sexual activities."

Entering one of these bars, going on to climb the rickety stairs, then gradually making our way down a dark dirty corridor which serviced many bedrooms. On entering one of these rooms, the army NCO and I came upon a scene still imprinted in my memory.

On top of a filthy mattress, was a young naked soldier. Performing what I would describe as energetic and rather violent exercise on top of an Asian female. I had difficulty containing my laughter when the Sergeant Major tapped the young man on his white buttocks and said:

"What the fuck do you think you are doing lad?"

Looking over his shoulder, the young soldier replied:

"What the fuck do you think I am doing, SIR?"

The culprit was then removed from the female and sent back to his barracks. We continued the patrol without further amusement.

During my stay in Singapore, young National Servicemen, just as today, found it fashionable to visit tattoo parlours. Many of them had been tattooed unknowingly with an insignia of Singapore's criminal Tongs. These Tongs were gangs of vicious thugs who dealt in many criminal activities. We had to carry out a mass inspection of National Servicemen, and then ensure that any Tong insignia were removed. The Tong's preferred weapon at the time was an electric light bulb. These bulbs were filled with acid, then thrown at their unfortunate victims. I am delighted to say, my desire for a tattoo is still non-existent.

A nightly attraction, pre-Lee Kuan Yew days, took place in Bougie Street. At 10 pm each night, a group from the community of transvestite men, would appear in the street, then parade up and down. These people had undergone the full conversion treatment. They were absolutely beautiful; one would never have guessed their original sexuality. Just as it is today, it was a most popular attraction for tourists...

During my deployment, race riots were becoming prevalent. The plan for riot control was initiated by certain signals from sirens across the city. Although on temporary duty, I was fully involved.

On the given signal, a team comprising of an Officer, a couple of NCOs, a sniper, a medic, and armed troops were bussed to strategic locations. These included Government buildings, road junctions and utility sites.

When a mob approached, my orders were to telephone a Magistrate for him to arrive and read the Riot Act. Somehow, I doubted whether that gentleman would arrive in time. Should the mob continue towards us, the sniper was to be brought into action.

Unlike in the movies, the order of, "fire over their heads" was never used. Instead, I had to instruct my sniper to kill a selected person in the front rank of the mob.

Once again, being in a new country and to my misery and disgust, another bug attacked me. Ensuing I ended up in sick quarters for seven days with my bowels in uproar. Once fully recovered, I returned to the UK with the group I went out with. We boarded an RAF Transport Command aircraft at RAF Changi, making an overnight transit stop at RAF El Adem in Libya. What an infamous, violent country that has now turned out to be.

I look back with pleasant memories, having enjoyed a most interesting time in the "Lion City".

The RAF's 45 Squadron finally received its new Canberra PR9 aircraft, and operated them successfully, due to the team's efforts.

Chapter 8.

Divided Land.

Officers on ground tours who are not on flying duties were often deployed to other services or RAF units, primarily for liaison and familiarisation experience. These were considered a necessity in the development of one's career. During 1964, I was sent to RAF Ballykelly, in Northern Island.

The troubles in this part of the United Kingdom were still ongoing. I viewed the assignment with some trepidation, knowing full well of the activities and horrific alleged bombings by the Irish Republican Army.

After crossing a calm Irish Sea, taking the Stena Line Ferry from Holyhead and disembarking, I travelled by Irish Railways to the town of Limavady, situated close to RAF Ballykelly.

The Irish Railways train had a unique dining car. This was operated by two, large and cheerful Irish ladies, unusually wearing floral aprons. They served a large, delicious meal, the equivalent of an oversize English Breakfast.

The resident squadron at Ballykelly was the 204 Maritime Reconnaissance Squadron equipped with the AVRO Shackleton MR MK 2, similar to the WW2 Lancaster bomber.

Thankfully, I was made very welcome but unfortunately had to sleep in a corrugated iron Nissen hut. This damn hut annoyingly had loose sheets on its roof, which kept me awake most nights due to the high winds.

During my visit to 204 Squadron HQ, I met an old friend named Dennis Brooks. Dennis was a Shackleton aircraft captain, who had enlisted in the RAF at the same time as me. I had not seen Dennis for many years, it was marvellous to have the chance of spending a very convivial evening with him in the Officer's Mess bar, consuming a significant amount of alcohol, and wallowing in nostalgia.

Dennis, to my delight, suggested that I flew on a supply operation with him.

204 Squadron aircraft amongst other duties, flew supplies to Weather Ships. The ships were converted Castle Class Naval frigates. Having completed their working lives, they were now permanently moored in the North Atlantic.

The ships also assisted in search & rescue and monitored for possible marine pollution. They also provided weather forecasts. Ballykelly was responsible for two of these ships at locations named "Juliet" and "India," situated to the west of Northern Ireland. Essential supplies were dropped in suitable containers approximately every two weeks as near to the ships as possible.

Having agreed to join Dennis, and after a flight of two hours we located the Weather Ship "Juliet." We descended almost to sea level, the bomb bay doors were opened, and the waterproof containers were dropped alongside the vessel. After pleasantries were exchanged by radio with the crew, we returned to Ballykelly. Due to the airfield's tricky approach between the mountains, we landed with radar assistance.

Some of the entertainment at Ballykelly was provided in the nearby town of Limavady. The Orange Hall as it was called, held a weekly dance. The hall supplied a well-stocked bar, along with an Irish accordion band providing the music. At the end of the evening, as an officer and gentleman, and in an attempt to foster Anglo-Irish relations. I enquired of an attractive young lady if I may offer her a lift home, obviously with the most dishonourable intentions. I was taken aback by her reply when she asked,

"Are you Protestant or Catholic?"

For the record, I guessed correctly and will draw a veil over subsequent proceedings. I certainly was in a divided land.

The second half of my liaison deployment found me attached to the Army. I travelled to Belfast, to the Head Quarters of 3 Para of the Parachute Regiment. The following morning, their Adjutant, asked:

"Roy, would you like to accompany a section of paratroops engaged on a mobile patrol into the city? I must warn you; the patrol will include both Catholic and Protestant enclaves."

Knowing of the current civil unrest, and clashes between the religious groups, I agreed but with some trepidation.

We departed the heavily fortified Head Quarters of 3 Para and entered the city centre in an open Land Rover. All was normal until we entered a street of terraced houses which were part of a Catholic community. A large group of females emerged from the houses, they were armed with dustbin lids, saucepans, and other metal utensils. Banging then together they created a cacophony of noise and screaming expletives about Britain in general, and the British Army in particular.

We ignored the mob and drove slowly down the street. The paratroops and I had been seated on metal benches in the rear of our Land Rover, facing inwards and knee to knee.

Without warning, one of the harridans approached the vehicle and spat at one of the young paratroopers. His weapon was horizontal against his thigh. Imperceptibly, he slid the weapon backwards over the side of the Land Rover. The butt striking the face of the obnoxious female, spreading her nose across her face. The Platoon Commander, his men and I, made a point of looking away. Our driver then drove rapidly out of the street. We returned to Head Quarters without further incident.

After what had been a most interesting liaison deployment, I returned to the UK by road, rail, and sea with mixed views. My personal thoughts being that very little has changed from the days of Elizabeth I to Elizabeth II about the Divided Land.

Chapter 9

University Respite

One of the responsibilities of the RAF Education Branch was to assist in the training of new personnel. The year was now 1966. With it, brought an increase in diverse technical equipment, plus a rapid rise in the complexity of technology. The young men and women who were destined for employment in servicing and maintenance of aircraft required substantial improvement in their technical training. The Branch had a preponderance of arts graduates and a shortage of engineering graduates.

Their Lordships found a unique solution. The solution caused a seismic shift in my RAF career.

With my engineering qualifications, and together with five other Officers, I was summoned for an interview at the Ministry of Defence in London. To our collective amazement, we were informed we were to be sent north for 12 months. Our destination was to be the Victoria College of Education at Manchester University. By attending the University, would allow us to obtain a Diploma in Education. Before we left the room the Senior Officer added:

"Gentlemen. We expect you to do well." No pressure there!

Attending the university meant one year out of uniform and away from normal military duties. This project sounded like a very interesting and pleasant assignment, more interesting than even I expected.

The RAF had found my family and me, a comfortable new bungalow in the village of Egerton. Situated a few miles north of Bolton. Little did I realise at that time, that one day I would return to what is now known as the Greater Manchester area for personal reasons. Our bungalow was set on the grounds of an old farmhouse.

The landlord had been a farmer who had previously sold off most of his land. He had retained a sufficient piece of land, enough on which to graze a couple of sheep.

As it turned out, these sheep provided him with tax relief and subsidies. He was also conducting, it seems, a number of running battles with the local authorities, as well as the tax office.

On returning home from the university each day, I would stop to have very interesting chats with him. He would inform me of the self-generating war he had started.

First, by not declaring the income he accumulated over the years, and secondly, he had not obtained the necessary planning permission to build the bungalow which was most definitely required. Thirdly, he persisted in submitting many frivolous applications, to seek permission for many ridiculous things. One utterly stupid request was to be allowed the siting of a burger van adjacent to the village war memorial...

One of the particular tales he told me, I found most amusing. His wife would purchase new suits for him at least three times a year from Kendal's, one of Manchester's top stores. The morning after, to annoy her, and to my great amusement, I would see him in his brand-new suit, mucking out his pigeons. Sadly, I never found out the results of his battles with either the taxman or the local authorities. I look back with fondness, as he was both a wonderful character and an excellent landlord.

Other events that took place that year, were not as amusing. I have no idea how, but at the age of 36, I found myself having to endure the miseries of a childhood ailment. Chicken Pox to be precise...

I must admit there was a lighter side to my maladie. The local doctor insisted that I must stay at home, and not have contact with the outside world. Perfect advice, which I was most grateful for, though not for my wife, as it gave me the opportunity to sit and watch England win the world cup football tournament.

Sadly, in the autumn of that year, my mother at 59, passed away. She had suffered from lung cancer. I travelled down to Leicestershire for her funeral feeling incredibly lonely and sad.

Life slowly returned to normal, though naturally, never quite the same again.

Unlike a number of civilian students, our RAF Group of six officers knew when to work hard, and then enjoy suitable relaxation.

I thoroughly enjoyed those 12 months, apart from the two periods of practice teaching. I was sent for two periods of three weeks to technical colleges in both Oldham and Moss Side Manchester. Moss Side, at the time, was awash with gang violence. I could well have been on the streets of New York...

I found teaching young trade apprentices along with coal miners, far from an easy task. At times I felt like a circus Ringmaster, who should have entered the classroom with a whip and a chair.

The year passed quickly enough, with final examinations soon upon us. Remembering the remarks in London about what was required of our performance, I went on to obtain a Diploma in Education. Adding to my pleasure, gaining a Distinction in Teaching Practice and a

Credit in Teaching Theory. Annoyingly, the only disappointment was the fact I had to share the top place with a female law graduate, who was not even pretty! All the degrees in the world would not have helped her change that fact.

By December life returned to normality. My fellow officers and I now wondered as to where our new postings would be. Orders eventually came through, and I was sent to No 2 School of Technical Training at RAF Cosford, near Wolverhampton. I began my final tour in the RAF in January 1967.

My new duties involved teaching Foreign & Commonwealth Officers, from such countries as Iran and Nigeria. Obviously at that time, having no knowledge that fate would one day ensure I would work in Africa.

For relaxation and having been a long-standing member of the RAF Amateur Radio Society, I would go on to enjoy operating from several countries including Australia, Iraq and Pakistan. Also, Malaysia, Morocco and Nigeria.

This brought me the privilege, to be involved in the first of two unique projects in the world of amateur radio. At that time, there existed a wanted list of countries from which there had never been any amateur radio activity.

The RAF Amateur Radio Society decided to mount an expedition to one of the top five such countries. One of the five chosen turned out to be Kamaran Island which is situated in the Red Sea, off the coast of the Yemen Arab Republic.

The Island, though small, holds a long history of great sadness. Most of it is flat with just a few hills to the south, the highest point is no more than 24 meters high.

The Portuguese established an outpost there during the 16th century. During the second part of the 19th century, the Island belonged to the Turks. They established a quarantine station for pilgrims from East Africa, the Persian Gulf, India, and other eastern countries who were travelling by sea to Mecca. By June 1915, Great Britain invaded the Island, and by the 30th of November 1967, Kamaran was returned to the People's Democratic Republic of South Yemen. (Previously known as Aden.) Only to be seized by the adjacent Yemen Arab Republic in 1972, and eventually became part of a unified Yemen...

A team of four RAF personnel flew out from RAF Lyneham, including a massive amount of radio equipment. Our flight was to take us to RAF Khormaksar in Aden.

There we were met by the fifth member of the team, who was a Master Air Signaler, serving in the RAF with 233 Squadron.

We were flown to Kamaran Island in a Vickers Valletta aircraft. From the air, the thought passed my mind that the landing strip looked a little on the short side for this type of aircraft. Thankfully, we landed safely, on our arrival, we were met by the British Political Officer. This officer was the sole resident apart from a few native fishermen and their families - his wife having returned to England many years previously.

We set up three radio stations and went on to operate continuously for ten days. Much to the delight of radio amateurs worldwide, we made over three thousand contacts. Then to our annoyance, after eight days had passed, our food supplies virtually ran out, leaving us to exist on tomato soup. Funnily enough, I still enjoy a bowl here and there. The relief and delight at seeing an aircraft arrive was obvious, which then proceeded to fly us back to Aden. From Aden we flew home to England, leaving our fifth member to continue his duty in Aden.

Once having returned home, the expedition was adjudged to have been a complete success, both for the amateur radio fraternity, and the RAF Amateur Radio Society.

Traditionally, dining-in nights were held monthly in the Officer's Mess. Strict rules were observed during these formal affairs. One particular rule which was enforced was that no one could leave the table during the meal. When mother nature made her demands, one could approach, and then ask the Mess President for permission to leave. The Mess President was a senior officer who sat at the top table. This request was rarely exercised, and most certainly frowned upon.

During one evening, having consumed a liberal quantity of alcohol. My colleagues bet me a bottle of wine, that I would not exercise the privilege.

I left my seat, marched up to the top table, stood to attention, and addressed the Mess President, stating,

"Sir, permission to pee!"

The President glared at me, never said a word, but nodded. I was ordered the next morning to his office, then warned in no uncertain terms about my future behaviour at dining-in nights. I certainly enjoyed the bottle of Australian Chardonnay I had won.

Another incident I remember well during my tour at RAF Cosford was on the day the base was to be awarded the privilege of being given the Freedom of the City of Wolverhampton.

This ancient rite permitted troops to march through

the city with bayonets fixed, flags flying, and drums beating. A ceremonial march followed by the presentation of a key at the Town Hall.

The day had been planned meticulously, the RAF's world-famous Queens Colour Squadron, was also that day on parade. Even today, they are known as a Squadron that does not ever make a mistake. Unfortunately, as they are human! On that day, one of their men fainted. To the amusement of all at Cosford, an unknown young airman sent the Colour Squadron a Get-Well Card.

The Parade was led by two mounted policemen, astride a pair of magnificent horses. Immediately behind them, came the Commanding Officer of RAF Cosford. He, in turn, was followed by myself, as Parade Adjutant, and a Warrant Officer. Behind us was the Flight Commander of the leading flight of airmen.

The march through Wolverhampton passed without incident until we were approaching the Town Hall. To our amusement, one of the Police horses lifted its tail and proceeded to evacuate its bowels. Depositing a significant pile of equine poo in the road ahead of the parade...

Our unfortunate Commanding Officer was unable to take evasive action and stepped into it. The result being that his shoes and lower legs were covered in horse manure, ruining his best uniform trousers.

The Commanding Officer proceeded to dismiss his officers and troops. He then turned to me and said,

"Come with me, Roy."

With swords still drawn, we approached the Police Officers astride their animals. The Commanding Officer, pointing his sword at them, and then went on to say,

"Officers, the next time you bring your animals to a

parade, take them for a fucking walk first. I have a good mind to stick this sword up its arse."

I managed to suppress a smile and we left the scene. I have often wondered which rose bed the poo eventually ended upon.

That evening, we entertained the Mayor and his Council Members to a reception at the Officer's Mess. The foyer had been beautifully decorated in the theme of a large ornamental fishpond. However, an unnamed Officer had emptied numerous packets of blue soap powder into the pond, creating waist high foam throughout the foyer, resulting in the Mayor having to use the rear entrance to both attend and leave. An eventful day in Wolverhampton.

Chapter 10

Anniversary

The Royal Air Force was formed on 1st April 1918, by the merger of the Royal Flying Corps, and the Royal Naval Air Service. The RAF celebrated its 50th Anniversary in 1968. During the same month one of the numerous events to celebrate this occasion, the RAF held a banquet and reception, hosted by the Air Board.

This was an event which was attended by Her Majesty Queen Elizabeth II, accompanied by HRH the Duke of Edinburgh, and other members of the Royal Family. Also included were various Members of the Government.

Also invited were 60 RAF personnel, myself included, all having for various reasons been selected to meet the Queen.

As the event that evening was to be held in Lancaster House, I travelled up to London from RAF Cosford, to my overnight accommodation at the RAF Club in Piccadilly.

My fellow officers and I were collected at the RAF Club, and then taken to Lancaster House. On arriving, the senior officer in charge, requested we assemble in small groups in a beautifully appointed large gallery, and then positioned around it.

Her Majesty had been invited to dine in the adjacent banqueting room, along with members of the Air Board. During that time, we were supplied with liberal amounts of excellent champagne and canapés. After a couple of hours and having consumed a significant amount of alcohol, I was ready to speak to anyone.

After the banquet, the Queen, accompanied by

members of her family, including Prince Charles, Princess Margaret, and various politicians, entered the gallery and circulated as they normally do. They proceeded to speak to individuals in each of the small groups that awaited them.

I was part of a group that consisted of a Senior Officer, another Flight Lieutenant like myself, as that was my rank at the time, together with a Sister from the Princess Mary's RAF Nursing Service.

As the Queen approached my group, she stopped, then spoke to the senior officer who stood next to me. Then to my utter delight, the Queen graciously extended her hand to me. I inclined my head at the required five-degree angle, and then very gently shook her hand in return. What a wonderful experience it was to speak to her. Knowing Her Majesty would ask mundane questions, it was still a unique moment. I had the joy of receiving one of her dazzling smiles and looking into the Queens beautiful corn blue eyes.

The Queen is naturally known for her knack for ensuring people are at ease in her company when speaking with her.

Meeting my Monarch without exception will always remain with me.

Seeing the wedding photographs this year of the Queens Granddaughter, Princess Beatrice, reminded me of the Tiara the Queen wore that evening, as well as her exquisite white gown.

I was fortunate enough in being able to shake hands with other members of the Royal family, including Prince Philip and Princess Margaret, who was very lovely and rather small, plus various members of the Government. Eventually, Prime Minister Harold Wilson approached.

He had obviously consumed a significant amount of alcohol and was a little unsteady on his feet. His speech was somewhat slurred, as he asked the Flight Lieutenant next to me where he worked. The officer explained that he was a gynecologist at RAF Halton Hospital. I should explain that all the domestic staff at the Prime Minister's official residence at Chequers, are RAF personnel from RAF Halton.

I was amazed when hearing the Prime Minister of the UK, reply to the Officer, stating,

"Ah! I was wondering why I keep losing my WRAF cooks, they keep getting pregnant you know, and I have to keep sending them to see you. Now I have solved the mystery. It was that bloody Corporal chef."

I could not believe that the Prime Minister, was having this conversation, making him as it should be. A very decent amusing human being...

The evening finally ended as her Majesty made her way to leave. Once she left the building, we proceeded to depart. We boarded an RAF coach which would take us back to the RAF Club. On leaving through the gates of Lancaster House, the Guard's sentry on duty presented arms as required. We could not help but notice the look of amazement on his face, on seeing so many very senior officers traveling by coach.

On the return journey to RAF Cosford, I was feeling very excited having helped celebrate the 50th Anniversary of the Royal Air Force. I felt truly thrilled and privileged to have shaken the hand of my Queen. The memory of that evening will always be with me, but at that time, my joy was short-lived. On returning home my wife had no wish to share with me the treasured memories of that wonderful evening. I think I knew at that moment my marriage was most definitely over.

Chapter 11

Entente Cordiale

The Royal Air Force No 2 School of Technical Training, was twinned with a similar French Air Force School based at BA 722 at Saintes, in the Charente Maritime Province, in southwest France. Regular exchange visits by staff and trainees were routinely carried out, and of course, were enjoyed by all.

Luckily, I found myself ordered to join one of these visits during the autumn of 1968. Along with other students, we flew in an RAF Andover aircraft from RAF Shawbury to the French Air Force base at Cognac.

After disembarking, we travelled by road to Saintes, courtesy of a French Airforce coach.

Once we arrived at the base, we were made extremely welcome. I thankfully found myself in a single comfortable room, with the same amenities as any RAF Officer is provided with in the UK. I must admit, I did appreciate the delicious French food on offer. We found the same hospitality was extended to us by the local townspeople, particularly in the shops.

From time to time, I would be seized by the hand which would then be shaken vigorously, along with repeated voluble thanks for the Allied liberation of France. I did not spoil the shopkeeper's obvious pleasure by revealing, I had been far too young to serve in WW2.

I was informed to my amazement, that French Officers are not provided with married quarters, either for themselves or their families on any base. I found this fact rather sad, as most Military personnel in all three services in the UK are offered married quarters.

The Base Commander, who went by the name of Colonel Berbier, insisted that all officers were to dine in the Officer's Mess at lunchtime. Continuous eating and drinking, followed by more drinking, usually took place until around 5 pm. Thus, ensuring each meal became a marathon event. Naturally, this in turn meant little or no work was carried out.

Colonel Berbier was a very charming man to all who knew him. During one afternoon session, while sitting next to me, he stated,

"Roy, if we fight alongside the RAF again, the RAF should bring the aircraft and guns. We, the French, will bring the food and wine."

I thought his remarks summed up the French attitude admirably.

Saintes, of course, is in wine country. Most weekends spent with French colleagues; I would enjoy particularly interesting outings. This was known as dégustation! We would drive around the vineyards in the local area, sampling their latest products. Limits on the amount of alcohol one was allowed to consume, were obviously more liberal in France than in the UK. Allowing one to drink and drive well over the legal requirement. Fortunately, often with a somewhat inebriated driver, we escaped without accident back to the base.

Prior to our departure, our host honoured us by laying on a splendid evening reception. As always with French food, it was superb, as was their wine. This in turn was followed by suitable music for dancing.

During the evening, I was approached by an attractive French Officer's wife, she was in fact very lovely indeed. Obviously, I was more delighted to keep her company for the evening. My dishonourable intentions were highly enhanced, as her delicious body was on display through her see-through shirt, and silk harem trousers. However, such intentions were very quickly destroyed, on finding out my company had only been sought to enable her to practice the English language. C'est la vie.

All too soon this delightful interlude came to an end. As the group and I prepared to return to RAF Cosford, we had a new appreciation of the French and their way of life.

Before returning home, we extended an invitation to our host, requesting they give us the pleasure of their company. An invitation they took up later in the year.

I can remember that reciprocal visit so clearly. During their visit, I had been given the pleasant task of escorting our visitors to the famous Wedgewood ceramic factory in Staffordshire.

On the journey there we had to cross a canal with recreational boats moored on the waterway.

My French was not as perfected back then as it is now, and so in limited French I informed the party that these boats were now used as,

"Un bateau de plaisir." (A boat of pleasure)

The French party leapt to their feet shouting,

"Magnifique! Arretez l'autobus, immediatement s'il vous plait." (Magnificent! Stop the boat, immediately please)

I had inadvertently described the boats as floating brothels. I should have said,

"Un bateau de pleasance." (A pleasure boat)

The reciprocal visit went well, and the French airmen

enjoyed their trip as we had in France.

Our return flight home was courtesy of the French Airforce in a Nord Atlas. We left Cognac for Birmingham hoping we had strengthened the Entente Cordiale.

Chapter 12

Change of Direction

During the late summer of 1971, I received a summons to report to the Ministry of Defence in London. As usual, one was not sure if this was to be for praise or a reprimand. On entering the imposing Ministry building, I was requested by a charming receptionist to go to a small room, which I thought looked very much like a Police interview room. The room was furnished with a rather tiny well-polished table, and two comfortable chairs.

Several minutes later, a senior officer entered the room. Under his arm was a large collection of pink files.

From previous experience, I recognized those files would contain confidential reports.

Unlike millions who work in civilian life, reports are written each year commenting on a military officer's performance.

As we exchanged pleasantries, the senior officer proceeded to take a seat at the small table, then cordially invited me to take one of the chairs opposite him.

Eventually to my relief, he informed me of the reason for my visit. Genially, he went on to explain that several officers were being shortlisted for promotion to Wing Commander. My excitement rose as he went on to say,

"Roy, running through your confidential reports, I detect that you do not suffer fools gladly."

Looking him straight in the eye, I replied,

"With respect Sir, I have no problem with fools. Unfortunately, it is the silly buggers that should know better, that I cannot stand." I then further stated,

"Sir, may I ask a question?"

With his affirmative answer, I went on to inquire,

"May I ask Sir; how many officers are you considering for promotion?" He replied.

"Sixty-four." I then asked,

"Sir, may I again inquire with respect, how many vacancies are there?"

The answer given was,

"Just two…"

I stood up, replaced my uniform hat, saluted, and asked permission to leave. Replying to his answer, I said,

"Sir, even If I was Jesus Christ, those odds on promotion are far too long." Looking at me astounded, he replied,

"Very well Roy, if that is how you feel." With that, I left the interview room.

Leaving the Ministry of Defence building, as you can imagine I felt somewhat rather disappointed. The following morning, having slept on the previous day's events, I made the momentous decision, that it was time to seek employment outside the Royal Air Force and see what the civilian world had to offer. A decision that changed my life, and career in no uncertain manner.

Setting a date for two years ahead, the year being1973. This would give me time to prepare my exit, from a life I had known and enjoyed for almost 30 years.

The Royal Air Force, like all military services, provides help and assistance for all personnel leaving the service. This service involves being given excellent advice, along with resettlement support, which personnel would require in their future everyday life. This service was designed naturally to ease their transition from military to civilian employment.

After the New Year, I was granted one day a week release from normal duties, enabling me to study at Wolverhampton Polytechnic, obtaining a Diploma in Management Studies, along with a Diploma in Advanced Business Studies.

Having achieved these qualifications, I would like now to try and obtain a Master's Degree. After some diligent research, and to my delight, I found out that if I attended Pennsylvania State University in America for one semester, (term) I could obtain a Master's Degree in Business Administration.

Obtaining the necessary permission from the RAF, and armed with a student visa, I found myself travelling to the States.

On the long-haul flight to Philadelphia, suddenly a strange thought crossed my mind. Had I not been married, how many lovely girls I may have met, or even found someone who would have healed the chasm of loneliness I now felt.

Pennsylvania State University was founded in 1855. The university claims to provide the same quality standard of education, as that obtained at Ivy League universities.

I attended Smeal College of Business on one of the 24 campuses. Luckily for me, I was provided with a single room of my own, probably due to my age, or being a Brit. I must admit to eating, or should I say overeating in the college dining facilities, as I loved American food.

Studies were not arduous and at a standard not higher than those experienced at Wolverhampton Polytechnic.

After the necessary three months, I said goodbye to

America, having accomplished what I came for. The Master's Degree in Business Administration would prove to be of great value to me in the future.

I returned to the UK later that year, flying into Birmingham with many mixed emotions. I continued my service at RAF Cosford, knowing with both excitement and trepidation, this would be my last year in the Royal Air Force.

1973 would be filled even further with certain emotions I do not normally succumb to.

As I went to attend my last dining-in night at the Officer's Mess, my thoughts reflected some sadness. This would indeed, be the last time I would have the opportunity of enjoying such an evening. After the dining out ceremony, which is an RAF tradition, I departed into the civilian world clutching an engraved silver tankard.

Having no idea what my future work life would provide, maybe it would make a difference to my married life. Only time would tell.

Chapter 13

Faux Pas

After almost thirty years as man and boy, having opted for premature retirement unable to find the legendary Air Marshall's baton in my knapsack. Their Lordship's and I agreed that we should part company.

During September, prior to the magic date of my departure from a life I had thoroughly enjoyed, my Sunday mornings were spent closeted with the appointments section of the Sunday Times. Replying to various jobs I quite fancied, was not as easy as I thought it would be.

Some 324 letters and several interviews later, my two-finger typing agony ended. To my delight, I was rewarded with a summons to attend an interview at the Foreign and Commonwealth Office in London.

The interview was to be held in another rather imposing edifice, situated in Grosvenor Gardens, London SW1. Apparently, this building had been the Free French headquarters of General de Gaulle and his staff during WW2. I had to smile, as the French it seems must have enjoyed the ancient toilet facilities that had not undergone modernisation in the following 30 years!

My interview took place in a large, elegant room.

Obviously not furnished according to normal Civil Service regulations. After the messenger escorted me into this room, I sat nervously at the end of an enormous, highly polished table; confronted by at least a dozen people. I realised later that some of those present did not manage to ask a single question!

The chairman was William Bell, CMG. Silver-haired and urbane (known irreverently, by his staff, as "Call me

God"). Bill had at one time, been the High Commissioner of some Caribbean Island or other. He may well have been Sir William, had not the British Government given his island independence before Queen Elizabeth could tap him on the shoulder with her sword.

The job I was hoping for; I did not expect to get. Principally because, after giving my explanation at some length, including the fact I regarded RAF Officers were required to be highly intelligent, far more qualified than Army infantry, or cavalry officers. Due to the excellent technical qualifications of other ranks in the RAF.

Bill Bell went on to remark dryly, he had been a Major in the Light Infantry! After this faux pas, I really thought the game was up.

I managed a weak smile and departed. To my utter amazement, a week later I was offered a position as a Principal Scientific Officer, in H.M. Civil Service.

My Royal Air Force salary doubled overnight, and I was also entitled to the Inner London Weighting Allowance... whatever that was. Sometime after that, the realisation hit me. I was about to enter a whole new world - "Civvy Street."

Back then as today, considering the salary I earned, purchasing a house in central London was out of the question. So, my search for a home had to be within a radius of thirty miles of the capital.

After a laborious search, I ended up purchasing a bungalow in Flitwick near Bedford.

Within a month while waiting in the rain at my local rail station for the 7.50 am service to St Pancras, I smiled to myself, realising I had joined the commuter brigade, complete with the morning newspaper and the obligatory umbrella. This journey, I carried out daily for the better part of the next four years. How I endured the torture of four hours of travel on British Rail, and then the London Underground, even to this day, I am still not quite sure.

I did though in my innocence, plan to use the time effectively. Having a moment of madness, I decided I would learn of all languages, Arabic. Plus, improve my knowledge by reading, and so on. Reality soon set in, the overcrowded, noisy commuter trains between Bedford, and St Pancras were full of sweaty (and often damp) bodies.

Frequently, I was deprived of a seat making these journeys quite horrendous. Suffice to say, that in the evenings on the return trek, I would scan the London Evening News in an attempt to do the "Quick" crossword. I would often fall asleep before half the journey was over.

I survived several one-day strikes, which Trade Unions and the staff of British Rail had perfected. Particularly, the go-slow weapon, along with other various tactics they would employ from time to time. Bringing chaos to the rail services, simply by strict adherence to the rule book. A railway guard had no problem inflicting pain and frustration, on his passengers. He would simply count the carriages, then go on to ensure that all couplings between each carriage were secure. All, of course, specified in his rule book. This often became common practice to leave home in the mornings, not knowing what time one would return home that evening.

Despite the daily horrors of rail travel, I must admit, I was pleased to leave behind my military career. Finding to my amazement I actually enjoyed my employment in the public sector as a Principal Scientific Officer, including being a member of H.M. Civil Service.

My duties involved the provision of advice to the Ministry of Overseas Development. This involved the identification of various projects, including the allocation of aid funds, to foreign and commonwealth countries.

My immediate boss was a Chief Scientific Officer. The two of us being responsible for aid projects worldwide.

With my new standard-issue briefcase, bearing the ER cypher. I felt ready to take on The World, or at least part of the Third World.

Naturally, as the new boy, I was given the less attractive parts, ending up with most of Africa as my geographical responsibility, along with all its problems. Before Africa, with my induction complete, came Gibraltar.

Chapter 14

Gibraltar

Just before Christmas, in December 1973, I flew to Gibraltar on my first solo assignment for H.M. Government, which would find me away from home for nearly a week.

I had been instructed to conduct an Industrial Training Survey of Gibraltar, better known as "The Rock."

Spain, as history tells us, had coveted this small territory of real estate that jutted out into the Mediterranean.

Spain, having lost Gibraltar in 1704, after owning it since 1502. The combined forces of the English and Dutch fleets captured it during the war of the Spanish Succession.

The acquisition was formalised by the Treaty of Peace of Utrecht in 1713, and Gibraltar was named a Crown Colony in 1830.

During 1964, the UK handed over complete control to the Government of Gibraltar. Spain contended that under the terms of the Peace Treaty of Utrecht, she should once again be given back the sovereignty over Gibraltar.

Relations with Spain, since the days of Elizabeth the First, had always been strained. This act by the British Government, further strained issues between the two countries...

A referendum was held in 1967. Gibraltarians voted overwhelmingly to remain under British rule.

Unfortunately, much to the embarrassment of H.M. Government, who would probably have not been too upset to once again hand over responsibility to Spain.

During the late sixties, the Spanish threatened, and finally closed the border between the colony and mainland

Spain. History reveals, that the British never actually closed their gates. These gates are of course situated on the narrow isthmus of land, connecting the two territories.

Each day, Gibraltarian officials duly went through the ceremony of opening, and closing the border, at dawn and dusk.

Despite the fact that nobody could enter Spain or leave it by that route. The only means possible for a person to enter Spain from Gibraltar was to take the ferry to Tangier in Morocco and disembark at Algeceiras port on mainland Spain. They would then have to return home the same way.

The closure of the frontier continued to be a problem. Unfortunately, this means that the Bay of Algeceiras, is seen as disputed territory. The practice for the Spanish Navy was to park an ancient WW2 aircraft carrier in the Bay of Gibraltar, to claim its waters for Spain.

The story continues, that in the face of this action, the Royal Navy would then board the carrier. Once onboard, a senior Officer would politely inform the captain that he had violated British territorial waters. Formalities completed, both parties would retire to the wardroom and consume copious quantities of Jerez sherry. The following month, a Royal Navy frigate, would then take up a similar position in the bay. The procedure would then be repeated, only this time with pink gin, replacing the Jerez sherry.

The Gibraltarians, have Moorish and Castilian roots. They are very proud and somewhat lazy! This is illustrated by the fact that before the gates were closed, some 5000 Spaniards crossed the border daily to work on The Rock.

The morning after the closure, Gibraltar awoke to find that the colony did not possess painters, welders, auto mechanics etc. Hence, my mission was to identify training needs and recommend methods of UK assistance.

To remedy the shortage of manpower, Gibraltar imported 3000 Moroccans to replace the 5000 Spaniards. The ratio may indicate the difference in productivity levels. 1980 saw an agreement being reached for re-opening the border.

This was delayed until 1981, due to the Prince and Princess of Wales having selected The Rock as the first stop of their honeymoon cruise in the Royal yacht Britannia.

A choice regarded as an affront by Spain. The border finally opened in February 1985, 16 years after its closure.

By 1974, at the time of my visit, Gibraltar's strategic position had lost its importance, and most of the British forces had left. An infantry battalion remained, its 600 personnel were left to assist the economy, rather than defend the place. The historic naval dockyard had at one time been the major source of employment. Sadly, it was now virtually closed. Ensuring the facility remained open, the Ministry of Defence periodically sent a frigate to be overhauled.

Leaving a wintry England, for what I hoped would be warmer climes once I reached Gibraltar. Flying out from Heathrow, on a Trident 111 aircraft belonging to British European Airways. The flight took 2 hours, 45 minutes.

Never having flown into Gibraltar, I was of course curious about the landing facilities. On our approach, I found it fascinating that the runway extends out into the Mediterranean. Another unusual feature is the fact the main road crosses the damn runway. A misjudged landing could mean passengers burning or drowning!

Traffic lights are required when aircraft are landing.

Delighted this does not happen at Heathrow.

Minister of Public Works met me, and who thank goodness, was a very pleasant man. He kindly took me to my accommodation at the Holiday Inn. My room had the most wonderful views of the town and harbour.

Gibraltar was almost like a time warp with its red Victorian mailboxes, old fashioned British telephone kiosks, and policemen still dressed like London "Bobbies." Main Street is the social concourse of the place. With its entire population, it seemed would stroll up and down its length in the evenings. Everyone knew everyone... and I dare say, were probably related.

As a guest of the Gibraltar Government, I was fortunate enough to visit interesting places which were no longer open to tourists. Until the 1920s, the water supply for the town had been a potage system. This system relied on the collection of rainwater. The rainwater being collected from one face of The Rock, then going on to be diverted into enormous limestone caverns, situated inside the apex of the Rock itself. The water being stored in large stone vats, then fed down to the town by gravity. No pumps were required for the process.

The system had been sufficient to meet the needs of the population until after WW2. After that date, and until the opening of the present desalination plant, water had been imported by sea.

Gibraltar has affectionately always been known as The Rock. There is more to The Rock than meets the eye.

There was a small railway across the apex of The Rock, which had been opened to tourists, but sadly is now closed for reasons of hygiene.

The base of The Rock surprisingly is also

honeycombed with tunnels. These are used by the military for storage purposes. One of my hosts was also a member of the Royal Naval Reserve. This gentleman provided me with access to such facilities. On one invitation he extended to me which I remember well, was to a convivial evening in the wardroom of HMS Rooke - the naval shore establishment.

Another privilege extended to me was to observe a session of the Gibraltar Parliament, which is naturally modelled on British lines.

This proved to be a very interesting episode, which I doubt would not happen in the British House of Commons. On witnessing an Honourable Member presenting budget estimates. When suddenly, he was interrupted by another Honourable Member. This member went on to suggest rudely that the arithmetic given out by the first member was wrong! I fell about laughing together with the rest of the members.

This type of rude behaviour is not it seems, limited to the Gibraltar Parliament, after having witnessed similar behaviour in the House of Commons, during the latest Brexit debates.

December 23rd. It was now time to depart as I was anxious to be home for Christmas. As we taxied away from the ramp in the British Airways Vanguard turboprop, I noticed from my window seat, a plume of fluid from one of the engines. My Royal Air Force background suggested the venting of fuel, came from an over-filled wing tank.

As we continued to taxi, the fluid continued to flow. I knew I had a dilemma. Over the years since leaving the Royal Air Force, I had cringed on numerous occasions. Especially when neurotic passengers had insisted that flight attendants inform the captain, that an engine was on fire, or about to drop off. I was saved as there came an announcement from the captain,

"Ladies and Gentlemen... we have a problem... we are returning to the terminal."

We spent the night in a hotel and were bussed back to the airport the following morning being Christmas Eve!

With the previous night's flight having been cancelled, there were now double the passengers for the daily aircraft. I could see Christmas on The Rock, staring me in the face.

Fortunately, (Rank hath its privilege) and with the assistance of a new friend, the Minister of Public Works, who just happened at that moment to be at the airport, came to my assistance. He thankfully had a word in the appropriate ear, and I was on the flight, bound for the UK.

With my report written and its recommendations accepted. I was now ready for further challenges to be given to me throughout the remnants of the British Empire.

Chapter 15

The Mountain Kingdom of Lesotho

After the Christmas break, like everyone else, I returned to work. Little did I realise that by the midsummer, I would be on my way to Africa. Once again, I would be unaccompanied, and perhaps a little nervous with this being my first trip to this vast continent that I knew so little about.

I left England, taking an evening flight from Heathrow onboard a British Airways Boeing 747. My destination for the first part of the journey was to be Nairobi. Having endured an eight-hour flight, our plane touched down at Eastleigh Airport. After a short transit stop, I flew on to Jan Smuts Airport Johannesburg.

I had to laugh to myself, it was like stepping back in time to Britain in the sixties. Female airport staff sported bouffant hairstyles and wore miniskirts, which I had not seen for ten years. South Africa's isolation, due unfortunately to its apartheid policies, was obviously having an effect on fashion if nothing else.

My destination was to be the tiny country of Lesotho. This mountain kingdom is the only country in the world, with all its territory at 1,000 metres above sea level. Formally, the British Protectorate of Basutoland. The kingdom is one of the few monarchies left in Africa, that is bordered on all sides by the Republic of South Africa.

After Britain resumed full control of the formally named, Cape Colony in 1884, subsequently re-named South Africa. Our government left the Basuto to themselves, assuming their eventual incorporation into South Africa. The Basuto rejected this, and such incorporation became impossible, after the introduction of apartheid in 1948. Full independence was finally achieved in 1966, after one hundred years of British rule.

Enabling me to make the final part of my journey. I flew out of Jan Smuts Airport, as a passenger on South African Airlines, to the small capital of Maseru, landing at Leabua Jonathan Airport. Maseru was certainly a one-horse town, appearing desperately in need of the United Kingdom's aid.

Once again, I found myself as a guest of the Holiday Inn, having been met by a Lesotho Government Official. Fortunately for me, this gentleman was most pleasant to talk to, easing the tension I first felt.

My mission was to identify possible U.K. aid projects and to do this, I needed to have various meetings with several Lesotho Government Agencies.

Ironically, despite the official opposition to apartheid, 20 percent of the Lesotho workforce, actually worked over the border in South Africa.

These so-called Remittance men were the main source of income for Lesotho. They contributed around $200,000,000, to the national economy. Some of the do-gooders, who preached anti-apartheid from a standpoint of ignorance, would find it difficult to accept, that all abled bodied-men in Lesotho, were not only grateful, but they were also delighted to obtain work in the Republic, whether this was considered exploitation or otherwise.

The South African State of Transvaal is adjacent to Lesotho. During weekends, a steady stream of Boers would cross the border to indulge themselves at the Holiday Inn Casino. Here they would purchase pornographic material and enjoy the pleasurable services of the local female populous. No doubt these activities were frowned upon by the Dutch Reform Church in South Africa.

Such was the volume of these activities, that the management of the Holiday Inn, made a practice of raising room rates at the weekends. Presumably, this practice continues today. After a mild altercation with the front desk, I was exempted from the additional surcharge.

During my stay, the advertised highlight was a performance of the rock musical Hair. This was staged by a combined American, and White South African cast. The musical had been a smash hit in London sometime previously, having raised eyebrows with its scenes of nudity.

On the night of its premiere that evening, the occasion was graced by the presence of His Majesty King Moshoeshoe ll. His Majesties Royal entourage also accompanied him.

At the end of the first act, the final scene saw the entire cast lined up on stage, hand in hand, and totally nude. To preserve dignity, the plan was to immediately dim all stage and auditorium lights.

Unfortunately, or fortunately, depending on one's personal point of view, the Lesotho electrician, confused no doubt by such a scene, switched on every floodlight and house light in the theatre. The King and his party, being seated on the front row of the stalls, were indeed treated to a full-frontal view of the 20 to 30 nubile nude bodies on the stage. There is no record of what his Majesty, or those who accompanied him that night thought.

On completion of my mission, having taken thirteen days, of which I was delighted about. The journey home was to prove more complicated. I departed from the Joseph

Leabua Johnson airport in Maseru, for Johannesburg, once again courtesy of South African airlines.

On arriving in Johannesburg, I transferred to an Air Malawi flight to Blantyre in Malawi. Followed by another flight, this time onboard a British Airways aircraft to Nairobi, and then annoyingly once more needing to change aircraft to fly home. Pleased to say, once having done so, there were no further problems, at least until reaching Heathrow.

Arriving back in London at three-thirty in the morning feeling totally exhausted, only to find I then had to queue for a taxi. I most certainly by then was looking forward to my bed and a decent night's sleep.

I had a passing thought, which reminded me of Dr Henry Kissinger, who was America's previous Secretary of State. Dr Kissinger commented on leaving Bangladesh, during one of his many diplomatic shuttles around the world. Remarking this country has no apparent military, political, or economic significance.

Lesotho, although a very pleasant place, was obviously very much like Bangladesh. However, UK aid would be welcome in the near future.

Chapter 16

Swaziland

Less than one year after visiting Lesotho, I was once again onboard a British Airways aircraft. Only this time, to find myself heading south once again to Johannesburg. The difference in this journey was to take me en route to the independent monarchy of Swaziland, which geographically adjoins Mozambique in southeast Africa.

On this occasion, I was accompanied by George Gee. George was a Senior Training Adviser from the United Kingdom's Road Industry Training Board (RITB).

Our mission was to evaluate the Swazi Government's Central Transport Organisation (CTO) and recommend possible UK aid.

With an estimated population of 800,000, Swaziland had gained full independence in 1968, with King Sobhuza II as its Head of State.

Two years prior to our visit, the King had suspended the constitution and banned all political activity. I suppose if you are a King, all is possible.

After an overnight stay in Johannesburg, which was most welcome, we then took a 70-minute flight by Air Botswana, after which we were deposited at Manzini Airport. This airport served Mbabane, the principal town and administrative centre of Swaziland.

The town's limited entertainment included an ancient cinema that was open all hours. During our visit, it was showing (continuously) "A Clockwork Orange". A film which had shocked and been banned by several town councils in the UK.

In the 1960s, the view on what constituted

pornography was rather different to the present day.

Our survey of the CTO occupied us for the next week. The CTO was much as we had anticipated and was typical of similar organisations in the Third World. Facilities and systems were ancient, or non-existent.

The fleet of decaying vehicles was unbelievable, as was the diversity of manufacturers and models represented. No two were the same, and the provision of spares and servicing was proving an impossible task. The terms rationalisation, and standardisation, figured prominently in our report to our masters in the Foreign Office in London.

To our delight, we managed to enjoy some sightseeing, in what is a very pleasant and green country. The climate of Swaziland supports sugarcane, cotton, citrus fruits, and pineapples. Visiting a small town on the Mozambique border, we enjoyed the largest king prawns I had ever seen. George, who was to fly home direct to London, bought an enormous bag of avocado for the princely sum of 50 pence. Hoping he would not be contravening import regulations on arrival at Heathrow.

Before leaving London, it had been decided that I should return via Malawi, which would give me the opportunity to familiarise myself when I visited that country.

Twelve days after our arrival in Swaziland, I departed Jan Smuts Airport in Johannesburg, for Chileka Airport, Malawi.

All was going far too well, until 30 minutes after take-off, our captain announced a diversion to Salisbury in Southern Rhodesia, (Now called Zimbabwe) had to be made. This was due to the closure of the airport in Malawi.

Apparently, Dr Hastings Banda who was the President of Malawi was returning home after a visit to the UK, and Chileka was closed for security reasons.

I was somewhat nervous!

Presumably, I would only be in transit for a very short time. Should things go wrong, I could plead it was only an emergency. Nothing untoward thank goodness happened in the airport lounge, and once again I was able to breathe more easily.

During 1965, Southern Rhodesia had declared unilateral independence (illegally) from Britain. Relations between the two countries were strained to say the least. Visits to Salisbury, or Harare as it became by UK Government officials, were not exactly welcomed.

As things turned out, this was to prove to be a disastrous decision by the former Prime Minister, Ian Smith. Both politically and economically, with thousands of people eventually murdered under the regime of Robert Mugabe.

Copper was a major product of the country. I ventured into the souvenir shop with every intention of buying a copper jug. Unfortunately, only to find that I did not have sufficient local currency. I was considering my problem, and about to abandon the purchase, when a dear old lady handed me the required amount, saying,

"Never mind the politicians.... we are still friends."

Bless her!

After a further 35-minute flight, I made it to Malawi without provoking a major diplomatic incident. Dr Banda's entourage had by this time departed the airport. The celebrations continued led by his personal bodyguards.

These were a large body of ladies. The operative word

being "large". They all wore the standard African mama's headdress and matching cotton dresses, printed on them was Banda's portrait. Although unarmed, one would not wish to argue with them!

The journey into the capital, Lilongwe, was uneventful. The High Commission's official did warn me not to say anything derogatory or otherwise in front of the driver. Sensible advice I adhered to.

Five days of familiarisation now over, I was airborne once again and heading home via Nairobi. The excitement was not quite over, as we annoyingly had to divert to Rome, due to mechanical problems. After the Italian ground crew solved the issue, we arrived home into a very murky Heathrow, with the cloud base below 500 feet. I had survived another three weeks in darkest Africa, only to return to darkest England.

Chapter 17

South American Adventure

My first visit to Central and South America took place in July 1975. I flew with Air France to Mexico City, on a somewhat circuitous route from London, via Paris and Houston, Texas.

Charles de Gaulle airport may look futuristic, being very modern in design, and although aesthetically and architecturally pleasing, I am afraid to say, it is an awful international airport. Should it have to cope with the volume of passengers handled by Heathrow, or Chicago's O'Hare, it would simply stop working.

Attempting to board the flight to Houston was a nightmare. Air France's passengers were boarding several Boeing 747 "Jumbo" jets through one small security gateway. Given our European neighbours' refusal to queue anywhere, total chaos reigned. A loud and noisy German basketball team made matters infinitely worse. The Krauts, all more than 2 metres tall, forced aside diminutive Frenchmen, enabling them to gain entry first. Had I not been a Diplomat, I would have reminded them who had won two world wars!

Apart from a technical fault that delayed departure from Texas, the flight to Mexico City was uneventful having taken over twelve hours.

The next day, I boarded a very small Hawker Siddeley HS248 aircraft, of AEROMEXICO. This was for a short internal flight to Lazaro Cardenas via Uruapan in southeast Mexico. My final destination was Las Truchas south of Acapulco, on the Pacific coast. There, H.M. Government were considering aid to a steel producing facility.

Las Truchas itself was nothing more than a small shanty town with inhabitants living in abject poverty. It seemed to me that a new steel mill for the state-owned organisation SICARTSA would do little to alleviate the suffering of the locals.

Thank goodness I did not have the need to stay overnight, taking a return flight back to Mexico City late that evening. Thinking back, maybe I should have stayed, as the return flight became a nightmare.

Heavy tropical storms are normal in the rainy season, and the small aircraft we were flying in was tossed around the sky. Allowing us to gaze at the spectacular display of lightning, accompanied with a crescendo of thunder, all of which added to the uncomfortable ride. Several of the passengers turned an interesting shade of green. To make matters worse, our destination was a small grass airfield, which had minimal airfield lighting and elementary landing aids. With visibility down to a minimum, it was certainly by "Guess and God" that we made it down to earth in one piece.

Little did I realise, that the remainder of my trip would go on to get even worse! The next morning, I presented myself at Mexico City airport, for the flight to Miami in Florida. I would then need to change aircraft and take another flight for the onward journey to Brazil.

As I made my way to the Aeroméxico check-in desk, 50 or so would-be passengers were milling around the counter. Besides all the shouting, and to my amazement, they were all waving money. With commendable British patience, I waited for the scrum to subside. I was enlightened by my host, who went on to explain that the flight was (as normal) overbooked. Hence the punters waving pesos and US dollars. Taking on board his wise advice, and minus $20, I finally boarded the DC 10. Collapsing with relief into my business class seat and happily clutching a gin and tonic. Such are the vagaries of air travel in Central America.

The USA was a most welcome sight, at least until I reached an Immigration desk. US Customs and Immigration officials are amongst the rudest in the world; particularly to US citizens, which I suppose is some comfort. With the required deference, I handed over my British passport.

My polite "Good Morning," was totally ignored. At this point, I should mention that prior to my departure as was routine, I had enquired of my Office Manager about visa requirements for this trip. He was adamant that I did not need one for the USA, and in any case, I was only in transit in Miami. He could not have been more wrong!

With a resigned look; no doubt as a result of dealing with many visa-less morons; the vastly overweight US Immigration Officer growled, as he informed me,

"You ain't gotta visa."

My feeble explanation about being British, and not requiring a visa etc, was cut short. His reply was,

"Stand over there," he said.

I stood over there... Then found myself joined by a very large Deputy Sheriff, complete with Stetson and the biggest Colt 45 revolver I had seen outside the movies. At that moment I thought to myself, shame I did not have my 0.38 revolver I sometimes carried on operations. Realisation was swiftly followed by panic. I had been arrested!

My new gum-chewing friend was a little short on

conversation as he escorted me to my embarrassment, through the busy airport concourse to a detention room. Fortunately, I was only detained for a few short hours. The large lawman never left my side, even accompanying me to the men's room. At the appointed time I was taken to the aircraft, my passport and I were then handed over to a member of the cabin crew. I could not wait to board my onward flight to Brazil and could barely believe I was actually being deported! My thoughts on what I would say to a certain Office Manager on my return to London must remain censored.

Once having left Miami, the flight south to Brasilia was thank goodness uneventful allowing me a couple of hours to unwind.

On my arrival in Brazil, it was still daylight. Sitting in the back of the taxi, gave me a chance to observe the city which I was not impressed with. The new capital of Brasilia, like all "artificial" capitals, was faceless; lacking in character and appeared to have been designed only for motor vehicles with no thought for pedestrians. Such was the attraction of the place, that most of its residents joined a mass exodus for the fleshpots of Rio at the weekends.

As demanded by Foreign Office protocol, I made the required visit to the British Embassy, there to present myself to His Excellency the British Ambassador. A very friendly First Secretary informed me that he, meaning the Ambassador, was still in Rio and promptly invited me to a cocktail party. The next morning, after completing my briefing with Brazilian officials on possible aid schemes, I departed (somewhat hungover) for Sao Paulo in a Lockheed "Electra" aircraft, which has a dubious safety record.

I should have realised after the events in Miami, that this trip was not going well!

His Excellency, on his return from Rio, was annoyed that I had not waited for him and promptly sent a strongly worded telegram to London. He decided to complain of my apparent disregard for Foreign Office protocol. My boss, William Bell CMG was not best pleased, resulting in me receiving an earful on my return. I was told in a rather forceful fashion that a mere Principal Scientific Officer does not upset Her Majesty's Ambassadors.

Sao Paulo is in a natural hollow surrounded by mountains. The domestic airport has a frightening approach, which involves climbing above local buildings and then landing on a raised runway. The city boasts some of the worst pollution in the world, pedestrians needing to wear surgical masks in the same fashion as the Japanese do in Tokyo.

After discussions with senior officials regarding the funding for a UK consultancy with SIDERBRAS, which is the state-owned shipbuilding organisation. I was glad to leave for the flight to Rio. The flight was an aviation thrill in an ancient Lockheed Electra, whose safety record makes the Russian Airline – AEROFLOT – look like one of the safest in the world!

My first night in Rio was spent in the salubrious hotel Ouro Verde. I was hoping for a quiet evening despite the persistent attention of a posse of very attractive prostitutes in the foyer.

As the hotel overlooked the world-famous Copacabana Beach, the view was indeed stunning, enabling one to admire the barely clad golden bronzed females cavorting on the beach. Making any healthy man's blood pressure rise, though unfortunately that first evening I was much too tired…

However, at the rear of the hotel, were the worse slums I had seen outside Africa and India. I wondered how many of those beautiful women came from the filthy shantytown.

Regardless of staying in a luxury hotel and having beautiful women to constantly gaze at. I must admit, I was glad to see the end of this eventful mission and totally relieved to board a Brazilian Boeing 707 for the flight to London via Lisbon. 12 hours later, I delighted in conveying to my Office Manager about his illegitimacy! Perhaps further missions to the Americas would be less eventful and there might be a new Ambassador in Brasilia…

Chapter 18

Green Monkey Disease

The film The Four Feathers had been a great favourite of mine having watched it many times as a teenage boy. The film of course was set in Sudan. Based on true facts of 1882, during the British Army's action against Muhammad Ahmad. He was the self-proclaimed Mad Mahdi by his fanatical followers, known as Dervishes. The Mahdi, according to Muslim tradition, is a person who is divinely guided. He believes he will restore justice on earth and establish a Universal Islam.

The Dervishes won successive victories. Eventually, they besieged Khartoum, the capital of Sudan. The British commander at that time, General Gordon, withstood the siege for ten months until finally, the Mahdi's forces entered Khartoum. Once having done so, they massacred both General Gordon and the entire Anglo Egyptian garrison.

On a miserable grey morning in November 1976, I boarded a British Airways aircraft on a direct flight from London Heathrow to the Republic of Sudan. Little did I realise that I would stand on the bank of the river Nile near the confluence where the Blue Nile, coming from Ethiopia, and the White Nile, coming from Lake Victoria meet. The Nile then flows northwards to Egypt, and ultimately to the Mediterranean.

Evidence of family photographs shows my stepfather had also stood on the same spot fifty years previously, during his service with the Royal Air Force. No doubt a promising trip lay ahead of me.

Sudan is divided into three natural regions. These

range from the desert in the north, through vast semi-arid steppes and low mountains, in central Sudan. To the south lay swamps, and rain forests. These regional contrasts are mirrored by its population. Consisting of Arabs in the north, and Africans in the south. I was to have the privilege of seeing most of these areas during the following two weeks.

During my stay, I took the opportunity to visit the imposing White Palace, which General Gordon occupied as Governor. The Palace is situated on the banks of the River Nile. History tells us, General Gordon was hacked to death on a staircase in the northwest part of his palace. As I stood on this infamous staircase, the thought of, "could I possibly be standing on the very spot that General Gordon had lost his life?" crossed my mind.

Khartoum was eventually recaptured by a British expeditionary force at the Battle of Omdurman. This force was led by General Lord Kitchener in 1898. Khartoum was the capital of the Anglo Egyptian Sudan, until 1956. Later becoming the capital of the newly independent Republic of Sudan.

My first journey outside the capital was delayed due to a countrywide lack of petrol. At the time, Sudan was an impoverished country with almost nil economic growth. President Nimeiry had first seized power with the Army in 1969. He had initially turned to the USSR, along with Libya for support. The honeymoon turned sour, when an attempted coup in 1976, allegedly backed by Libya failed. This prompted a new approach for aid from Egypt, including various Arab States and the West.

The British Government had been a major aid donor to that country for many years. My mission was to discuss possible new aid projects, specifically, for the southern region of the country.

Fuel shortages were an accepted part of life in Khartoum. Citizens would commence queuing at filling stations, anticipating the arrival of fuel. Desperate motorists would leave their vehicles in queues, which were often many kilometres long. Government vehicles naturally had priority, which meant that once fuel arrived in Khartoum, I was able to leave and commence my tour.

The town of El Obeid was to be my first stopping off point for a few hours. This town in Kordofan Province was reputedly the place from which the Mahdi commenced his march on Khartoum.

Like most people who travel overseas, I had a weak spot and loved buying souvenirs to add to my collection. Taking the opportunity so few people are afforded, I visited the local bazaar and strolling through it, I came across an enterprising trader who went on to sell me a couple of birds carved from horn. His story went, that an inmate in the local prison awaiting execution on death row, had carved the items. True or not, it added a novel twist making it a good story and allowing him to add a few piastres to the price.

The second purchase was an Ostrich egg. This overly large egg had been hand-painted with scenes of rural Kordofan. Not your usual gift from Frinton on Sea!

Leaving El Obeid delighted with my purchases, I returned to Khartoum. Having been booked into the Khartoum Club, which by now was a faded and decaying relic of colonial times. My parting memory of the place besides that of a hovel was the expatriates at a weekly Scottish dancing class. I find myself smiling when thinking about them performing their strange rituals by the swimming pool in temperatures approaching thirty-five degrees. Noel Coward's famous song came to mind,

"Only mad dogs and Englishman go out in the midday sun."

A Boeing 737 of Sudan Airways, named White Nile, flew me to the city of Wadi Madani, en route to southern Sudan.

Cynical ex-patriates have labelled the airline as the White-Knuckle Airline. A reference to its terrified passengers gripping armrests and producing the bloodless knuckles. The 737, is also the personal transport of the President.

Disruption of airline schedules was often common when he called for its services. Another irreverent tag is the IBM airline. This is derived from the Arabic Words Inshallah, Bukra and Mallish. Which loosely translated means, God Willing. Tomorrow and maybe.

On reaching Madani without incident, or interference from the President, the city was and still is, the headquarters of the Sudanese Irrigation Organization. The city is also the centre of the Aljazirah region, and its Gezira Project.

The latter is something akin to the famous Tennessee Valley Scheme in America. The Gezira Project commenced in 1925 and was part-financed by the British Government. This project is one of the largest in the world and has made the desert bloom in no uncertain fashion. This scheme included two huge dams, along with a vast network of canals and ditches which are fed by gravity and has brought over one million hectares of desert into cultivation. The main crop surprisingly being cotton. Not just any cotton, it produces the finest cotton in the world, known as Egyptian cotton.

My hotel - the only hotel - if that is what one could have called it, was situated on the banks of the Nile, and did not have the luxury of air conditioning.

On the one night I stayed there, I decided to move my bed out onto the balcony to spend the night under the stars in a cooler temperature. To my immense misfortune, I found myself sharing the night air with a million or so mosquitoes and other assorted nameless bugs.

The next morning, after covering myself in calamine lotion, turning my body into a pretty shade of pink, I flew onto the city of Juba in Equatoria Province, which is adjacent to the border with Uganda.

Sudan had the misfortune to endure a civil war from 1955 until 1972. The southern African population feared dominance from the northern Muslims.

President Nimeiry had ended the war in 1972 and had granted the south a measure of autonomy. Unfortunately, the conflict flared again in 1983. Due, this time, to the Sudanese Government's attempt to impose Islamic Law over the entire country. At least on this mission, I was not about to enter another war zone, however, there were other problems.

During the months prior to my visit, a mysterious fever had claimed many lives, not only in Equatoria Province but in Zaire itself.

The estimated number of casualties at that time was around 300 people. The exact number would never be known, as many of the victims had fled back to their remote villages or simply died in the jungle.

Until formally identified, the outbreak had been

given the name, Green Monkey Disease.

The reference to monkeys is unclear, based upon an early theory that the virus was animal-borne. Very much the same theory in regard to the Aids virus many years later.

My destination was to be Juba, staying at the Juba Regency Hotel. Regrettably, it had been quarantined for several weeks. The ban on movements both in and out of the city had only been lifted a week prior to my visit. By the time of my arrival, research establishments in Atlanta, in the United States of America, and Porton Down, in England, I am pleased to say had fortunately identified the virus as Marburg Fever.

The latter was one of several rare fevers, which were identified in 1970. This list also included Lassa fever, Ebola, Bunya and Chikungunya fevers. All of these fevers are found predominately in tropical regions. Sadly, back in 1976, there were few antidotes.

The nature of these fevers caused a person to die by massive haemorrhaging from their internal organs. In other words, one literally drowns to death, in one's own blood.

After weeks of isolation, Juba had become vile. The city was utterly filthy to see and sickening to one's nose. To say I felt uneasy, was the understatement of the year. Over the next few days, I met with officials at the British Consulate to discuss possible aid requirements. Talks concluded; I was greatly relieved to return to civilization. Boarding an aircraft belonging to Sudan Airways, I returned to Khartoum.

The next place on my itinerary was Port Sudan on the Red Sea coast. Port Sudan is 70 minutes flying time from the capital. The return journey eventually proved somewhat longer. I should have known that omens were not good.

After completing my tour of the water purification plants, I returned to the local airport for the early evening flight back to Khartoum. By the time I should have boarded the planned flight, the Boeing 737 White Nile was ominously nowhere to be seen. The answer to my obvious question as to where the aircraft was, revealed that the aircraft had been commandeered by the President. The aircraft was still in Saudi Arabia, which is situated just across the Red Sea.

The Haj, which is a religious pilgrimage to Mecca, takes place once a year and had come to an end. All able-bodied Muslims are required to make the pilgrimage at least once in their lifetime. The President had decided to use the White Nile, in helping the vast number of pilgrims return home. Many returning to Sudan from Jeddah.

The White Nile landed and took off repeatedly for the following eight hours as we sweated it out in the small airport, which naturally had no air conditioning.

Almost ten hours behind schedule, I finally departed from Port Sudan, arriving in Khartoum at some obscene hour in the morning.

Fourteen days after leaving London, I returned on a miserable grey day, worse than the one I had left. As the British airways VC 10, came to a standstill, over the tannoy came an announcement from the captain of the aircraft. His voice very clearly stated,

"Will Mr Roy Harrington-Brown make himself known to a member of the cabin crew and prepare to leave the aircraft first."

At last! Recognition for my services to H.M.

Government. My euphoria was short-lived. As the plane door opened and stepping onto the ramp, I was seized by a very large Irish nursing sister. This very well-proportioned lady hauled me off to the Medical Centre in the bowels of Terminal Three.

After routine tests, there was no sign of the Green Monkey Disease. Having thankfully been given the all-clear, my blood pressure returned to normal. I was then released, but only after having been given strict instructions to contact my local Department of Health in Bedford.

The next day, the local medical officer telephoned me. He was an excitable Indian doctor, who it turned out I am convinced, envisaged medical fame with his first-ever Marburg Fever victim.

I was ordered to contact him every day for the following month. He stated quite clearly, I was to report any variation in my temperature or condition. I sensed the disappointment in his voice after I failed to produce any symptoms of the dreaded disease. Sadly, for him, the planned article he had in mind on the disease for the British Medical Journal, would never be published.

Reminiscing about this chapter of my life, in particular of Khartoum, brought back memories once again of my dear friend and colleague Dennis Brooks.

I remember during one of his overseas postings, Dennis found himself serving in Aden, with a Maritime Reconnaissance Squadron. Dennis at that time was the Captain of a Shackleton Mk 2 aircraft.

During the Queen's South African visit, Dennis was scheduled to operate a security patrol, over the route of the Royal aircraft.

Unfortunately, the Shackleton aircraft he was flying,

lost one of its four engines over the African coast.

His aircraft had to make an emergency landing at Khartoum. A replacement engine was flown out from the UK, enabling an engine change. Dennis and his crew performed an amazing engineering feat. They did this using minimum tools, along with inappropriate ground equipment in temperatures exceeding 100 degrees. Once this task had been completed the aircraft was able to return to Aden. After his RAF service, Dennis became Training Captain for Air UK.

Chapter 19

An Indian Affair

1976 had been a very busy year. At the beginning having returned after the Christmas break, H.M. Government had made the decision to aid the development of a shipyard and dry dock facilities at Cochin in southern India.

Excited at the prospect of returning to the sub-continent, only this time instead of Pakistan, I was to travel to India.

My boss at that time was a gentleman named Leslie Kemp. Leslie had been born and bred in London. By the time I joined the Foreign Office, he had achieved the position of Senior Principal Scientific Officer, having spent most of his working life in Kenya and was not your typical Civil Servant. He had, unfortunately, a strident Cockney accent, with an attitude to non-Brits, honed by innumerable years of working in Africa.

Leslie had decided he would like my company and politely stated, I would be accompanying him without giving me the choice.

Our flight to India meant we would be going via Tehran and would take the best part of seven hours. Eventually landing at Palam Airport New Delhi.

With 16 percent of the world's population inhabiting this continent, on my arrival I found it to be exceedingly noisy, certainly unpleasantly smelly, and naturally very overcrowded.

New Delhi surprised me by being one of the cleaner cities, poverty is less apparent there than in such places as Calcutta or Bombay. Even so, the collection of cardboard boxes at the side of the road from the airport, unfortunately, had become home for several families as was the norm.

The taxi Leslie and I shared, was the Hindustan model, based on the British Morris Oxford design of the 1950s, and still manufactured in India today. Amongst the traffic, I spotted several motorcyclists riding Royal Enfield 500cc Bullets.. which I believe are still produced locally, already I was knee-deep in nostalgia!

Reaching relative civilisation, by at last checking into the Sheraton Hotel. I had so far survived the pollution and traffic antics seen only in India. Leslie decided tea was required. Gin and tonic are permitted in the British Empire, (or ex- British Empire only after sunset) Lesley summoned a turbaned waiter, who enquired,

"Would Sahib prefer Darjeeling, or Earl Grey tea, or......?"

Leslie stopped him in his tracks by stating,

"No... I would like coffee, none of your silly decaffeinated stuff .... Nescafé is what I like."

While listening to his strident cockney tones, I found myself cringing. Our waiter bowed deferentially and disappeared. After several embarrassing minutes, the waiter reappeared, bearing a magnificent silver salver. The salver contained; a beautiful silver teapot, together with two bone China teacups, and a jar of bloody Nescafé. Together with the teacups, there was a newly opened tin of condensed milk. I collapsed in a fit of giggles when Leslie then stated with a straight face,

"One doesn't get this service at home anymore."

On our second night there, the High Commission invited us to a reception. I had undergone this social ritual many times in the Royal Air Force. One enters, collects a drink, and circulates; naturally exchanging pleasantries and inane small talk. After a couple of hours, you begin suffering acute cocktail legs and would kill to sit down. This is most certainly not allowed, and one must suffer pain by remaining to stand until such time the senior guest has left.

The Diplomatic Service is probably even worse than the Royal Air Force, especially when it comes to its rank-conscious wives. They were out in full force that evening. Delhi, being high on the list of posts should they wished their husband to aspire promotion to Paris, or Bonn. I was introduced to one such female. Her first words of conversation were,

"And what grade are you?"

She left hurriedly when I attempted to say, "Principal..."

I learned later that her husband was a Clerical Officer, which unfortunately placed him well below me in the pecking order of things.

The following day, Leslie and I officially presented ourselves to the High Commission. There, we would be given a briefing for our long trip south to Kerala State, and the State Capital of Cochin, situated in southern India. On leaving the High Commission, Leslie summed up our treatment, by a rather patronising First Secretary, when he stated,

"I don't think any of the bastards have even been to Cochin."

The following morning, I awoke in acute pain with the dreaded realisation that India, (as expected) had got to my bowels, and an attack of "Delhi Belly" was imminent. Panic ensued, as we were due to fly south, changing flights at Bombay. The day would now require detailed planning. Enthroned in the bathroom, I considered the situation carefully. Breakfast was of course out of the question, with the necessity of having to remain within easy reach of facilities. Having had the foresight to bring certain types of medication with me, especially including my bung up pills to help one's bowels, I decided that the 20-minute trip to the airport was possible, given the present frequency of visits to the ceramic throne. Toilets would be available at the airport. Once airborne, I hoped all would be well until we reached Bombay.

All went according to plan, even though our arrival at Santa Cruz Airport was late. That is until the necessity of requiring the bathroom came to the forefront. Had the Olympic coach been present and seen me sprinting through the transit lounge in search of facilities, including pushing aside several gentlemen in my eagerness to reach a cubicle, he may well have chosen me for the British team.

The facility was in eastern design, where one squats over a ceramic hole, rather than that of a western toilet, this did not concern me at that instant. However, on the completion of one's actions, using water rather than conventional toilet paper to ensure one's bottom was respectable, did cause various problems.

Airborne once again, this time with Indian Airlines, I was able to relax, hoping by the time we landed in Cochin, my bowels would be relatively stable. Keeping my fingers crossed, I had generated sufficient antibodies to avoid such excitement on the return trip!

On my arrival in Cochin, I was surprised to find how beautiful the city is. There are palm trees everywhere, also a great many canals feeding picturesque lagoons.

Kerala State is one of the richest states in India. Known for producing tea, rubber, and spices, it is also known as a progressive state, having the highest literacy rate in the sub-continent. The city of Cochin, being at the southernmost tip of India, has over history been visited by many explorers heading east. Evidence remains allowing us to see the occupation by several of these nationalities including Romans, Greeks, Arabs, Dutch, and French. Even to this day, there is a tabernacle still in use for worship by the tiny Jewish community.

The Malabar coast is the Spice Coast of India. I had the privilege of wandering around the city, marvelling at the smells permeating from warehouses that were situated on the waterfront. These warehouses contained every spice imaginable. I must admit, I had never seen such quantities anywhere during my travels from that day to this. My previous experience of such things, having been limited to small jars of delicious spices on the local supermarket shelf.

Due to its parlous economy at that time, having suffered increases in oil prices and an overabundance of coal. India had mothballed its diesel railway locomotives and had returned to steam. As a bit of a transport freak, I took the opportunity to visit Cochin railway station and engine yards. There, I found huge steam locomotives, normally associated with the heyday of steam in the United States. As a non-aficionado, I cannot recall the wheel combinations; by which steam enthusiasts classify these huge beasts. Figures like 4-10-0, (which identify the number of huge driving wheels) came to mind.

Cochin is the southern terminus of such steam exotica as the Madras Mail, it is here these monsters are fed and watered. Modern steam technology meets ancient material handling techniques. The coaling of the locomotive involves a team of ladies with wicker baskets full of coal, amazingly balanced on their heads.

Remarkably, their job consists of climbing a flimsy wooden ladder, enabling them to tip coal into the tender, returning down a second equally unsafe ladder to the ground. Labour overheads were obviously minimal!

Over the weekend, our hosts at the High Commission insisted that we visit a guest house in the mountains. We drove for hours over what can only be described as appalling roads, hoping they would eventually take us to a government bungalow in the Periyar National Park.

Once we arrived at the bungalow and had taken a quick look around, although clean, it provided the hardest bed I had ever slept on. Adding insult to injury, we were awakened at 4 am to make a trip that had been organised for us.

We had been informed a safari boat trip had been organised, this was to visit Lake Periyar. One we hoped would turn out to be enjoyable, after having been woken up so early. The lake and the national park supported thirty-three species of wildlife. Consisting of I was told of various animals including wild boar, tigers and elephants, also a number of exotic birds. Unfortunately, we did not see a single animal or bird!

As its latest visitors, it mattered not, as Leslie and I were not sufficiently awake to spot them regardless. Despite our host's obvious embarrassment, we thoroughly enjoyed the trip and were pleased to return safely to Cochin.

The following day we visited the Cochin proposed dry dock and shipyard development, both were very interesting projects. Our visit was intended to give us the opportunity to see the progress that we hoped was steadily being made. The whole thing was being funded by the Ministry of Overseas Development.

Progress was adequate, my only concern was that the labour productivity figures had been based on Japanese work ethics. Somehow in my estimation, and with my experience of Indian workers, I felt the figures given were not realistic.

They had been asked to produce cost estimates, labour requirements, construction timescale along with giving an undertaking of a completion date. The figures provided were of course based on other projects the Japanese had previously undertaken. Returning to London, we made our opinion very clearly known.

Our stay in Cochin was to last for nine days until it was time to return to Bombay. By then I am delighted to say, the bowels were now stabilised.

The next stop on our itinerary was to fly to Delhi, then on to Tehran. We boarded an Air India 747. As the aircraft lumbered onto the departure runway, going on to accelerate into its take-off run. As usual, I was mentally checking our progress. Speed V1 is the point in a take-off where the pilot pulls the aircraft up off its nose wheel, quickly followed by rotation at speed V2. Which at that speed the aircraft leaves the ground. Abruptly, the whine of the turbines decreased, and we slowed down rapidly.

The captain informed us that we had struck another damn bird... quite a large one! Probably a Kite Hawk (or in the vernacular of British troops a "Shite Hawk!") The bird had been most unobliging, apart from making a mess of the radome. This being the circular cover on the nose of the 747, which protected the weather radar. The bird was still spread-eagled on the nose! There was no other alternative than to return to the ramp, remove the bird and inspect for damage. I said a silent prayer, hoping that the damage inflicted by the bird was not serious. At least not serious enough to impair the aerodynamics and delay us further.

My hopes were swiftly dashed. We were de-planed into Bombay Airport's transit lounge. The place was dimly lit, the air-conditioning had failed, and to make matters worse, there were no refreshments available.

The toilets were indescribable. Bombay Airport is unlikely to be voted as "Airport of the Year." I watched the proceedings from a window in the lounge. The bird and the damaged radome were removed quite quickly by the engineering staff of Air India. Within a matter of three hours, the replacement had been fitted, or almost...they managed to fit the blasted thing upside down!

I will draw a veil over the next four hours spent in that dreadful place. Suffice to say, that seven hours later, we were once again on the runway, and I fervently hoped that darkness had grounded all the bloody shite hawks at Bombay International Airport. Or at least those who lived around runway 28R.

1996, Air India reported a trading loss of many millions. Maybe bird scarers at Bombay might decrease the consumption of Boeing 747 radomes. It is unlikely that further economies could be made in facilities in the transit lounge.

A four-hour flight with British Airways took us from Delhi, and then on to Tehran where we stayed the night. I was thankful that in those days we were treated in a civilised manner. I doubt sadly the same thing would happen today. The day after we flew from Tehran to Tabriz, boarding an aircraft belonging to Iran Air.

Our mission there was to investigate the possibility of UK aid to assist in the development of a vocational training centre, in the northern city of Tabriz. Plans had been agreed that the centre would be built on a cold windswept hillside outside the city. Construction was for the Imperial Organisation of Social Services. After a visit in sub-zero temperatures, we flew back to Tehran.

The Patron of the Imperial Organisation was none other than the sister of the Shah. The Shah, Muhammed Reza Pahlavi, was still on the Peacock throne at the time of our visit. The monarchy having been restored in 1953, with the aid of the United States. He was formally crowned in 1967, after tragically having divorced his first wife whom he loved desperately, and sadly having no option but to remarry. Thus, enabling him to produce the male heir required...

He remained as Shah until 1978. Riots by then were being orchestrated by a Muslim cleric, who was exiled in France. The cleric in question went by the name of Ayatollah Ruhollah Khomeini, considered to be one of the most evil men in history. His escape overseas was due to his demands that the country returned to fundamental Islamic law. He eventually returned in triumph and became President of the country.

In 1976, Iran was a most liberal Muslim country, with alcohol and other pleasures readily available. Despite sub-zero temperatures in the north, our visit was interesting and marked by warm hospitality. Tehran was an impressive capital but suffered from horrendous pollution problems. During our briefing, we had been informed of many important facts, including there were 1.5 million automobiles in the country, with 42% of them in Tehran itself!

Life as a pedestrian was decidedly dangerous. We soon learnt that the hordes of scooters, and small motorcycle drivers, totally ignored traffic lights. This made crossing at a busy junction suicidal! After dark, all drivers ignored the traffic lights.

Conditions at the international airport were somewhat chaotic, as the roof of the terminal had collapsed under the weight of a recent snowfall. Having been constructed by a British contractor, we wisely made a low-key withdrawal from Iran.

With the subsequent political upheaval in 1978, the centre in Tabriz did not receive UK aid. I was very pleased with this overseas mission and looked forward to the next. I hoped it signified that my civilian career was destined to be most interesting.

As for Iran, sadly it has turned inward on itself away from the world. Fear and the love of war now seems very prevalent on the streets. Instead of swords, she now threatens to wage war against the world, by producing nuclear weapons.

Chapter 20

United Republic of Tanzania and Zanzibar

During my first two years with the Foreign Office, every overseas assignment I undertook, I endured terrible problems with my bowels. The parasites not only lurked in every territory, but they also appeared to know that by waiting patiently, they could invade my intestines ensuring I suffered from nausea and detestable diarrhoea. This virus was known colloquially, and probably still is today as, Singapore Screamers, Delhi Belly, Lesotho Lurgy or Malta Dog. Unfortunately for me, no matter where I went, I caught it!

My next mission from the start became quite an adventure. Far more than even I had anticipated. I was sent to the United Republic of Tanzania and Zanzibar. There were no direct routes at that time, so my flight to Tanzania would first find me flying out from Heathrow, then changing aircraft at Brussels. I flew with the Belgian airline Sabena, which sadly went into bankruptcy.

On arriving in Brussels, I had a few hours to kill, and so decided to take a look around the city. On returning to the airport via the shuttle train, having finally reached the airport departure lounge, I realised that I had left my jacket on the train. Airports naturally are a strictly one-way system. Passengers are processed via ticket desks, along with customs immigration and security in the outward direction. Fighting one's way against the flow is extremely difficult and causes great concern to the airport staff. I managed to reach the railway station and thankfully retrieved my jacket from the train before it returned to the city.

Boarding the aircraft and being of a polite nature, I most certainly was not over pleased to find that the aircraft was an ancient Boeing 707, which most airlines had retired due to noise and pollution issues. The damn thing was also a freighter, with half of the accommodation being taken over for cargo. My seat faced a cargo bulkhead, which I was forced to stare at for several hours. I most definitely was not impressed with the Belgian State Airline, and more than delighted by the time I reached Rome. Rome was not only to become the only transit stop but there would also be many more until I reached my final destination. Fate had already predestined, that Rome several years later would become my home for a period of time.

Leaving Rome, and to my disappointment, I found myself on the same aircraft... the next leg of my journey took six hours until at last, I arrived in Africa. Entebbe Airport to be precise, though this too was only another temporary stop. My journey continued as the aircraft headed south to Nairobi.

Would you believe it; I was still on the same damn plane, with still another transit stop to go? The only difference being this time, thank goodness, I actually changed aircraft. The aircraft I now boarded was a DC9 of East African Airways. Once again, another shortstop, this time it was to be Kilimanjaro, and then on to Mombasa. How I wished that stop could have been a great deal longer. Unfortunately, I was not that lucky. After an hour the plane headed for my final destination.

At long last, I arrived in Dar-es-Salaam, once the capital of our ex-colony Tanganyika. The entire journey from leaving Heathrow had taken eleven hours. By that time, I was looking forward to my bed at the Giraffe hotel.

Not the finest place in the world, even if it was complete with ugly prostitutes in the bar.

My mission to the country was made at the request of the Ministry of Works (Ujenzi) and stemmed from the British Aid Mission in October 1975. The moment I arrived; a particularly nasty bug once more found its way into my poor susceptible system. For the first three days, embarrassingly, I found myself making my apologies a number of times when having to leave from various important meetings.

These meetings consisted of officials from the British High Commission, the British Council, and a number of Directors. These Directors represented most of the country's vital services. Energy, Water and Manpower Development. By excusing myself, this enabled me to rush away to visit what was becoming a familiar sight to several interesting bathrooms, including the manicured lawns of various buildings.

These facilities, allowing me the pure joy of vomiting or purging my lower colon. This procedure continued over a period of four days.

After having taken liberal doses of "bung-up" pills and no food, the four days passed, and slowly the feeling of becoming almost human again came into effect. I was most grateful knowing on the fifth morning, everything was back to normal, and I would be leaving Dar-es-Salaam in the company of a senior civil servant, along with our driver. We were heading north to visit the Ministry of Works training school at Mgulani.

Our night stop turned out to be in a strange town. The only reason for its existence was the railway junction. Naturally, there was only one hotel known as the Railway

Hotel, what else!

The accommodation one could only describe as primitive, on closer examination of my room, the suspect dining room, including the prevailing hygiene standards. I decided that neither water nor food would pass my lips that night. Gordon's Gin was readily available, allowing me thank heavens to clean my teeth in comparative safety. A gin and tonic today, occasionally takes me back to that strange little town.

The following day found us on the road at dawn, to make our return to Dar es Salaam. My precautions were soon justified. After we had covered 50 Km, my African colleague turning a strange colour, instructed our driver to stop. He hurtled from the vehicle in the direction of the bush. Noises of bodily fluids were clearly heard being evacuated from his body.

The stricken party eventually returned to the car and proceeded in his native tongue to say something like,

"Fuck me. Must be the altitude!"

This smug Brit made no comment.

Two days later, once again I found myself in the air. Flying north to Tabora, accompanied this time by a member of the Ministry of Works. Our accommodation was to be another Railway Hotel. This one thank goodness had acceptable standards of hygiene. My insides by now had produced the necessary antibodies against the Tanzanian Trots.

The hotel had been built in 1914, its claim to fame was that it had been built for Kaiser Wilhelm. Tanzania, at that time, was a German colony. The reason for the Kaiser's visit being, he had decided to open a new railway line. World War 1 prevented his arrival and after Germany surrendered, he was exiled in the Netherlands and never lived to see it.

While in Tabora, I visited many of the new building projects along with attending meetings with the Regional Staff from the Ministry of Works. Another visit on my agenda was the Igombe Dam and pumping facility.

The wet season most certainly lived up to its reputation. After two days of continuous torrential rain, the local airstrip had been washed away. My host conveyed his thoughts by stating,

"Please not to worry Mr Roy, we will return by rail."

Enquiries revealed that Tanzan Rail (now no longer East African Railways), was scheduled to leave in 48 hours for Dodoma, at least we knew we could travel from there by air to Dar es Salaam.

Dodoma was destined to be the new capital of Tanzania. This seemed in line with the current vogue of moving capitals once the British had handed over the country and left. We bought first class-soft seats, having been informed they were so much more comfortable. We were also advised to report to the nearby railway station at 7.00 am in 48 hours' time.

I will admit, I was less than happy with the added comment, that departure times were of course, provisional.

To my relief, Tanzania Rail did appear, only being ninety minutes late. By their standards not late at all.

After boarding, we were met by a smiling, white-coated steward, who immediately insisted we remove our shoes for cleaning.

The faded glory of the old East African Railways was

indeed very evident. Even if the sheets on the two bunks were a little threadbare.

The monogrammed crockery sadly had seen better days, as most of it was somewhat chipped. The train stopped at every tiny hamlet and village, and I dare say probably never exceeded 25mph.

Arriving at each stop, we were swamped by hordes of hawkers offering food, drinks, and medicine. Added to all that, you could buy live chickens, along with clothing, and naturally your proverbial souvenirs. With only a couple of trains per week, the cash flow for these entrepreneurs must have been problematical.

Our route skirted the magnificent Rift Valley. This spectacular natural cleft in the earth's surface is of course now a national park. The Great Rift Valley extends more than 3000 miles from Syria to Mozambique. The valley is believed to have been formed by the sinking and tearing apart of the earth's crust, along a 50-million-year-old zone of weakness.

Dodoma was a welcome sight. Part of the mission there was to check on the availability of clean water. On visiting several villages in the region, I found myself utterly appalled at the lack of any clean water whatsoever.

Disease from the filthy streams and rivers, polluted by animal and human waste was rampant. Even today, despite UK aid. The problem has not and will not be remedied. Regardless of TV advertisements appealing for money for the Water Aid programme which we are led to believe is matched by UK water companies. The way forward is not simply throwing money at a project like this, as education is just as vital in this current situation.

From there we returned by air to Dar-es-Salaam with

unspoken relief. The city is also the end of the line for the Tanzam railway. A railway project providing nearby landlocked Zambia, with an export route for its copper. When political problems arose in South Africa, its border with Zambia was closed. This prevented the export of copper and caused many problems.

Rebuffed by the West, the Zambians turned to China. Despite all the odds, the Chinese built a railway measuring, 1,860Km in length. This links Zambia with the port of Dar-es-Salaam.

The suburbs of Dar-es-Salaam are indescribable. One can only state they are no better than filthy shantytowns, which houses the eastern terminal built by the Chinese.

Amongst the corrugated iron hovels, stands an imposing marble railway station with immaculate lawns, fountains, and ornamental lamps. A copy it is said, of Peking Central station.

Departure day arrived. My host who was a government official, and had spent all his time accompanying me, suggested we should be at the airport at 5 am. This being the time of the first flight to Nairobi, which was due to take off at 6.50 am. Why do airlines have to leave at these uncivilised times?

We duly arrived at Dar-es-Salaam airport, only to find the check-in area deserted. My host went on to inform me by stating,

"Not to worry Roy, we will have a coffee upstairs in the airport restaurant."

We awoke one of the supine waiters, still draped over one of the unpolished tables, and ordered coffee.

By 6.15 am I was getting distinctly nervous. The total lack of activity downstairs, along with the deafening absence of any loudspeaker announcements, was becoming very worrying. I received further placation from my companion, with the assurance that all was normal.

At 6.45 am my nerves eventually snapped. I rushed down to the check-in area. Several check-in desks were obviously open and again manned by sleepy locals. My flight number was conspicuously absent from above any desk and in a state of near panic, I enquired of the nearest desk about my East African Airways Flight EC 634 to Nairobi.

"Sorry Massa, it am left" I sensed the colour draining from my face and my stomach felt it had turned over.

Feebly, I asked,

"Where the HELL is the check-in desk, for flight EC 634 to Nairobi?"

Looking at me with practically a blank expression, the half-asleep chap replied,

"As they had not been able to find all the numbers required, they had not been displayed."

He further went on to say,

"By the way, the airport tannoy system was quenched." (broken)

Almost speechless, I asked if the flight had actually departed.

"No Boss, it out dere," he answered, pointing out of the window at an aircraft with its engines running, the ground crew preparing to remove the stairs from the door.

This was no time for indecision. I grabbed my suitcase, hurdled the luggage carousel, and sprinted for the aircraft. I made it to the top of the stairway, managing to persuade a startled flight attendant to re-open the partially closed door.

Eventually arriving in Nairobi, my blood pressure which I hoped had now returned to normal, was assisted by the splendour of the Norfolk Hotel. This hotel indeed was very lovely, it dated back from colonial times, the accommodation ranges from a single room in the main building, to spacious bungalows in lush green grounds. One thing is for sure, it serves the best curry luncheon in East Africa. After that, the flight home via Zurich with British Airways was almost an anti-climax.

My report on the need to aid a Clean Water Project for 500 villages in Northern Tanzania, naturally, was received by the Overseas Development Ministry with the normal level of enthusiasm. The dead hand of Civil Service bureaucracy was applied. The file would be passed over a dozen person's desks. Returned with lengthy comments, decisions would then be implemented. That way, a possible wrong decision was untraceable. With a GDP, equivalent to $100 per head, Tanzania was one of the poorest countries in the world, most definitely needing all the help it could receive!

Chapter 21

The Horn of Africa, Somalia

Returning to work after the Christmas holidays, the New Year was to find me once more bound for Africa. My boss informed me I was to travel to Somalia of all places. At that time, I knew precisely zero about the country or its people.

Naturally, the next step was to research as much as I could about both. To my surprise, my research revealed that apart from an estimated 20 million goats, 13 million sheep, 5 million cattle and around 7 million camels, Somalia produces sugarcane, sorghum, corn, along with bananas and sesame seed. The most surprising of all was the fact that the Cushitic people of that area, have not had the benefit of a written script until well into the 20th Century. What was I heading for?

History tells us that in 1882, the Government of Egypt at that time withdrew from their territory of Somalia. The reason for this withdrawal was to help sort out the Mahdi rebels in Sudan. British and Italian administrations had over a period of years been in and out of Somalia. Resulting in turn, that the territory had been known as British Somaliland, or Italian Somaliland, Italian East Africa, and a UN Trusteeship.

Britain first arrived in 1869. Establishing a presence to protect the sea route to India via the Suez Canal which had opened in that year. By various treaties with local Sultans and conventions with Britain. Ethiopia, and Zanzibar. The Italians also acquired a foothold on the Indian Ocean coast of Somalia, extending her rights by signing the Treaty of London in 1915, along with various other post WW1 agreements.

In 1936, Italy merged its Italian Somaliland with Eritrea and the newly conquered Ethiopia, going on to form a colony, known as Italian East Africa.

Flushed with success, the Italians then invaded the British part of Somaliland, leaving Britain to return again in 1942. Unfortunately, the merry-go-round continued even after WW2, when Italy was required to renounce all title to her African territories.

The Allies (USA, USSR, France, and Britain) could not make up their minds what to do with this part of Italy's territory.

Eventually, the United Nations decided that the ex-Italian Somaliland, should become independent, then after a further 10 years had passed, it became a UN Trust territory. During 1960, the merry-go-round eventually stopped. Both the former British and Italian Somaliland's were granted independence, becoming the state of Somalia. Going on to become the Somali Democratic Republic as we know today.

My journey to Somalia started badly. The British Airways flight into Rome's Fiumicino Airport was two hours late due to fog. The Italian staff of Alitalia offered to rush me to their waiting DC8 aircraft, but could not guarantee when my baggage would join me. I declined the offer and opted for an overnight stop in Rome. Having survived two terrifying trips in Italian taxis, I eventually departed on Alitalia's Flight AZ868, in another DC8 bearing the name "Luigi Cherubini" on its nose. I had often wondered who that gentleman was. Thanks to the miracle of modern-day computers, I now know he was a classical composer.

It seemed a somewhat circuitous route to Mogadishu,

via Khartoum and Addis Ababa. In fact, I suppose I was very lucky to find any route to that obscure part of the world.

After arriving in Khartoum, we stopped briefly in Addis Ababa, before the final 2-hour leg to Mogadishu. The airport was crowded with troops, waiting to board several large transport aircraft. Many of them appeared to be attending to bodily functions at the edge of the taxiway. Then realisation struck, I was heading for a country at war!

The province of Ogaden in southeast Ethiopia had been returned to that country in 1948. Since the 1960s, Somalia had disputed Ethiopia's claim to that province. By the middle of 1977, this long-standing conflict had now escalated into an all-out war. I had indeed picked a bad time for my visit.

My hotel in the capital of Mogadishu was named the Croce del Sud. Meaning the Southern Cross. Or nicknamed by the uncouth expatriates, the "Sweaty Crotch." Comfortable enough, after a fashion. Any deficiencies the hotel may have had were compensated by the fact it stood in an idyllic spot on a beach adjacent to the Indian Ocean.

The capital was desperately poor, and terribly rundown. I found it difficult to know whether a particular building was under construction, or in the process of falling down. The previous Italian influence was very apparent, leaving many very fair-skinned Somali ladies, as well as vast amounts of pasta consumed at lunchtime.

During one evening, the First Secretary at the Embassy asked,

"Roy, would you care to join me for an evening out in the capital?"

Being polite, I accepted his invitation, though a little curious as to where he would take me. As it turned out, our destination was to be a nightclub. Mogadishu of course being the capital of a Muslim country, I kept my thoughts to myself, as it would be a rare entity in any Muslim country to have such a place.

Entering the building, and to all appearances as well as to my deep surprise, it was indeed a nightclub. Further surprises were in store for me. I was offered alcohol, and there were beautiful women present. I could only surmise these women, who were Somali and may well have had a little Italian blood in them, being both tall and fair-skinned.

After a very convivial evening over drinks, I was amazed when two of the women invited my companion and me, to continue our evening with them. One of the women informed us, that due to certain factors, we should wait outside for a vehicle that would drive us to their home.

Amusingly we followed their advice, and in due course, we were driven to a large villa set in its own grounds and surrounded by high walls. Once inside we were served aromatic black coffee. Shortly afterwards, there was a cacophony of noise coming from outside. The dogs started barking their heads off, followed by the gates being thrown open. Then the sound of dustbins being knocked over greeted our ears… one of the women then uttered the word,

"Police," indicating we should leave.

Regardless of any indecent intentions we may have had, we left rapidly through the back door. Running like hell across the courtyard, then through the rear gate. Had we been chosen for the Olympics; we could not have sprinted any faster up the street and headed towards the lights of central Mogadishu.

Due to the ongoing hostilities, travel restrictions on foreigners were very strict. British, and other diplomatic staff were only permitted to travel within a 50 Km radius of the capital. I was naturally concerned, as my mission was to look at possible aid for the Somali Government. Thankfully, I was exempt from these restrictions. I must admit, much to the envy of the staff at the British Embassy.

Diplomats could apply for special permits to travel further afield. One day, I was regaled with the story (by junior staff) of the recent experience of our own Ambassador.

His Excellency had applied to fly to Hargeisa, a city in the north of the country. Not having received permission before the date of his intended journey, he decided to travel anyway. The Ambassador made it to the aircraft, only to be removed in an unceremonious fashion by Somali security personnel. Then invited in the strongest terms, to leave the airport in his Rolls Royce.

Apparently, His Excellency was so put out with this, that he returned to the Embassy, locked all doors, and refused to see anyone. It was not revealed to me what the Somalis or HM Government made of his actions. I suspected at that time, that our man in Somalia, would not go on to be considered a candidate for a similar post, should one arise in Washington or Paris!

My reason for being in town was that a British company named Booker McConnell had been awarded a contract. They had been asked to develop a new sugar plantation in Jubba Valley. The valley was situated in southern Somalia. My survey was to assess the UK Government's possible aid for a vocational training centre, in support of the project. The proposed site was in the jungle, several hundred Kilometres south of Mogadishu. There was no alternative for me, but to travel by road to view this site. My briefing had indicated that of the 17,200 Kilometres of roads in Somalia, 1600 of them, were unpaved, guess where these were situated?

Leaving the "Sweaty Crotch" at dawn, a member of the embassy staff and I were still travelling as darkness fell. The road was unpaved and at times resembled a sandy beach. Vehicles, even at a snail's pace, produced dense clouds of dust that reduced visibility to a few metres. The terrifying part was to come up behind a truck, invariably minus rear lights, and then attempt to overtake it. This manoeuvre was by "Guess and God," as there was no way of knowing what was in the impenetrable dust cloud ahead. After several hours of this nightmare journey, my nerve ends were raw. Leaving me to feel as though bones were growing out of my rear end, due naturally to the hard seats, and rigid suspension of the four-wheel-drive vehicle.

Eventually, we turned off the main road into what one can only describe as a dense jungle. Somalia, though almost on the Equator, has an arid dry north, as well as a tropical region to the south.

Around midnight, we found the Booker survey camp, meeting the cheerful Brit, who was the sole ex-pat. Meeting this man left me to feel I had just re-run the Stanley and Dr Livingstone's meeting in darkest Africa. The camp was a collection of ridge tents, and lean-to palm leaf shelters. I was shown to my residence, which turned out to be a tent with open ends and a palm frond cover. Out of curiosity, I enquired about the marks in the sand, resembling bicycle tyre tracks.

"Oh, nothing to worry about, it is only those of a python that comes through the site at night," said the Brit, in a matter-of-fact voice.

Somehow, I knew that I was not going to have a good night! The continual insect attacks, thoughts of pythons, and the noise made by the night watchman setting off firecrackers to scare away wild animals. Sleep in fact completely evaded me. The next morning, the good news was that the python had not visited us, but some other creature had eaten several of the chickens.

The trial planting of sugarcane had already begun, and the site already had a unique problem. Elephant trails crisscrossed the entire area, those mighty pachyderms, were not about to change the habits of a lifetime to avoid our newly planted sugarcane. Fences were out of the question, and Booker would have to accommodate the elephants and plant accordingly.

The entire Jubba Valley is a natural and unspoilt area teeming with wildlife. Tourists are banned in Somalia, and the herds of zebra, giraffe along with elephants, roam at will without fear or hindrance. The number of hippo wallowing in the Juba River was quite unbelievable. On many occasions, we had to stop the vehicle to allow a herd of giraffe, or elephants to cross the road ahead. Fortunately, none took offence, obviously not having noticed us. The only threat to wildlife were the ivory poachers from across the border in Kenya. After seeing the rotting remains of magnificent beasts, minus tusks, I remain an ardent supporter of the ban on the international trade in ivory.

At one point during the tour, our road actually crossed the Equator. I have now walked, driven sailed, and flown across this imaginary line many times.

We parked, then went on to take the obligatory photographs. Having seen sharks in the Indian Ocean, I considered swimming across the line was not for me. I was privileged to visit a refugee camp in the valley, which housed a staggering total of 250,000 unfortunates.

The Russians had moved these people from the war zone in the north; no doubt combining humanitarian with military exercise needs.

There were no permanent buildings. All in the camp, lived, slept, ate, and attended school under huge trees, their branches bent down like enormous umbrellas, some even touching the ground.

There was a marked absence of international aid agencies. Which I suppose, is the difference between 1977, and today's proliferation of such organisations. On my return to Mogadishu, I met the local United Nations Commissioner for Refugees; a man with an impossible task in Somalia.

We took our leave of the brave Booker Brit, then headed for the airport at Kismayo. Sadly, our Booker Brit, later contracted a severe dose of cerebral malaria, almost losing his life in the Jubba Valley. Such are the risks of expatriates who work around the world.

Often, they work in hostile environments, as valuable and invisible exports in many capacities for the United Kingdom.

Having left the camp at dawn, we stopped for refreshments at a local café. I use the word in its loosest form. Under a tree, we were offered goats meat, most of it in a slimy and gristly form. Hungry and with my stomach heaving, I would have attempted to eat the ghastly offering, had I been able to reach the food through the dense cloud of enormous flies.

I departed Kismayo, which is the largest airport in southern Somalia. The aircraft this time, being a Fokker 27 of Somali Airlines. Fortunately making it safely back to the comparative comfort of the "Croce del Sud." That night it felt wonderful as I drifted off to sleep, to the sounds of the Indian Ocean, wondering if my friend the python was looking for me.

The next day I was confronted with an immediate crisis. East African Airways, which was a conglomerate of Kenya, Uganda, and Tanzania airways, had dissolved the alliance and ceased flying. My problem was to reach Nairobi in Kenya, for my connection back to London.

Enquires revealed that the only service remaining, was one operated by Somali Airlines. This airline was flying direct to the Seychelles. From there a flight to Nairobi presented no problem.

I departed the "Horn of Africa" on Flight HH312 onboard a Boeing 720. This was a rare variant of the Boeing 707 series (the first commercial jetliner.) Obviously, this was not an oversubscribed service, as the crew outnumbered the passengers on the flight south to Victoria, on Mahé Island in the Seychelles Group.

To my dismay, the next onward flight to Nairobi was five days away. There was nothing to do but grit my teeth and suffer for five days, by trying to act like a tourist on a beautiful island in the Indian Ocean. Sometimes, it is a tough job, but someone has to do it!

After a brief stay at the Norfolk Hotel in Nairobi, which incidentally serves the finest curry lunch buffet in Africa, British Airways deposited me safely at London Heathrow. As the aircraft stopped at the ramp, there was an announcement.

"Will Mr Harrington – Brown make himself known to a member of the cabin crew."

I could not believe it! This was Sudan all over again. I was met at the top of the ramp by a similar (large) Irish Nursing Sister, who then hustled me off once again to the BA Medical Centre, located as usual in the bowels of Heathrow airport. I began to feel at home in this place.

Apparently, a new strain of smallpox had appeared in Somalia. No spots – one simply died! After being checked over and then released, as I had previously been for the green monkey disease. Once again, I was given strict instructions to contact my GP if my condition changed, or in this case, the inevitable happened!

I learned while waiting to be checked over, that drug smugglers, suspected of having swallowed heroin in condoms, were detained in the same Medical Centre. Such miscreants were held until nature took its course, and the drugs were naturally expelled from the body. I had been informed during this time, that it was common practice for a junior Customs Officer to be detailed, to rummage in the expelled shit in order to extract any of the drug-filled condoms. All part of an everyday job.

Back at the Ministry, my only problem was explaining my inflated expense account. How does one explain five extra days spent on a tropical island?

Almost twenty years later, I watched newsreels recording the landing of US Forces on the beach at Mogadishu. They were the vanguard, of a United Nations Peacekeeping force. An abortive attempt as it turned out, to intervene in a civil war, and protect international aid agencies attempting to distribute food supplies in Somalia.

I doubt whether they had as an interesting time as I did in the "Horn of Africa." With the civil war continuing, I did not manage a return trip to the Jubba Valley.

Chapter 22

The Khyber Pass

A further trip in 1977, saw me preparing to fly off once again to another part of the world. Within a week I boarded a VC-10 of British Airways. My flight was to take me en route, firstly to Amman, then on to Islamabad.

Islamabad was the new capital of the Islamic Republic of Pakistan. Like all new capitals, I found it quite faceless, and certainly unlike the noisy and more colourful adjacent city of Rawalpindi.

After a flight of four and a half hours, eventually going through the normal procedure of security, then checking into my hotel, it was already evening. This of course was not my first visit to the country, as I have previously stated, having been on loan from the Royal Air Force to the Royal Pakistan Air Force from 1952-1954, based near Karachi.

My mission this time, was the standard exercise intended to identify and gather information about certain projects, suitable for H.M. Government aid funding.

After meeting a number of Government officials in various Ministries, my only interesting recollection is the road journey north from Islamabad to Peshawar and onwards via the famous historic Khyber Pass.

The Khyber Pass of course, is more than just a road... few passes have such continuing strategic importance. History tells us through it have passed the Persians, Greeks, Mughals, Afghans and British.

The name Khyber is a range of arid broken hills through which the pass runs. On either side of the connecting ridge are the sources of two small streams. The beds form the Khyber Gorge, which in turn forms the Khyber Pass, winds its way between cliffs of shale and limestone.

After a steep ascent, the pass continues to rise, flanked by imposing and precipitous walls, eventually widening into a valley with forts villages and scattered cultivation plots.

The path drops as it eventually leads to the Afghanistan border.

Apart from the manic driving of both our driver and the other road users, we were involved in an accident which had some frightening moments.

Travelling through one small village in Baluchistan. Our vehicle hit a young cyclist who darted from a side street, giving our driver no chance of missing him. Dozing in the rear, my first recollection was of a heavy thump. I came around to see a body descending vertically onto the bonnet of the car. Against our advice our driver jumped out to see if the young cyclist was still alive. Having foolishly done so, he was then immediately surrounded by a crowd of angry villagers, receiving a blow to his face for his troubles.

Unable to drive on, we sat in the car as the crowd grew around it, frighteningly pressing their faces against the windows and mouthing threats and obscenities in Urdu. The scene was ugly and gradually grew worse becoming more menacing by the minute.

One of the wing mirrors and a wind screen wiper was torn from the car then disappeared. The next couple of seconds saw some of the crowd picking up rocks from the side of the road. I could see the headlines: "Diplomat stoned and killed in Pakistan!"

Fortunately, an older man appeared, obviously an elder of the village. He eventually managed to restore some calm and after several tense minutes of negotiation, we agreed to take the cyclist to seek medical attention, thankfully escaping what was by now a hostile scene. We took the young man to what turned out to be a primitive building. I did notice outside of the building, there were dozens of veiled women with tiny babies waiting for attention. Fortunately, the young cyclist was only bruised, and we continued our journey after the exchange of a number of rupees.

Eventually we arrived in Peshawar, it was still the "Wild West" of Pakistan, also the gateway to tribal territory. Entering the city, we observed a large sign which read,

"No weapons to be carried in the Cantonment."

The first local we saw was a very tall Pathan tribesman. He, like most of the other men, was wearing two bandoliers of cartridges, two curved daggers, and carrying an AK 47 automatic rifle.

After a short stay and fortified by tea and samosas, we then continued north passing signs which clearly informed us. I must mention, the tea contained the requisite mutton fat.

"You are now entering Tribal Territory"

To say I felt nervous would be an understatement.

We continued to drive up the historic Khyber Pass… one could almost smell the history as we negotiated it.

The Khyber Pass led us on through the mountains to Landi Khotal (3,518 feet) the highest point on the pass, and then on to the Afghan border...

Regimental signs carved in the rock faces around

Landi Khotal Fort, were reminders of the British Army, and their skirmishes with the local tribesmen. Here, I saw turbaned heads behind every rock. Was it my imagination, I wonder?

Landi Khotal was a typical Pakistani town. Overcrowded, appallingly smelly with interesting odours. Or maybe I should say, disgusting odours of open sewers, and the ubiquitous curry, as well as extremely noisy.

The town's bazaar sold everything from food to clothing. What amazed me was the unique weapons facility producing superb handguns along with automatic weapons. All were exquisitely made, and one was able to buy them at any time. Personally, I feel many ended up in the hands of terrorists during the recent conflicts in Afghanistan.

During my entire visit to Landi Khotal, though there was no immediate danger, I constantly felt uneasy. Particularly when coming into close contact or passing by any member of the public. This of course, was due to their personal reaction on seeing an English man in close proximity to them.

I was relieved at the thought of leaving, but before doing so, the Government official who had accompanied me, suggested we ate in a local establishment. The meal consisted of rice and spicy meat of unknown origin. My main thoughts being, what the possible effects would it be, on my well-known sensitive bowels.

After what was a most intriguing visit, we commenced the return journey back to Peshawar. As it turned out, it was uneventful, especially after having survived the antics of the mad men driving the ancient buses through the Khyber Pass. These vintage vehicles were actually works of art, regardless they emitted dense black smoke from there ancient engines. The beauty of the paintings on the bodywork, reflected religious slogans, as well as the type of art of the region.

The busses were all dangerously overloaded, not only with passengers inside. There were a number clinging outside, together with others traveling precariously on the roof amongst the baggage.

We left in the late afternoon, having a second opportunity to travel one of the world's most unique roads. I found it a wonderful experience, regardless of it being very frightening.

My journey to Pakistan was drawing to a close. I flew with Pakistan Airways, back to Lahore in an ancient Boeing 720 (a variant of Boeing's first jetliner – the 707).

The mission ended on a sleepless night, due to the locals having decided to have a riot quite close to my hotel. Like most demonstrations, it is immaterial if one was staying at the Hilton or in a mud hut.

British Airways returned me via Amman in Jordan, and then on to Heathrow and civilization. Most definitely a unique experience and one I will never forget.

Chapter 23

Costa Rica

Spring had arrived and the country was full of excitement as Her Majesty the Queen was about to celebrate her Silver Jubilee. My boss had invited me a little earlier into his office, he informed me I was required to visit Costa Rica in Central America. The journey was to take place with me flying out on my 47th birthday. Not bad for an unusual birthday present, or maybe not a coincidence. As I left Heathrow, the weather was perfect that year, allowing the Queen to enjoy her special day, unlike the incessant rain on her Coronation.

Boarding a VC10 of British Airways, I knew I would need to make myself comfortable, as the flight ahead to Mexico City, would take approximately twelve and half hours, with two transit stops in Bermuda and Nassau. Coming into land, I must admit, both transit stops were indeed on beautiful Caribbean Islands, which I intended at some time in the future to re-visit.

On arriving in Mexico City, by now feeling both dirty and tired. I was most certainly ready for a shower and bed. Staying the one night at the airport hotel, ensured I did not have long to wait for either. Early the following morning after having enjoyed a good breakfast, I made my way back to a check-in desk, this time to catch another flight.

My flight was to be a BAC 1-11 of the national airline of Costa Rica. Firstly, taking me to San Salvador, then onto my destination of San José, the capital of Costa Rica.

One of the attractions of flying with LACSA was the serving of free cocktails to all passengers. These drinks were quite a lethal concoction, served in a very large glass with a profusion of fruit and other items. Passengers became ever increasingly boisterous as we approached San José. While strictly against regulations, the flight crew also thoroughly enjoyed some of these alcoholic time bombs. The flight path into San José airport is along a very narrow valley. There are steep hills on both sides, covered in dense vegetation making this a dangerous approach at that best of times. Needless to say, we had a wobbly descent due to the cocktails consumed on the flight deck. I wonder if this practice is still prevalent in that part of the world even today.

Obviously, I needed to know a little about this rather small central American country. After doing my normal amount of research, I was quite surprised to read that Costa Rica is a sovereign state and classed as the jewel in Central America. Bordered by Nicaragua to the north, the Caribbean Sea to the northeast, and Panama to the southeast. The Pacific Ocean lies to the southwest and Ecuador to the south of Cocos Island.

The mountains of this amazing country, have one hundred volcanic cores separating the coastal plains. There are also four volcanoes, two are still unfortunately active, and rise near the capital of San José. The largest is named Irazú. Last erupted in 1965 with disastrous results. The country has a wonderful tropical climate, capable of growing coffee, sugar, and cocoa. This ensured Costa Rica's principle source of wealth.

Costa Rica has generally enjoyed greater peace and more consistent political stability than many of its fellow Latin American nations. The country at present has no military forces, along with a relatively small Police Force. The only real problem it sadly endures is the transhipment of drugs from South America to the USA.

Due to both its climate and political stable situation. The diversity of the flora and fauna enhances eco-tourism, adding to the national economy. Costa Rica I am delighted to say, even before I set foot in the country, has successfully managed to diminish deforestation to almost zero. One of her parks, in particular, Corcovado National Park, is internationally renowned for the protection of its wildlife.

The reason for my visit at that time, H.M. Government was in the process of funding a training facility for the development of a construction trades training school. I had been tasked with a quality audit of this establishment. After a comprehensive inspection of the school and with my audit completed, I could relax and act like a tourist.

My female host Maria was a member of the management team and laid on a very interesting trip. She had arranged that she and I should visit the summit of the Irazú volcano. As we drove up the mountain, one could see the path of the molten lava and rocks that had spewed from a previous eruption.

Reaching the summit, we then descended into the mouth of the crater. With black ash underfoot, and strangely silent. I found that most eerie. Naturally, there were no birds or vegetation, only this strange Englishman and his guide. The only volcanic evidence being a small plume of steam rising from the centre of the crater. Certainly, a unique experience.

On completion of the audit and talks with Management to discuss my findings. Just as I was preparing to leave, Maria turned to me and asked,

"Roy, are you free this evening?"

Before I could give her my answer, she continued to say.

"As a token of our gratitude for all your efforts, I would like to invite you to dinner."

Somewhat taken aback, I replied,

"Thank you, that would be most welcome."

We arranged that Maria would pick me up at my hotel at seven that evening. Sure, enough at seven precisely, Maria entered the foyer. I could not believe the transformation. Gone was the hard hat that hid her dark hair. The Hi-Vis jacket and jeans were now all replaced by a scarlet, floor-length silk evening gown. A garment that did little to hide the curvaceous body beneath!

All the male heads in the room turned, obviously taking in the low cut of her gown and the stupendous cleavage it revealed.

My male hormones went into overdrive as she extended her hand for me to shake and said in her soft voice,

"Buena noche hombre hermosa."

Then going on to plant kisses on both cheeks. Her large brown eyes made me feel she was already promising so much.

Preparing to leave the hotel car park in her Mercedes, Maria placed her hand on my thigh and gave me a most friendly kiss. At that point, I decided if the lady harboured indecent thoughts, I was not the man to deny them!

On arriving at our destination, we entered one of the most fashionable restaurants in San José. The restaurant provided ostentatious evidence of the gap between the super-rich and have-nots. Which characterised Costa Rican society back then, and I dare say is virtually the same today.

The head waiter who obviously knew Maria, seated us at a table in a discreet corner, maybe having done so many times before. Going on to order our food, Maria asked,

"Would you mind Roy if I ordered the wine, as I would like you to experience one of our excellent red wines?"

The food and wine were indeed superb and impeccably served. After coffee had been served, Maria reached across the table, gently took my hand in hers, choosing her words most carefully, she stated,

"You are probably aware that I am married."

I sat listening intently as she continued,

"I was married at a very young age to an older man. He is an architect and of course very wealthy, we have no children, and I am now trapped in a loveless marriage."

A statement that explained very clearly her exciting current behaviour.

Driving back to my hotel, my excitement rose. Only to be crushed on arrival as the night receptionist reminded me, that guests were not allowed in one's bedroom after 6 pm. My acute disappointment was eased when Maria asked,

"Roy, would you like to have lunch with me tomorrow?"

Unsurprisingly, my excitement returned. Raising her hand to my lips, kissing it, I then answered her by saying,

"I would love to."

At noon the following day, I found myself being driven in Maria's white Mercedes, to an elegant villa in one of San José's fashionable suburbs.

On my arrival, I was instantly greeted by Maria's

maid. As she invited me in, she asked if I would follow her through what was a cool white and gold elegant hall. Walking further into the villa, my feet sinking into the white carpet I noticed the artwork hanging from the walls, also the exquisite white and gold furniture that must have cost a king's ransom.

At last, we reached a magnificent dining room, it was there Maria greeted me warmly. She was dressed in a white silk shirt and tight-fitting black silk trousers. Extending her hand, she then gracefully indicated to me to sit beside her at the magnificent antique carved wooden table. We talked of many interesting things while enjoying a superb lunch served by Maria's maid. Our meal ended with Maria's maid serving a rich aromatic coffee, after which she discreetly left not only the room but the villa.

After having enjoyed our coffee, Maria led me to her bedroom. As with the rest of the house, it was luxuriously furnished, the colour scheme following through in white and gold. Maria excused herself and walked towards what I imaged was her dressing room, then entering it for a few minutes leaving me alone with my indiscreet thoughts. At the time, I had been wearing an open-necked white shirt and cream-coloured slacks. Not quite sure what Maria had in mind, I decided to sit on her bed in high anticipation and wait for her return.

The time dragged interminably, though it was only a few minutes. Maria, at last, reappeared, taking my breath away. Gone was the silk shirt and trousers, they had been replaced by a white diaphanous silk chemise, tied at her breast and which left nothing to the imagination. As she walked halfway across the room, Maria untied the ribbons of the tiny chemise, allowing it to drop on the richly carpeted floor, revealing her near-perfect body...

Her pert breasts, and smooth flat tummy, joined her statuesque thighs and long legs. My blood pressure soared. I could smell the perfume Maria was wearing, it was intoxicating as she came closer, reaching my side she then proceeded to undress me. There was certainly no objection on my part to her perfume.

The next two hours remain a blur of sexual passion, as we explored each other bodies. Up till then, I never quite knew I was such a good lover. Maria enforced that fact as she climaxed noisily several times, ensuring she in turn had given me a great deal of pleasure. I had never experienced up until then what real lust was, now I most certainly did. Sadly, time was not on my side, and after having enjoyed so much pleasure, I had to leave the villa before Maria's husband returned home from work. After a tearful parting, Maria ensured I was driven back to my hotel once again in her Mercedes. She promised to come and visit me in the UK, I must admit I doubted that would happen, Costa Rica being a long way from England.

Another lively diversion was a party at the British Embassy. The reason it had being given, for the moment, escapes me, not that it matters. His Excellency the British Ambassador, I found to be an amazing character. His penchant for the local ladies had earned him the nickname. The Cork. I do not think you need me to expand on that. His wife had long gone back to England and given his present appointment as Ambassador. With Costa Rica's position on the Diplomatic Corps league table, it would be unlikely that he along with other Ambassadors, would find his next posting to be, New York or Paris.

His Excellency had served with the British Army in

the Coldstream Guards. With my military background, we got on famously. The evening as I remember was an alcoholic blur. However, I recall marching with him around his residence to the strains of military music at three a.m. in the morning.

Costa Ricans in general, are a happy race of people and totally laid back. This is clearly evident in their joi de vivre. Their liberal attitude to marriage shows up very well in their behaviour towards extramarital relationships on a regular basis.

I was told that most Government officials and politicians etc. Enjoyed the pleasure of a mistress, as if enjoying a glass of wine each evening with dinner.

To cater for such activities, San José has numerous high-class brothels. These establishments are normally housed in impressive buildings set in large palatial grounds. The approach to them is a long drive lined by tall dense trees and hedges. The object being complete privacy to screen arrivals.

My informant further explained that the interior possessed a number of vast luxurious bedrooms. Each bedroom having a telephone and a hatch in one wall. These enabled customers to order food and drink, without fear of contact with brothel staff. Obviously, a model for other nations, enabling them to learn about being discreet.

I was offered such a service, and though very tempted as the women are incredibly beautiful. On this trip I declined, having had my liaison with Maria.

My mission complete, LACSA flew me back to Miami minus cocktails. After previous experiences with immigration authorities, I made sure this time I had a USA visa. I continued my ten-hour flight home with British

Airways without incident, though my thoughts turned to the wonderful afternoon I had spent with Maria. Those thoughts also gave way to deeper feelings. I realised for the first time in a very long time, that I had missed the touch or the kiss of a woman. Holding Maria in my arms, not just the sex, but the warmth of another human being lying next to me. I returned home, to what is still regarded as the best summer England has ever enjoyed.

Chapter 24

Yemen Arab Republic

During the summer of 1978, once again found me leaving England on what was a hot sultry summer's day. I had boarded an aircraft belonging to Middle East Airlines, en route to Yemen, via Beirut and Jeddah in Saudi Arabia.

The Ministry of Overseas Development required a visit to the Yemen Ministry of Interior. This visit was to be part of a survey for that country's application for UK aid. Naturally, I felt a little uneasy at the thought of transit through Beirut Airport, particularly, as it had recently only just been opened after continued fighting in Lebanon's civil war.

Fighting had broken out during 1975, between the Lebanese Muslims and the Christian Phalange factions. The Palestine Liberation Organisation (PLO) in 1976, had joined the conflict in support of the Muslims. Neighbouring Syria in the same year had intervened against the PLO.

Later that year, the Arab League brokered an uneasy truce by creating a Syrian-led Arab Peacekeeping force, and by 1978, Israel decided to invade troubled Lebanon in order to destroy PLO terrorist bases in the south of the country. Had the world given a great deal more support to Israel, the world may have become a great deal safer than it is at present.

The ravages of war were very evident from the air as we approached Beirut International Airport. The devastation I observed, reminded me of so many photographs I had seen as a schoolboy of the appalling aftermath of German bombings, of cities in World War II.

All of which was a tragedy for a city like Beirut, which

had been known as the "Paris of the Middle East" under its former French masters.

After a brief transit stop and a change of an aircraft to an elderly Boeing 707, I was back in the air bound for Jeddah in Saudi Arabia. I felt very relieved, though deeply saddened at what I had witnessed on leaving the war zone. Little did I know, just how eventful the rest of my trip was to be!

After a brief transit stop in Jeddah wasting a couple of hours, then changing to Saudi Airlines (soft drinks only) I finally arrived at Sa'ana, the Yemeni capital, only to find I was minus my damn luggage!

Attempting to resolve the problem by communication with useless airport officials. I can only describe what was an exercise in great patience, as they were extremely slow, or better still, in fact, you could say exasperating. After a period of time, the officials at long last informed me, that my precious luggage had been shipped back to London from Jeddah.

The month was June, it was midday, and I was in the desert Kingdom of Yemen. The temperature at that time was hovering on the 35 degrees' centigrade mark. I laughed to myself when thinking back about that having left England, in what I thought was a hot and sultry day. Now I knew what hot was; as well as sultry. Plus, things did not appear too promising, for this angry, hot, and tired Brit!

After checking into the only hotel, which had definitely seen better days, I stormed into the Saudi Airlines office, which was located in the centre of Sa'ana, demanding some kind of assistance as well as compensation for my desperately needed lost luggage.

As is usual in such cases, and as I expected, the local

agent recited the small print on the back of my airline ticket, then went on to offer me the statutory sum of $25 for my inconvenience. Having travelled extensively and having been in this type of situation in other countries. I was more than ready for battle.

With commendable British restraint, I pointed out in polite fashion, that with the number of limited flights to such a God-forsaken hole, I was unlikely to see my luggage and a change of clothes for at least a week, and by then I would smell worse than the sewers in the street outside.

The grossly overweight Saudi agent repeated the party line, by re-offering the paltry $25. This Brit decided it was time for sterner tactics. I went on to inform him, that under no circumstances would I leave his office until I was in possession of sufficient local currency. Enough to enable me to buy a change of clothing and toiletries in the local souk. (market)

The stand-off, annoyingly continued until British resolve triumphed, and his ample stomach reminded him that it was lunchtime. I left clutching a suitable amount of cash and headed to the market. For the record, my luggage did not reach Yemen, but luckily, I did manage to retrieve it at Heathrow airport on my return.

My hotel was definitely not good, but at least acceptable. I survived several nights in the capital, though I did not get much sleep. The receptionist had at least located me in a room on the third floor. I thought he was being generous until I realised it was above an alleyway. This alleyway was the receptacle into which the hotel and others deposited their garbage.

Refuse collection services in the city, were either on strike or non-existent. This was appallingly evident by the piles of smelly rubbish which had reached the level of the second-floor windows, it was not the fragrance that disturbed me, but the cats, dogs and assorted vermin scavenging and fighting for delicacies amongst the rotting food.

As required, I was well received by the Honourable Minister of Interior and his subordinates. The Kingdom appeared to be in a time warp. Words such as "Feudal", and "Medieval" came readily to mind. Hospitality was generous in the Arab manner, and we consumed innumerable cups of fierce Arabic coffee, together with local fish, lamb, and curry dishes.

During my tour, it was evident that poverty was incredibly widespread. This left me debating how the United Kingdom, would decide which sector of the Yemeni economy, should receive priority for aid funds. Also, whether such funds could even scratch the surface of Yemen's needs.

After two weeks, it was time to return home. My flight home commenced with Egypt Air from Sa'ana to Cairo. The plan was to then transfer to an onward flight by British Airways to London. The old saying of: 'the best-laid plans of mice and men, can often go astray' came to mind. Unfortunately, my plan to return home without any hitches came unstuck thanks to Egypt Air.

Annoyingly, being several hours late arriving in Sa'ana, and even later returning to Cairo. The flight of BA 150 had long since departed by the time we arrived. Why did I feel that this mission was jinxed?

Economy class, along with the business class passengers, were bussed off to a hotel in Cairo. First-class passengers were directed to the airport terminal, with the promise of beds at the airport hotel.

A large, uniformed gentleman, who stood behind one of the terminal desks, commenced handing out room keys to the passengers from Sa'ana. Politely, as the others had done, I held out my hand.

This oversized official examined his clipboard, then announced,

"Mr Harrington-Brown, you are not on this flight."

I felt my blood pressure rising even further after all I had already been through. Still, I continued to show my stiff upper English lip, I went on to reply.

"Sir, I have just walked from that Egypt Air aircraft, the one you see over there," indicating the Boeing 737 that had brought us to Cairo.

The official then re-examined my ticket, then answered,

"You are not confirmed on the flight; you must pay for bed."

Logic was obviously not the solution to this problem.

The fact that I had just disembarked from the Sa'ana aircraft, and must therefore have been confirmed, and accepted on the flight; appeared foreign to the stupid man's brain. I must admit, I was more than tempted to introduce him to a number of old-fashioned choice English words. Instead, I reached for my wallet and gave him several US Dollars.

Hotel or not, none of us managed very much sleep anyway as the hotel was built in the centre of the airport, it seemed from the noise as if each jet aircraft taxied through the room.

Two eventful weeks from first leaving England, British Airways deposited me safely, and on time at

Heathrow. Reunited with my much-travelled luggage, I headed home hoping it would be some time before I saw the Kingdom of Yemen, or Cairo again. At least they collect the garbage in England – most of the time! Rapidly though, we appear to be heading for a Yemeni style garbage collection.

I was finding the "Dead Hand of Bureaucracy" frustrating. I would return from overseas missions, full of enthusiasm for a new aid project. My written report after publication would be circulated among Desk Officers in the Administration Branch.

The officers were responsible for overseas territories. These individuals would add comments, being careful to avoid any possible personal criticism of themselves or be made responsible for any contentious comments. Finally, I decided, it was time for me to leave the public sector and find employment elsewhere.

Chapter 25

Bailbrook College

After considerable thought and taking into consideration the official reaction to my hard work, plus the long hours spent travelling overseas, I no longer felt happy at the end result. I decided therefore to resign my position from the Foreign Office. Once again, I would have to go through the monotonous task of seeking employment. The thought of having to apply, probably for an untold number of jobs, did nothing to enhance my mood. Giving the normal thirty days' notice, I commenced the task of seeking a new position.

Reading through the Sunday Times, I spotted and replied to an advert by (International Aeradio Ltd.) which was a subsidiary of British Airways. This was a position I quite fancied and immediately applied for. Being the first advert I replied to, I did not hold my breath.

Within a week, I was asked to attend an interview in central London. A few days later, I was invited back to attend a further interview, this time in Southall. Never having been in that area, I thought I had stepped back onto the Asian continent.

The second interview must have gone well. I was informed that the position, should I wish to take it, was mine. Surprised, greatly relieved, and delighted, one could say expressed the emotions I felt. Surprised, as the job I had just been offered, was not only that of Principal, but General Manager of a proposed new training facility by British Airways. Greatly relieved, as I did not have to apply for dozens and dozens of other positions. Delighted, as the new facility was to be known as, Bailbrook College.

Bailbrook was one of the finest buildings of its time. Built in 1790, for a Royal Navy Surgeon Commander, serving in the Caribbean. Very little, unfortunately, is known about this man as he misappropriated Government funds to build for what he felt was a necessary mental asylum. Wealthy patients were accommodated on its upper floors. Sadly, paupers were chained in its cellars.

British Airways purchased the mansion in 1976 for the sum of £2,000,000. Up till then, the mansion had been owned by many wealthy people over the centuries.

I.A.L. decided to centralise its U.K. based training services and opened Bailbrook College in 1977. The College of Air Traffic Services at Kidlington, near Oxford and Southall College of Radio Engineering, completed their move by the end of 1978. Bailbrook College, apart from the Civil Aviation Authority, had the unique permission, to issue ATC licenses. Allowing a person to obtain employment as an air traffic controller.

My next step was to move my family from Bedford. I bought a beautiful bungalow adjacent to the college. Little did I foresee, that I would lose my home within two years.

I took up my appointment in 1978. The initial role of the college was to provide training in air traffic control, radio engineering and meteorology. This training was for I.A.L. and its customers, both home and overseas.

The arrival of Bailbrook College in the area, as well as her new Principal, provoked considerable interest. I was invited to give an interview on Points West, the regional TV channel. A smart young reporter, with obvious and devious intent knowing we had Arab students, asked what my reaction would be, should I be asked to receive Jewish students. As politely as I could manage, I reminded him

Bailbrook was an educational establishment, and students of any nationality would receive the world-class training normally expected of British Airways.

As a new boy in any school or business, there were always politics. Being of a sensitive nature, you could say during my lifetime on various dangerous missions, I had developed an acute sense of awareness when all was not as it should be.

This awareness came into being when first meeting the two Chief Instructors. Both men, who were from Kidlington and Southall, having lost their ability to run their departments as they so wished, much to their annoyance, now found themselves under my authority. The resulting situation was not to their liking and did not go down well. They were not on their own regarding that feeling, as the Administration Manager had expected to be appointed as Principal and of course, was overlooked. Apparently, this animosity was to build and lead to more serious consequences later. So much so, that in the end, they were to make huge changes to my life.

I soon realised that the college had further potential than existed at that present time. I felt with both my RAF and Foreign Office work experience, the college could be capable of facilitating industrial training for overseas nationals. I am pleased to say; this came into being. I had asked an old friend who had served with me at the Foreign Office if he would care to assist me in this adventure as he had a great deal of experience in the field.

Delighted to say, he took up my invitation.

We received a group of Saudi meteorology students, all with relatives connected to the Saudi Royal family. One particular Sunday morning, I received a telephone call from the local police. The officer informed me that several Saudi students had been arrested, were now in custody; and would be charged with causing an affray. Worried about hearing this news, I immediately hurried down to the police station, and organised their bail. I was also informed they were to appear at the magistrates court the following morning.

I attended court the following day to seek mitigation on the students' behalf.

Unfortunately, the hearing was before an elderly and rather unpleasant magistrate. After hearing the evidence, and to my horror, the dreadful woman sentenced the group to fourteen days in prison, along with instant deportation after having once served their time. As a result of this decision, one can imagine how red hot the telephone lines between London and Riyadh became. Fortunately, the legal department of British Airways became involved. They instantly ensured an appeal hearing was obtained before a High Court Judge.

The hearing was held within a couple of days, and to my utter relief, the judge quashed the prison sentence. He also rescinded the deportation order. The students were immediately released from Bristol Prison, where they had been held. Having completed their course within two weeks they then returned to Saudi Arabia.

Several weeks after that event, out of the blue, I received a telephone call. The call took the wind out of my sails, leaving me to feel totally amazed.

The voice on the other end was no other than Maria's. She asked how I was, then said,

"Roy I am here in Bath and would very much like to see you. Please may we meet?"

Quickly gathering my thoughts, my first reaction was to say no. Then remembering the passionate afternoon, we had spent together, I thought what the hell; why not. Replying as calmly as I could, I said,

"Hello Maria, you sound well, and yes I would love to meet you. May I ask where you are staying?"

Maria informed me that she was staying at the Royal Hotel in Central Bath. I then asked,

"Maria, would you like to meet me in the hotel foyer, or should I come directly to your room?"

Maria requested I went direct to her room, giving me the number in the process. We arranged to meet after lunch.

Making my excuses enabling me to leave the college, I drove into central Bath already feeling aroused. Entering the hotel, I noticed the lift was directly ahead which took only seconds to reach the first floor that Maria's room was situated on. Gently knocking on her door, Maria opened it throwing her arms around my neck drawing me close to her. I could not help but smile to myself, as Maria was already partially undressed and wearing only a flimsy white dressing gown.

I found myself enjoying a repeat performance of Costa Rica. After two further hours of what one can only describe as, pure unadulterated sex, it was time for me to leave. Maria returned to London to make her way back to Costa Rica. I returned home.

While Maria had fulfilled my sexual needs as a man, the emotions I felt came to light while putting the key into the lock of my front door and opening it. I immediately came to realise how empty and alone my life had become, and that I had to further endure my sterile marriage. It was at that moment I decided my marriage was now no longer worth saving.

I made an appointment to see a solicitor, and in the meantime, I told Diane I wanted to have a serious discussion with her when I returned home from work the following day.

I dreaded going home, wondering what would be said once I divulged to Diane I would be moving out. As was to be expected, at first, Diane was naturally distressed, though I felt like me she was relieved. Diane like myself was living in a cold empty marriage or so I thought. Cold as far as I was concerned, but not empty of love for her. At that time, she was running her own small business. I had heard rumours from time to time, about the liaison she and the man who worked for her were having. Logically thinking, it was a perfect reason she had no wish to share the warmth of my bed.

I left the bungalow with a few personal possessions and moved temporarily into a bed and breakfast establishment. Leaving behind almost everything I owned, including the majority of my photos and my RAF uniforms.

As is normal when couples divorce and property is involved, I placed the bungalow on the market.

In the meantime, life at the college continued, in fact, went swimmingly well.

The college went into substantial profit within the second year of operation.

Bath was a genteel city, and still full of retired Admirals and Colonels. Therefore, I was anxious to maintain good relations with the city of Bath. Accordingly, I allowed such organisations as Rotary International, the Red Cross etc, to hold formal events using the college facilities. Bath being popular, gave me hope it would not take long for the bungalow to be sold. Any thoughts I may have had for a quick sale were soon dashed. Within a few weeks, I received a phone call from the estate agent. He informed me that my wife was being totally uncooperative. Not only uncooperative, but she was also being downright offensive to prospective buyers, plus the house was a complete mess. Diane thought by behaving in this manner; the bungalow would not be sold.

    I drove over to inform Diane, that it would be in both our interests if she would be reasonable and allow the prospective buyers to feel welcome. My comments fell on stony ground, leaving me to feel a little concerned. Despite Diane's determination to be unpleasant, the bungalow thank goodness was eventually sold.

    To be rid of Diane as soon as was humanly possible, I admitted adultery. I also promised to look after our son, ensuring he had a home. Therefore, Diane had no alternative but to inform me she wanted to move closer to her older sister who lived in Salisbury.

    With the proceeds of the bungalow, I bought Diane a house. Fortunately, there was enough revenue to buy Diane the house she wanted. I ensured she did not need a mortgage paying for the house outright, including giving her all the furniture we owned from the bungalow. I also made arrangements for Diane to have a very good monthly maintenance payment for our son until he was either eighteen or completed his education no matter what age he may be.

    Once Diane moved, I never knew what happened to my clothes and the rest of the personal belongings that I had left behind. She denied me not only entry to the new house, and my personal belongings. The worse thing she did. She ensured should I want to see my son; I would have to meet him somewhere else.

The divorce absolute eventually came through. I thought I was now free, and with luck, I may now find someone who would give me the love and warmth I truly craved for. Diane, unfortunately, had not completed her revenge. Her venom it seems, went a great deal further, even beyond the grave.

While not only refusing to allow me to see our only son at the home I had bought for him, and his mother. The maintenance payments I had arranged to ensure he was financially secure while at university, she had withheld telling our son I had never sent a penny. This action left our son to believe I did not care what happened to him.

The result of that action was to cause a chasm between us for practically the rest of my life.

Being a meticulous person regarding keeping records. I had kept all the paperwork, which proved, that indeed I had paid her many thousands of pounds for both him and his welfare.

Fate is strange, as Diane collapsed and died while shopping a number of years later. The money from the sale of the house added to my son's financial stability.

Life at the college continued normally until one particular event took place. The Red Cross had held a very successful dinner. Once the event had ended, my Catering Manager informed me several bottles of wine remained unopened. I decided to give my hard-working staff the residue of the wine, as a reward to show my thanks and appreciation.

A couple of days later to my amazement and anger, I

was summoned to Southall. There I was accused like a criminal, of conduct prejudicial to the good name of the college.

To say I was extremely upset, would be an understatement. I felt my integrity and honour had been compromised, particularly as the college had just moved into profit. Under those circumstances and as its Principal, I returned to Bath and submitted my immediate resignation. I served out the required thirty days' notice period. The thought of going back once more to the drawing board to search for pastures new was not at that time to my liking.

Before this unfortunate incident, I had decided to visit Cairo. I wanted to have discussions with the Arab Organisation for Industry, about the provision of industrial training in the U.K. for Egyptian nationals.

The departure of my British Airway's flight from Heathrow was delayed for an hour. Italian air traffic controllers were responsible for this delay, apparently due to congestion over Europe.

On arriving in Cairo, I found it to be not only dirty and full of flies. It was extremely noisy and not the most pleasant of places, including the rancid smells. The traffic was unbelievable, with vehicles parked four deep. The inner vehicles looked as if they had never been moved in years as they were covered in layers of dust. Certainly, no respect for any traffic signals was shown whatsoever. When the outer cars were driven, the habits of the drivers were similar to those of Nigeria. Thankfully, my hotel was situated some miles outside the city. On arriving at the hotel, I found it to be an oasis of green gardens and tranquillity.

Due to an Israeli delegation who were also using the hotel, the whole place was surrounded by a cordon of tanks and troops. At least this made me feel very safe. The Israelis occupied several floors of the hotel, making those particular floors restricted to the rest of the hotel's guests. Mossad, the Israeli secret service, had their agents everywhere.

Discussions complete, I was able to act like a tourist, visiting the Pyramids and Sphinx. I found myself cajoled into riding a camel at the site. A particular ugly beast was offered to me, taking me on a circular tour of the Pyramids. At one point of the journey, the camel managed to place its feet in a large pile of camel dung, almost unsaddling me over its head.

With consummate skill, I managed to stay onboard completing the circuit. Unfortunately, this incident dislodged an expensive gold pen from my pocket, which now resides in the camel's saddlebag in Egypt. I was also invited to climb the Great Pyramid but declined on the basis of age.

I loved seeing the Sphinx and the Pyramids. Sadly, though very obvious for all to see. The Egyptian Department of Antiquities was doing a less than a perfect job, in either preserving or restoring its priceless legacy.

Without further incident, I returned to London onboard a Super, VC10 of British Airways. Fortified by several large gin and tonics, savouring every drop. Mentally I was removing Cairo, from my top ten of possible holiday destinations.

Following Cairo in the November, found me once again catching another aircraft. This time to attend the Eighth International Federation of Training and Development Officers in Manilla. This ensured that I had to endure a fifteen-hour flight, courtesy of both British Airways and Cathay Pacific. Flying from Heathrow, via Dubai, Bangkok, and Hong Kong to reach my destination in Manilla. As usual, for the first few days, I suffered horrendous jet lag. Even pilots unfortunately can suffer as do normal passengers on long haul flights.

Spain ceded the Republic of the Philippines to America, together with Cuba and Puerto Rica after Spain's defeat in the Spanish American war of 1898. Independence was gained in 1946. At the time of my visit, it was still under the dictatorship of Ferdinand Marcos. He remained in total power until 1986. His wife, of course, became very notorious for the number of shoes she had acquired during his years of power. Some reports stated from 5,000, to around just under 1,000. These figures do not include her fantastic collection of clothes, which were found when Marcos lost power.

During 1979, air travellers arriving at foreign airports had to produce international inoculation certificates, in addition to a normal passport. On arriving in Manilla, I was informed that my yellow fever document was out of date. The official did not seem overly concerned, suggesting to two other passengers, and of course myself, that $50 would solve the problem. He further stated,

"I will provide you with the necessary injection."

The three of us then followed the official to an office within the airport.

My suspicions were aroused when we entered a rather dirty, extremely untidy office. Obviously, as far removed from a medical facility as one could ask for. Such doubts were confirmed, when a hypodermic syringe, plus a vial of colourless liquid, or vile liquid!

Depending on your choice of thought, were produced from a desk drawer. At this point, I handed over the suggested $50 dollars and declined further treatment. I hoped my fellow passengers, did not suffer any unwanted condition from their injection of tap water, from a dirty previously used syringe.

The conference itself was particularly uninteresting. So much so, I have no lasting recollection of the actual proceedings.

The country itself is a mixture of the super-rich and the desperately poor. Foul slums at that time were located next to palatial country clubs. This sadly could still be the case even today. No matter where I travelled, I found abject poverty in the rural areas. Manila had large districts which were solely devoted to strip clubs, along with sleazy bars. These bars were populated mainly by teenage girls, known as bar girls. I was to learn, that these girls, were solely provided to cater for the hordes of Japanese and Australian tourists.

These tourists, having flown in via their respective airlines, for what was known as so-called sex tours. The girls it seemed were more than happy to provide their services, allowing them to make a substantial income for their families. Tourists wishing to avail themselves of the services of these girls were firstly required to hand over a certain sum of money to the bar owner. This in turn allowed them to then take the girl to either their hotel or some such place.

An interesting and welcomed diversion provided by the conference organisers had been a trip to the island of Corregidor. Corregidor is a small fertile island, 48 kilometres west of Manila. There had previously been a base there, known as Fort Mills. This having been a United States Army Base since the early 1900s. This base was strategically located at the entrance of Manila Bay. During WW2, the island was a key base of the Allies, when the Japanese invaded the Philippines in 1941.

The Japanese air attacks on December the 8th 1941, seriously crippled the American forces. After the Japanese landed south of Manilla and other parts of the Philippines. The Supreme Commander, General Douglas MacArthur, withdrew his forces. The Japanese entered Manila, which had been declared an open city on the 24th of December that year. Corregidor, like Malta, suffered badly from air attacks. Unlike the devastation Malta went through, Corregidor also sustained continual artillery bombardment until forced to surrender on May the 6th 1942. Before that date, General MacArthur had been ordered to depart with his staff to Australia. Leaving with the famous words,

"I shall return."

Those words were certainly not much comfort to those remaining who had suffered from the atrocious treatment they underwent at the hands of the Japanese. Especially in the Japanese POW Camps. History tells us, that the Republic of the Philippines was not liberated, until March 1945.

Today, the island remains a memorial to one of the fiercest battles in the Pacific region.

During my visit, I found Corregidor quite an eerie place, almost resembling a museum. The remains of US Military buildings and gun emplacements are still there to be seen.

The conference drew to a close after a week, allowing me a few days' site seeing. All in all, after ten days my visit ended. I embarked on a seventeen-hour flight back to London. This time via Hong Kong, Bangkok, Delhi, and Frankfurt.

On returning to Bailbrook, I felt down and alone. Fate once again stepped in.

During the following morning as I started to go through my sensitive papers, preparing to clear my desk in readiness for my departure. The phone disturbed my concentration. Picking it up, instantly recognising the soft sensual voice on the other end, it was of course Maria.

"Hello Roy, I have missed you, I will be in London for a few days, would you care to meet me."

Would I care to meet her; Maria's invitation could not have come at a better moment.

Trying to be calm as I generally am, though today I felt rotten. I replied,

"Of course, I would love to meet up with you." What I truly wanted to tell her was. Of course, I cannot wait to see you. Instead, I asked,

"Where will you be staying?"

Maria informed me she had booked into the Cumberland Hotel in central London. At that time, I had no idea fate was to draw me there in the future for a totally different reason. We arranged to meet in a few days, then continued our conversation for a further few minutes. Replacing the phone, the dark clouds of feeling low disappeared, replaced by excitement with thoughts of seeing Maria once again.

As I walked for the last time through the doors of the college, leaving behind the job I loved; my first feelings of danger came to mind. Politics and small-minded men had claimed another victim. The world of loyalty, and companionship, I had known in the RAF, and the diplomatic service. Certainly, did not exist in the world of Bailbrook College.

Chapter 26

The Brides Fair

1979 had indeed been an eventful, yet deeply unhappy year; resigning from the job I loved, on top of having made the decision to end my marriage. Which sadly meant giving up my home and family and spending that first Christmas holidays on my own. Something I had never done before, and I will admit, left me to feel pretty low. Meeting up with Maria again would be the only highlight which I looked forward to for many months.

Arriving at the Cumberland in the early evening, I wondered what Maria would be wearing, or not wearing as such. This time Maria met me in the foyer, giving me a passionate kiss. She looked as lovely as ever wearing a fashionable black hugging cocktail dress. The thought passed my mind, I would like to remove it there and then. As it was, once we reached her bedroom, with her dress being so tight, our passion ignited and overcame us, we actually struggled to remove our clothing.

Maria being Maria, as usual was wearing nothing under her dress. After giving me a further couple of hours of untold pleasure, we took a shower, dressed, and went to have dinner in a small intimate Italian restaurant in Soho. Returning to the Cumberland, Maria decided a repeat performance of love making would be to her liking. Not a single word of protest passed my lips.

Before leaving, Maria gave me a present of a superb and I should imagine, a very expensive maroon leather jacket. For reasons unknown to me, this was our final meeting. A liaison I look back on with unadulterated pleasure.

Once having left Bailbrook, my search for a new position started in earnest. The monotonous chore of applying for various jobs continued through 1980. My batteries needed re-charging, so I was not too concerned as the rest would do me good. The year passed and another Christmas break came and went. So far there had been nothing I fancied in the world of work.

1981 arrived, and it was not until the spring of that year, while browsing as normal through the Sunday Times, that I saw and applied for a position which at last attracted my interest. Answering the advert, I received an invitation which as usual took me up to London for an interview.

Shortly after the interview, I received the confirmation I had hoped for. To my amazement and delight, I was offered the position of Personnel and Training Director with the American Company Westinghouse, USA, Inc. The Radar Division of Westinghouse based in Boston, had been awarded a lucrative contract. This was to both design and build an Air Defence System for the Royal Moroccan Air Force. I would now have the opportunity to fly and live in a country, I had so far not set foot in.

On June 1st, I boarded a British Airways Tristar flight BA316, bound for Paris. I made an error, by attempting to fly direct to Rabat, instead of using the recommended route direct to Casablanca. Not taking the correct flight, meant I had to change from Charles de Gaulle airport in Paris, to the older Orly airport, situated south of the French capital.

Despite struggling with the heat, plus a mountain of luggage - as there was a shortage of luggage trolleys - a French taxi, and total grid lock of the Paris ring road, I eventually made the Royal Air Maroc flight by the skin of my teeth, arriving in Rabat, the Moroccan capital, almost five hours later.

After living for a month in a smart apartment in central Rabat, I flew home to collect not only my three dogs but a lady friend I had met and who I had grown quite fond of. I would eventually come to marry this very beautiful woman; whose name was Helen. Fate though once again was to play her hand regarding my happiness, but more of that later.

With a heavily laden estate car, we drove from Llandudno, crossing the English Channel and into France. The documentation I required for the three dogs, ironically was more than a human being required and never once inspected.

Once arriving in France, our journey continued, as we drove the full length of the country and then into Spain. Arriving at last in Algeciras, there to stay in the Hotel Reina del Mar. The journey was long and tiring, but extremely interesting, having it appeared no effect on the three dogs.

The following morning after a good Spanish breakfast, our journey to Rabat continued as we crossed the straits of Gibraltar. Going by ferry to the Spanish enclave of Melilla, situated on the northwest coast of Morocco. This being the normal route to enter Morocco, we found ourselves joining a queue of vehicles at the frontier where we handed over the required 50 Dirhams to a gentleman who would smooth our way through Moroccan immigration. After another lengthy road journey, we finally reached the capital Rabat.

Westinghouse had provided us with a lovely villa on the Route des Zahers, on the outskirts of Rabat. We were also provided with a Volkswagen Golf vehicle.

The next day, I reported for duty at the Royal Moroccan Air Force base, situated just outside of Rabat, which became my main place of work. The Air Defence System comprised numerous radar sites with communication links to an underground command and control centre at Rabat. As Personal and Training Director, I was responsible for the training and career development of 1200 Moroccan Air Force personnel. Several radar sites had been built on the Atlas Mountains, with huge parabolic radar dishes. These antennae were intended to detect aircraft but were never used in anger.

Normally, new customers buying such systems would be asked to supply information on which to base the design they required. This would include such parameters as: Where is the threat likely to come from? Also, how many enemy aircraft intruders would you expect to shoot down?

The Royal Moroccan Air Force informed Westinghouse that such information did not exist, and the company should just build them an Air Defence System. This amazing statement meant that Westinghouse was effectively handed a blank cheque.

The system proved most useful; it was used to detect the movement of Polisario rebels in the West Sahara region. The rebels were seeking independence from Morocco. I was amused to learn from my RAF experience, that should the RMAF be required to launch aircraft against a threat, it had to first seek King Hassan's II's permission.

Unfortunately, most of the air force personnel were conscripts and did not possess the inclination or education to operate a high-tech defence system.

Attitudes were somewhat lackadaisical, and discipline was poor. One key remote site, situated high in the Atlas Mountains, appeared to be out of use from 7 pm each day. A helicopter crew sent to investigate reported back that the site crew were in the practice of switching off the equipment each night, as the power supply to the diesel generator kept them awake.

The Arab approach to flying and safety in their helicopters was also suspect. To the extent that several Westinghouse technicians refused to fly with Moroccan pilots after surviving hair raising incidents with them in the Atlas Mountains. They would overload their aircraft and poorly secure the cargo, which was dangerous. Preventing diplomatic problems, the US technicians were returned to the United States.

King Hassan committed many troops and resources to protect the phosphate mines and major towns from Polisario harassment. The radar sites in the Atlas Mountains, although intended for the detection of aircraft proved very useful in detecting ground movement of the Polisario guerrillas in the disputed territory. A role never envisaged by the designers of the radar system.

My new duties were not onerous and consisted mainly of the recruitment of RMAF technical personnel. Supervising the numerous technical training courses. My counterpart was a charming French-speaking Moroccan officer, who went on to improve my French very rapidly.

Rabat was a very pleasant city, its historical French connection still very much in evidence. Although a Muslim country, it was most liberal with alcohol freely available.

The northern coast of Morocco mirrors the climate found in the Bordeaux region of France. Much to my pleasure, Moroccan vineyards produced excellent red wine. Life was very pleasant.

I was one of four Brits employed by Westinghouse. We were something of a novelty to the rest of the 400 American employees. Americans in some cases are very insular, many of them finding employment in foreign countries difficult. This characteristic can cause marital and alcohol-related problems. Westinghouse had to provide an American style social centre. This centre provided the required ice cream, coca-cola and hotdogs, all part of the American psyche.

With my acceptable level of the French language, I enjoyed visiting and shopping in the local Medina, or market. My American colleagues seemed amazed at this, often enquiring if I felt safe, or was I ever worried about civil unrest.

One evening, I was invited to the American Embassy. The disgraced ex-President Richard Nixon had decided to make a visit. On arrival, I was asked if I would like my photograph taken alongside the ex-President, it would of course cost me $10 for the privilege. I explained politely, that in my country, a disgraced politician would have kept his head down, and would have not been visiting overseas embassies. Naturally, I declined the offer.

The American Ambassador at that time came from New England. His position having been a reward from the US President. The individual wore the loudest checked suits I had ever seen and was driven around in an armoured version of the yellow taxi cabs seen in New York. Wherever he went, he was accompanied by his photographer. Even to the Baptist church which I attended. He usually asked if we would like him to say a few words. One American custom I did enjoy, was the travelling brunch. On Sundays after church, we would visit numerous houses, each family producing a different course. Many consisting of wonderful pies, meat dishes, huge salads, and various types of ice cream. All harmful to one's figure.

The highlight of my entire visit was held in late September. Westinghouse organised a trip to the annual Bride's Fair or Moussem.

We left Rabat in a convoy of vehicles, the journey taking us several hours. Initially on good roads, followed by narrow rocky tracks which seemed to cling precariously to the sides of the Atlas Mountains. At the site of the fair, we were pleased to find a comfortable tented hotel.

For more than a thousand years, history informs us, the Berber people have lived in North Africa since the earliest records. Reference to them dates back from about 3, 000 BC. The Berbers inhabited the coast of North Africa, from Egypt to the Atlantic Ocean. They were driven inland to the Atlas Mountains when the Arabs conquered North Africa in the 8th century. Many were of Caucasian extraction with fair hair and blue eyes.

They have lived in small communities, which are spread out across the rugged Atlas Mountains. The people living in such tiny, remote communities have a hard time finding wives or husbands.

The Berber Bride Fair solved this problem. Each year, men and women looking for marriage partners would converge on the shrine of a Muslim Saint, near the village of Imilchil.

Once there, they have three days in which to select a marriage partner from among the hundreds of other single, divorced, or widowed fairgoers.

Although many people attend looking for mates, the Moussem also includes an open-air market. Berber people from many remote villages attend the fair, looking to buy tea, sugar, jewellery, carpets, pots and pans, hardware, spices and produce. A camel auction also takes place.

Berber women, identify prospective grooms by their white turbans. Men who wish to find a bride at the fair, often wear white djellabas. This is a garment that looks like a full-length white shirt. Grooms identify possible brides by their headdresses, and silver jewellery. Courtship consists of meeting and chatting with one another in public.

Holding hands signifies that a deal is in the making. Should one person drop the other person's hand, then the deal is off. Each person will then continue to keep looking.

When a woman decides to accept a man's offer, she declares,

"You have captured my liver."

In Morocco, the liver, rather than the heart, is believed to be the seat of emotion. The couple goes on to roam the fair together holding hands, it is then assumed by all, that they are now engaged.

Men can, of course, tell which ladies have been married previously, simply by examining the style of their headdress. Women who are divorced, or widowed, wear pointed or conical headdresses. First-time brides wear round, spangled headdresses, and heavy makeup. Some of them also veil their faces.

Brides wander through the fair wearing silver and amber jewellery. Folk tradition teaches that silver jewellery brings them good luck

After a couple have become engaged, they wait until the last day of the fair. On the last day, marriage contracts are then signed. A government official arrives, he then records and notarizes the couple's decisions. The men and women sit separately inside the officials' tent, waiting their turn to make these final arrangements. For some, these marriages may only last for twelve months.

After three days of a unique and wonderful experience, it was time for us to commence the return journey back to Rabat.

Crossing a sandy section of road, the vehicles threw up dense clouds of sand. Visibility was almost nil and driving behind the first vehicle, I was unable to avoid colliding with a large rock in the centre of the track. Disaster had struck. I knew immediately from the noise; we had severely damaged the engine of the Golf.

Inspection revealed that the engine had lost oil from a damaged sump. We managed somehow to tow the vehicle to the next village, hoping for a local blacksmith to weld the damaged item. As the village did not possess one, we decided to leave the vehicle with the villagers to be recovered later.

Much later than planned. we arrived safely back in Rabat. A fantastic experience, one so few white men see, only slightly marred by our accident.

During my stay, I amused myself by writing a weekly column for the Westinghouse Bugle. The company paper gave me the opportunity to poke gentle fun at the other Brits, along with the dress sense, and language of my American colleagues.

The title of the column was called 'The Ramblings of an Englishman in Morocco'. One such story went,

'My large white estate car, complete with the British flag, and a GB sticker, provoked strange responses from the locals in Rabat. While stopped at the traffic lights, a group of excited youths gesticulated at me and chanted,

"Liverpool, Liverpool."

For the uninitiated Americans, Liverpool is not only a city in England, it also is a leading soccer club. At that time, being the European Cup Winners.

I suppose it made a change from my RAF days, where the usual cry loosely translated would be,

"Go home Feelthy British."'

On the domestic front, my French sheepdog puppy, who we had called Sophie. Had taken to stealing the maid's underwear and burying it in the garden. This had caused my Muslim gardener a huge amount of embarrassment, and now, I required a new gardener.

I went on to write many more tales but was subjected to the rather strange US censorship. One item they censored, concerned a pet budgerigar.

The article read,

'My pet budgie suffered a fatal heart attack and was found dead on the floor of his cage. Apparently, he had structural failure in flight when performing aerial manoeuvres during fornication with his mate on the top perch.'

Strangely our American cousins censored it.

After two years in a most pleasant country. My Moroccan adventure and contract ended. King Hassan would probably be late giving any order to protect his country. He was the rudest of monarchs, having kept HM Queen Elizabeth waiting for over thirty minutes, in the aggressive heat of Rabat during a state visit. As for me, I left to return to England, and I hoped. pastures new...

After the tragic terrorist incident of 2018. I feel very sad that the Moroccan tourist industry has suffered so badly. Denying many tourists, the joys and pleasure of this lovely country.

Chapter 27

Land of the Big Sky

Returning home to England in 1984, Helen and I had some decisions to make as we were still not married. Helen decided she would return to Kings Lynn to see the completion of her divorce. Having previously bought a pink gentleman's cottage, set in three-quarters of an acre near Beccles, this was perfect for the dogs. The cottage became my home for the following two years.

I enjoyed the first few months doing as little as possible, and as normal, I became bored soon after. My thoughts once more turned to finding a new contract. The Sunday Times, always a good paper to find a perfect job, proved in this instant to be no different than it always had been, on that fine summer morning.

LM Ericsson, the worldwide telecommunications group, was advertising for an Executive Project Manager for their company in Saudi Arabia. This was for a multi-million US dollar contract.

Interesting indeed to my enquiring mind, that I replied to the advertisement immediately. Within two weeks they asked me to go for an interview. The interview was held no less at the Cumberland Hotel in London. Instantly, the recollections of the pleasurable hours I had spent with Maria came to mind. After a further two weeks and to my delight, I was asked to attend a second interview. Only this time, the second interview was to be held at Ericsson Headquarters in Stockholm.

I left England onboard a Boeing 757, from Gatwick to Arlanda courtesy of SAS. The flight taking no more than two hours fifteen minutes.

The Swedish people I met during that time were most pleasant. After three days of discussions, I then returned home.

I must admit, I really fancied that job, and yes. I was on tenterhooks. Not hearing a word for several weeks, I continued to wait until in the end, my patience became exhausted. I was about to call it a day, when out of the blue Ericsson at long last telephoned.

The caller explained that the other person who had been interviewed had been appointed to the position in Saudi Arabia. Apparently, he had managed to upset the project staff, to the point that four hundred of them had threatened to resign.

The caller then asked, was I still interested in the position. Had the caller been a woman, I would have told her I could kiss her. As the caller was a man, I could barely disguise my delight. With all my self-discipline, I informed him I would be happy to accept the position.

The journey proved to be interesting. Setting off from Heathrow, I flew back to Sweden landing at Arlanda airport at four in the afternoon. As was normal, I took the limousine service. By doing so, it gave me the opportunity to enjoy the local scenery until we reached the Sheraton Hotel. The hotel had previously been booked for me by Ericsson and was located in the centre of the city.

After enjoying an excellent evening meal, a good night's sleep, and the following morning an excellent breakfast; I felt ready for the next stage of my journey. Before leaving the hotel, a member of the International Assignment staff introduced himself. He informed me he would be joining me for the rest of the journey. We flew out from Arlanda having a brief stop in Zurich, then onto

Riyadh, entering the Islamic Kingdom of Saudi Arabia.

The ultra-modern airport in Riyadh provides the first shock to the "infidel" visitor. There are no separate "Red' or "Blue" channels in their Customs Hall. All baggage entering the Kingdom is first examined for forbidden items such as alcohol, drugs, or pornographic material. Customs Officers even sniff at bottles of aftershave and flip through magazines for suspect pictures. Even one's wallet is treated in a similar manner, which I found appalling. I often wonder how they would feel should the same courtesy be reciprocated to them when entering England.

They also have installed fast-view video machines, which check for pornographic material. This alone left me feeling disgusted.

With many international flights arriving at the same time, these searches make for long queues and a lengthy wait. To add to the frustration of tired travellers, everything stops when their citizens are called to prayer in the airport mosque.

After leaving the airport, my companion and I left for the Ericsson domestic compound in Riyadh, where we would be staying for the next two days. On arriving at the compound, I was delighted to see not only married quarters but a huge swimming pool. Along with the pool was an excellent restaurant, it was certainly comforting knowing I would be able to enjoy a large, varied menu, serving international food.

Having recharged our batteries, we left after the two days and travelled north by road. My new responsibility indeed turned out to be as interesting as I first thought. In fact, I would describe it as very demanding. As a turnkey communications contract worth $150,000,000, awaited my arrival at King Khalid Military City (KKMC).

When one leaves Riyadh and goes on to drive 250 miles due north, then continues by turning right, and drive for a further 300 miles, you will arrive at the town of Hafar-al-Batin, which is adjacent to the Kuwait border. (A town that figured prominently as a staging post for coalition forces during the first Gulf War.)

Presumably for strategic reasons, the Saudi Ministry of Defence and Aviation (MODA), aided by the US Corps of Engineers, had decided to build a military city some 50 miles from Hafar-al-Batin. Not just an ordinary city, but one which would go on to house 70,000 troops along with their dependents in the middle of nowhere.

The Korean workers employed at the site dubbed the area "Land of the Big Sky". An apt title, as the flat and featureless desert, had a 360-degree horizon.

This looked like the last place God made! The barren desert, scorched by the searing sun. The thought this was to be my home for the next two years filled me with trepidation.

The city site was enormous. Security was extremely tight, and one had to have a visa to enter or leave. Adjacent to the construction areas were the worker's camps. These camps housed some 15,000 multinationals.

My staff numbered 400 and came from all parts of the world including, Swedish, Australian, American, Pakistani, Filipino, Egyptian, and Korean nationals, and of course English.

The Ericsson domestic and office compounds naturally had all been provided with air-conditioning, along with double-skinned chalets. These were the envy of the other contractors.

As the "Boss" I had the privilege of my own accommodation, whereas the other staff lived two to a chalet. The Recreation Hall in the compound was equipped with a TV, a snooker table, and a soft drinks bar. Being a Swedish company, we even had a sauna, despite outside temperatures reaching 40 degrees Centigrade.

For entertainment, I decided to organise regular games nights which included the French game of Boules. This was played of course on the sand outside. The competition was fierce, on one occasion I had to separate a number of argumentative Swedes about to come to blows.

The Korean sub-contractors were not so fortunate. They had to live in wooden huts, 50 persons to each hut. They were treated worse than animals, as that is all that had been provided by the Saudi MODA. They carried out manual labour from 7 am to 7 pm in the searing heat. The pittance they earned, represented a life-saving remittance, which they sent home to their families back in Korea.

Unlike expatriates, they had to serve a minimum of two years in KKMC, before being allowed a vacation, or leave to return to Korea.

Unlike the Ericsson compound in Riyadh and Jeddah, in which home-brew liquor was tolerated to some extent, liquor, drugs and pornographic literature were strictly forbidden within the KKMC compound. We were annoyingly subjected to frequent searches by the Military Police. I must admit at the time, they made me feel very nervous. Knowing full well as the senior Ericsson representative on-site, should they have found any of the forbidden items as mentioned above, I would be held fully responsible for any breaches of their code of conduct, and find myself in one of their miserable prisons.

My nerves became a little frayed, naturally hoping that the police would not unearth any copies of the Playboy magazine in the compound. Talk about living life on the edge.

As it turned out, my eventual crime did not involve alcohol, drugs, or pornography. The MODA required me to have on my staff, two Saudi Liaison Officers.

Their duties were not defined, and I rarely saw either of them thank goodness, apart from when it came to paydays.

During one of my regular visits to Sweden, one of these unpleasant Saudis came on-site and demanded a pay rise. Quite correctly, my Administration Manager informed him that such a decision would have to await my return to KKMC. Unfortunately, my return coincided with my manager's departure and the matter was delayed.

The impatient obnoxious Saudi proceeded to report me to the Military Police. Only to then find myself being arrested and charged with insulting a Saudi citizen.

Within hours after being arrested, I found myself in a dirty, grimy smelly cell, situated in the town of Hafar-al-Batin. Some 50Km to the north of KKMC. It was not what one could call a pleasant experience, and I was most relieved to be rescued after several hours. I was eventually summoned to appear before a Sharia Court, which is of course a religious court. The magistrate ordered that I pay damages and increase the salary to the man who had just put me through hell.

I remain unconvinced about the impartiality of the magistrate, who had been kissed on both cheeks by my Saudi accuser, before giving evidence!

After that experience, it is my hope that current

thinking regarding Sharia Courts, results in them being forbidden in the United Kingdom. We are a Christian country, and our legal system is more than adequate.

Several Korean companies were building KKMC. Most buildings being constructed from prefabricated concrete sections. The mobile plant manufacturing these items at the time happened to be the largest in the world. Fatalities though were very common, with many unfortunate Korean workers falling under and being crushed by huge concrete panels.

The Ericsson sub-contractor was a Korean company called Dong Ah. They were responsible for all the civil engineering works that were associated with our MODA telecommunications contract.

My routine included daily progress meetings with a Mr Kim. Mr Kim was the Dong Ah General Manager.

I look back even today, with fond memories of the working relationship I had with Mr Kim. His Oriental manners were of course always perfect. As with most Asians, he had trouble pronouncing certain letters, which he never mastered. On entering my office, he would first bow, then go on to say accompanied by a gracious smile,

"Good morning Mr Loy."

Even when it became necessary for me to admonish him about certain matters, his manners would continue to be impeccable, and he would then go on to say,

"Solly Mr Loy."

Like most Asians, Mr Kim never mastered the ability to call me Roy. One memory, I will of course always treasure.

Our contract with the MODA involved the design and construction of all communications systems. These ranged from telephones to CCTV links.

All contracts at KKMC were supervised by the US Corps of Engineers. A quasi-military/civilian organization, part of the US Department of Defence. The Corps were normally engaged in civil engineering projects. This included the construction of roads, bridges, and other building works.

Their "bible" was a set of Federal Defence Regulations, written in pure Americanized English. The somewhat incomprehensible material in this publication was such; that Ericsson employed a US consultant who would act as my interpreter. Finally, we knew more about the regulations than the Corps, it certainly proved a very useful weapon when having regular meetings, enabling me to quote obscure references for Ericsson's benefit.

One of the Corp's obsessions concerned the allowable profit margin for all contractors.

Enabling a company to work in the Kingdom of Saudi Arabia, it was essential to have a Saudi agent, to win a contract. Preferably, one's agent should be a member of the Royal family. (At the time this numbered 5000 Royals)

By Royal decree, any commission paid to an agent was limited to 5% of the contract value. The Ericsson agent was of course a member of the Royal House of Saudi. This particular Prince also had the Mercedes Benz sole agency. Making him one of the wealthiest men in the country.

Our initial contract was worth $150,000,000, and as was normal, we paid him considerably above 5%.

Not that we ever saw him. The profit margin, permitted by US Federal Regulations, limited Ericsson to a paltry 7.5%. This naturally, was a figure not acceptable in Stockholm. Despite our creative accounting, the Corps was well aware that we were making more than the permitted profit, which became a constant irritant to them.

Consequently, in the end, they finally came to my office, demanding to see the companies accounts. A request which I politely refused. I then went on to inform them, that a journey to LM Ericsson HQ in Sweden, would perhaps meet their requirements. Knowing full well that, this would prove a total waste of time.

Their response to me was pathetic, as they then stated that they would sue Ericsson.

I took great delight by pointing out that Ericsson, was of course a Swedish Company, having a Royal patron to work in Saudi Arabia. Working under the supervision of the US Corps of Engineers.

Which country did they suggest as the location for any legal action they may wish to take? The grumbles continued, but I heard no more about legal action. (Our final profit came out as approximately 20% of $150,000,000. Although the initial Ericsson contract was for that vast amount, we were given additional work packages. These ranged in price from $1,000,000 to $30,000,000 each, as the city grew...)

The Change Orders I received, involved the submission to the Corps of our plans, and price. This necessitated a long and tedious meeting at which my staff and I, were grilled on every small detail of our submission. I spent many hours during these meetings, facing around fifteen specialists.

Explaining to them the fine details of the plans, and what the prices were to be. Unfortunately, their expertise was in pouring concrete, rather than the sophisticated communications systems, which they knew very little about. Annoyingly, this meant over-long sessions arguing about actual prices, were not helped by their suspicions over our profit margin.

On one particular occasion, totally exasperated by their behaviour, I suggested that we abandon the argument, and they make me a sporting offer. Needless to say, they did not appreciate my Anglo-Saxon humour.

The Corps was very strict (often paranoid) about safe working practices. Frustratingly, I found myself regularly summoned. Often in respect of having to look at a newly dug hole or trench. Sometimes it may have been due to a Korean Foreman not having arranged the correct colour, or amount of warning tape required. My standard response was to nod wisely, then leave the scene of our *crime* as quickly as was humanly possible.

Site safety meetings were held once a month in my office. These were attended by the Corps Safety Officer. He was a large man even by US standards and looked to be of Hawaiian origin.

Although a cheery person, he insisted on wearing his protective working jacket and safety helmet. After several meetings at which I dropped hints about this habit, eventually, I could no longer restrain myself and suggested that the structure which had been made in Finland, was quite sound and the roof was not likely to fall in. Needless to say, the irony was lost on the US citizen.

Each Friday is regarded as a Muslim Holy Day. Due to this factor, we only worked six days a week. Every two weeks Ericsson staff were therefore permitted to drive the 500 miles to Riyadh. Regardless of the fact the journey took several hours, it was essential to have a break for so-called rest and relaxation from the monotonous, and oppressive environment of KKMC...

Although the Company provided everything for one's personal needs, it was regarded by some, as therapeutic when able to go shopping in the big city. Personally, as there were no bars or women available, shopping was not at the top of my list of enjoyment.

Staff based in Riyadh enjoyed the facilities of the Ericsson compound, especially those who had been permitted to be accompanied by their families. Unlike KKMC, which was strictly "Bachelor Status."

Wives in Riyadh had to adhere to a strict dress and behaviour code. They were not allowed to drive a car and were required at all times to be escorted when out shopping. Public displays of affection were strictly forbidden. An unmarried couple found to be sharing a car or taxi were liable to arrest by the Religious Police.

Should the Saudis decide to allow tourism, then their attitude and laws must change considerably. I cannot foresee this happening in the short term without a major change in policy. They would do well to remember how they are treated by their hosts in non-Muslim countries.

Ericsson ensured I had the privilege of having my own company car. This vehicle was an enormous 7-litre Chevrolet Classic Caprice. One can only describe that beasty as a gas-gobbling monster, especially when driving to Riyadh.

From leaving the compound, I drove through the desert for two hundred and fifty miles until reaching a small town.

Driving into the town one needed to make a 90-degree turn, but before doing so, the town had a filling station and store where I refuelled and bought my favourite

Fig Rolls.

Continuing from there for another two hundred and fifty miles I eventually reached Riyadh. The temptation was to set the cruise control at 100mph and then sit back with feet up. The only real hazard was the numerous Bedouin tribesmen, herding camels and goats adjacent to the highway. With absolutely no appreciation of speed or distance, they were prone to drive the herd across the road in front of speeding vehicles. Apart from the risk to life and limb, the payment demanded for killing a camel, believe it or not, was an extortionate amount.

There did not seem to be an obvious Highway Code, and traffic accidents were frequent and spectacular.

Expatriates lived in fear of being involved in any accident, as the normal procedure was arrest and imprisonment. Concern about guilt or innocence did not enter the equation.

One of my Pakistani truck drivers, who was completely blameless, spent several weeks in one such prison after being hit head-on by an overtaking Saudi driver. Eventually returning to work without being tried. Saudi justice to this day remains abhorrent.

As Christmas drew close, I decided to return to England enabling me to join Helen. Straight after the New Year, I returned to Saudi Arabia.

1985 proved to be rather momentous. Global oil prices collapsed, and even cash-rich Saudi Arabia, felt the pinch as its oil revenues plummeted. The effect at KKMC was that MODA examined its budgets, finding the need to tighten its belt.

The result of this was the issue of work orders and the release of new sections of the city would be put on hold.

The large Ericsson workforce found itself running out of work, and I became increasingly concerned about this situation.

After a couple of months, with the situation worsening, I made the decision to fly to Stockholm to have urgent discussions with senior management. Once there, I had hoped I would be given positive guidance regarding this serious matter. Unfortunately, only to be met with typical laid-back, Swedish behaviour. As my bosses went on to suggest that I should make the decision for them.

On my return to Saudi Arabia, oil prices had fallen even further. After having spent several sleepless nights worrying, I took a deep breath and decided that Ericsson should abandon the contract.

Not an easy decision! Demobilisation naturally would be complex, time-consuming and require the most detailed planning.

We chose a Sunday, three months ahead and constructed a plan based on that date. On the given date, all four hundred personnel, our equipment, plus all vehicles would be gone. My Admin Manager and I would be the last two out of KKMC. The shortness of the timescale certainly focused the effort to achieve this plan.

I conveyed the news to a senior Saudi at MODA Headquarters, whose response was,

"Ericsson will never pull out of KKMC."

I thought we shall see. The next three months were more than nerve-wracking as we struggled to stay on schedule with the demobilization plan.

Under the terms of our contract, demobilization required us to dismantle the buildings on the worksite and return that site to the desert. Our domestic compound would be handed to MODA and used as accommodation for any future Saudi military personnel.

The office buildings, although prefabricated were of high quality and had cost several million dollars. Dismantling and any removal of them would also cost a large sum of money. With this in mind, I offered the buildings to MODA for $750,000. With a typical Saudi mentality, they commenced to haggle and attempted to reduce what was already a give-away price. I left their HQ, determined that MODA would not benefit from the situation.

Bearing in mind the high removal costs, I found another solution. I approached one of the Korean contractors who were in need of offices. They were in the process at that time of constructing a new hospital. We agreed on a deal where he would remove all the buildings from our site, level the area, returning it to the desert.

In return, he would receive all the buildings, FREE.

The Koreans most certainly did not hang about, and as I drove to work the following morning, I saw Korean workers swarming all over the office buildings like ants.

They were even sawing wooden buildings in half, then trucking them away! It was a most impressive operation, and within 48 hours, the site was no more. My contact at MODA drove by, and his double-take of the scene made my day.

"How much have they paid?" was his plaintive enquiry.

With delight, I said,

"Nothing, I gave them away free."

I smiled to myself thinking, this is one of my better days at KKMC. All personnel retreated to our domestic compound for the rest of our stay.

Our planned rundown continued on schedule; one last problem was the Ericsson vehicles. With one week remaining, and most of my staff having departed, we still had some 40 assorted vehicles. I decided to auction these remaining assets. After all bids were in, I opened them in my office on the Thursday morning, just three days before final departure. I then went on to notify the highest bidder, who very quickly removed the vehicles from the Ericsson site.

Within ten minutes of the vehicles having been driven away, an irate Saudi appeared. He was exceptionally rude, and in a forceful manner, accused me of fixing the sale. With commendable restraint, I informed him that the vehicles were my property, and as such. As far as I was concerned, the highest bidder had obtained them legally.

The angry Saudi departed, and shortly after I received a telephone call from the Military Police. I will be honest and say. That phone call left me panic-stricken. I had apparently, once again, insulted a Saudi citizen.

I was informed the auction was invalid and told to hold it again in thirty days. This statement coming within 72 hours, before we left!

My (good) Saudi Liaison Officer, being fully aware of the situation, advised that the only solution was to pay off the insulted party. We handed over the sum of thirty thousand dollars, then breathed a sigh of relief. I was informed later in the day, that the injured party and the successful bidder, had shared both the money and the vehicles. The whole situation reminded me of the tale about Ali Baba and the Forty Thieves.

Sunday arrived without further panic, and after all remaining staff had left on the Saturday evening, I left with my Admin Manager on the Sunday morning. To say we were relieved at the thought of leaving this difficult, stressful, environment. You may regard this as an understatement.

Our last farewell gesture was to wave a Union Jack flag out of my car window, first making sure that we were out of sight of the sentries at the gate. A gesture which 24 hours earlier, would have ensured we would have seen the inside of a prison.

As it transpired, the early departure from KKMC did not affect Ericsson's financial performance (or my reputation.) The company made a profit of $30,000,000 on the KKMC contract.

Postscript

Six years after the above events, KKMC reappeared in the news headlines, during the first Gulf War. The city, adjacent to the Kuwait border, played an important role as a staging post for the Coalition Forces, in the defeat of Saddam Hussein. I often wonder, did we make the right decision?

I returned home once more to England, only to find myself within a very short space of time, flying back to Stockholm.

Chapter 28
Down Under

Having achieved a significant profit for Ericsson and organised a successful departure from the King Khalid Military City contract, my reputation was now established within the Ericsson Organisation.

After spending a few months at home resting from having survived, what I will always regard as the worse posting of my life, I once again felt ready to take on new work.

I can only think my guardian angel, must have been in communication with someone at Ericsson, as the telephone rang at that moment in time.

I was asked to take a flight back to Stockholm. Only this time, not for an interview, but to visit the Railway Signalling Company (ERS) of Ericsson.

I was genuinely surprised to learn the company apparently were suffering problems in Australia. Presenting myself at the office of Bengt Gustavsson, who was the President of the Railway Signalling Company. Fortunately, I had been pre-warned by his staff, about the aggressive manner of the gentleman. On entering his office for the first time, he was sitting at his extremely large desk. As I drew closer, he stood up, though this made little difference as he was short in stature. He was known in Ericsson for his belligerent attitude to subordinates. One thoroughly unpleasant man.

As expected, I was greeted by him in a somewhat brusque fashion. I noticed he did not extend his hand for me to shake. Already not impressed by his attitude and bad manners. He sat himself down once again and went on to inform me in a very sarcastic manner,

"We have a problem in Australia. They tell me, you are capable enough to solve it!"

Politely, but firmly, I replied,

"Not without knowing the situation, and not from 12,000 bloody miles away!"

He looked at me for a glancing second or two, and then pulled from his desk drawer a large envelope which he practically threw across the desk. Carefully opening the envelope, I found it contained a huge amount of traveller's cheques, including a business class ticket to Brisbane, Australia. I must admit, it crossed my mind that I could abscond to Tahiti, and never be seen again by Ericsson.

The flight to Australia confirmed just how far it was from anywhere. 12 hours in the air to Singapore was long enough, without transferring onto another aircraft for a further 8 hours. Having said goodbye to Helen and the dogs, I departed from Heathrow on a Sunday afternoon, arriving in Brisbane the following Wednesday morning. Over the years, jet lag has always affected me badly.

I may have been exceptionally tired, but I did notice on entering the arrivals hall, there was a huge poster on one of the walls, which read,

'ALWAYS WEAR A CONDOM.'

Given this advice, I wore one for three weeks. Sadly, nothing happened.

Seven days passed before I approached anything resembling a normal human being.

Settling into a rather nice apartment situated on the banks of the Brisbane River, which is in the university suburb of St Lucia. Awaiting me was a Ford Holden company car. I now felt ready, to be able to address any of the problems being experienced by Ericsson Railway

Signalling.

Queensland Railways was engaged in the electrification of the mainline between Brisbane, Townsville, and Cairns to the north. A considerable distance of 1681 Km. Prior to electrification, it took 32 hours for a train to reach its destination. Ericsson had been awarded a contract, that was to replace the existing semaphore signalling. This new system had the capability of coping with the higher speeds provided by electrification.

The project in its final stages annoyingly had been bleeding money, but an Ericsson presence was essential in Queensland. Queensland Railways was about to award its first contract for Automatic Train Control. Ericsson was one of a limited number of companies worldwide who had the required technology, therefore, was in pole position to obtain the contract.

Therein lay the problem I had to solve.

First by stabilising, then try to stem the project losses, and finalise the work as soon as possible. My task was to ensure an Ericsson presence in Queensland, or at least until awarded the Automatic Train Control contract. Bengt Gustavsson was correct, there was a problem in Australia. One hell of a major problem.

Nervously, I started work as General Manager Projects but also felt optimistic. Very quickly it was obvious that sloppy work practices, the lack of supervision, plus attitudes to work, were the culprits. Australians naturally are very fond of sport, along with the pursuits of outdoor life. They found that work interfered with their weekends. To my further dismay, I realised several of my staff were ex-British Rail supervisors. Some having been junior managers, who had taken refuge in Australia. The word "profit" had always been a foreign word in the nationalised British rail system. Their attitudes were now obviously being transferred to Queensland.

One of the more pleasant ways my senior colleagues and I spent some time after work, would be in the Aussie equivalent of a British pub. We joined the Aussies in drinking Foster's Lager, served ice cold direct from a fridge. The lager came in a can and was known as a tinnie.

To my amusement, the Aussies would continuously bang on about the English drinking warm beer. A welcome diversion at weekends was the drive to the Gold Coast. Once there, we would visit a unique facility that bred crayfish in huge circular water tanks. One of the well-known delicacies of the farm was the tail of the crayfish. The farm had a wonderful restaurant, which served these tails. The word delicious is perhaps rather inadequate, to describe this particular delicacy.

The operations in the final stages of the signalling contract, involved work on the section from Gladstone on the coast of Queensland, into the interior. This was to a place called, Black Dog Halt.

From there, coal from opencast mines would be transported to the port of Gladstone, for shipment to Japan. Huge trains with four locomotives, and over a mile in length, ran 24 hours a day. Black Dog Halt was like the old Wild West in America; boasting a saloon, a motel, a house of dubious reputation, and a filling station.

Five months after my arrival, the 110Km section was completed, making the withdrawal of people and equipment necessary. As with all projects, unfortunately, it is much harder to escape from, than to set them up.

Vehicles, tools, and a mass of equipment, along with spares used in the project, were collected at the Ericsson depot in the town of Rockhampton. This being the nearest place of relative civilisation to Black Dog Halt. With my neck considerably extended, I announced that we would vacate the said depot on the 27th of June. Looking at the vast piles of junk, plus a great number of vehicles in the compound, in addition to spares and furniture in the buildings, I felt sure that I might regret my decision.

A relatively small amount was loaded onto a couple of trucks, then sent south for possible use in future projects. I was left with a mountain of junk, including some 20 vehicles that bore the scars of heavy use in the outback. I decided that the only solution was to scrap the lot or hold an auction. The auction option won. I appointed a local auctioneer and then advertised in the local press that our auction would be held on 26th June, 24 hours before my deadline.

Making preparations for the sale, the vehicles desperately needed valeting. I found an interesting solution in the shape of a local educational organisation. This organisation specialised in work placement for the mentally retarded. The principal was a charming man and delighted to help. A posse of young people descended on the compound. They went on to happily scrub the vehicles until even the most dilapidated looked almost pristine. I of course was delighted, the youngsters actually seemed thrilled at being allowed to help. The principal was naturally most grateful to receive a generous donation from Ericsson.

On June 26th, being a Saturday, I drove nervously to the depot. My worries were totally unfounded. People came in droves, both from town and the outback to the sale. By midday, it looked as though locusts had attacked the compound. There was literally nothing left except the fencing and buildings. Was I relieved? Most definitely indeed!

Standing with a representative of Queensland Railways, as we watched the last Aussie leave. I asked one tanned gentleman in shorts, who sported a wide-brimmed hat if he had had a good day.

"Too right, mate," he replied, as he held up several shovels. Unfortunately, they all bore the label 'Property of Queensland Rail' I smiled and left the scene.

With the project finalised on target, I prepared to leave for Brisbane. Flushed with success, I sent the following telex to the Head Office:

26/2/87

To: Managing Director & Staff, Ericsson Signalling Pty, Brisbane, Australia.

This is my final communication and may well become a collector's item. (I have several autographed copies, which may be auctioned in Head Office to further reduce the project costs)

The Ericsson outpost in Central Queensland is now closed. Fort Black Dog bears the scars of some particularly bloody skirmishes. The natives of Rockhampton have been pacified with gifts of vehicles, and spares. The enemy, Queensland Rail, is in full retreat, and I have been assured of safe passage to Brisbane by local tribesmen.

No significant casualties to report, and in the immortal words of General Macarthur of WW2 fame,

"I or we, shall not return. To all those that helped, thank you" To the others, no comment.

Signed.
The Non-Whingeing Pom.
Roy.

My communiqué it seems, fell on deaf ears. My British humour obviously not appreciated Down Under!

Eventually, Ericsson was awarded the new Automatic Train Control by Queensland Rail, and by early July I was the ex-General Manager (Projects) and bound for home. An interesting and often pleasant period in Australia was over, I was now ready for the next overseas adventure. I felt that I had solved Bengt's down under problem, and once again returned to England. However, fate was to deal me another hand, which I most certainly was not expecting.

Chapter 29

Head Hunted

After returning home from Australia, my thinking back then was that it may take some time for me to find work once again. Not too worried, as I decided an extended break may be just what I needed. Unfortunately, or fortunately, depending on how one may look at it, I received a phone call which deeply surprised me. I was being "head-hunted" for a job in the Federal Republic of Nigeria.

I had been requested to go up to London for the first interview. The interview took place in an apartment in Dolphin Square. SW1. This prestigious address is in a large block of flats, built in the 1930s and is the home to various nobility, along with the rich and famous.

The man I was interviewed by, was Lieutenant Colonel (Ret'd) Colin Mitchell. Better known as Mad Mitch. He was ex- Commanding Officer of the Argyll and Sutherland Highlanders, and a previous Member of Parliament. By coincidence, our paths had crossed in Aden during the early 1960s. Unfortunately, it was there that I had the misfortune to serve with the Royal Air Force, during Aden's bloody campaign for independence. During my stay terrorism was rife. The Adeni Police mutinied, ambushing an Army patrol, then took refuge in the Crater district (an extinct volcano area of the capital).

Contrary to orders from the UK Minister of Defence, and to the delight of every serviceman in Aden, Mad Mitch led the Argyll's into Crater, going on to disarm the mutineers. Sadly, he was later hounded out of the Army for this action. After a brief spell as Member of Parliament for West Aberdeen, he became an adviser in somewhat clandestine areas for the then Prime Minister (Margaret Thatcher).

During the interview, the Colonel told me about an amusing visit he had been on. The visit had enabled him to interview a Mujahadeen Rebel leader in Afghanistan. While waiting in the leader's outer office, he had been approached by one of the tall rebel bodyguards. Complete with bandoliers, daggers and an automatic AK47 rifle.

The tall, bearded gentleman asked the Colonel if he knew Margaret Thatcher. He replied,

"YES. I know the Prime Minister very well. Why?"

The rebel then told him,

"My brother lives in Leeds, and is having problems with his unemployment benefits... You have to speak to Mrs Thatcher!"

Obviously, these were grey areas of our foreign policy! What a small world we live in.

My initial interview went well, and I was summoned to a further meeting at the London headquarters of the International Signal Corporation (ISC) later to become Ferranti International. There I met Sir David Checketts KCVO, who at that time was the UK Managing Director of ISC. Checketts had previously served the Royal Family in the capacity as Private Secretary, to both HRH Duke of Edinburgh and the Prince of Wales. I was informed during my interview, that the position under recruitment was as Managing Director of ISC's Nigerian operations.

After this latest interview, it was suggested that I should meet the senior executives of ISC. This meant a trip to the United States of America. Naturally, I readily agreed!

Flying business class, I left London Heathrow in the September, onboard a British Airways Flight BA217 for

Washington. I was most impressed to be met at Dulles-Washington International airport, then continued my journey by being flown to Lancaster Pennsylvania, in a Cessna light aircraft, one of several owned by ISC. Two days later I was the new Managing Director, Nigeria. The return trip was not quite as smooth as my outgoing journey.

The ISC chauffeur, took me to Harrisburg airport, instead of the correct airport at Lancaster. Sufficient to say, I missed the BA flight to Heathrow. Having the need to spend an extra night at Dulles International Airport gave me the opportunity to have another night of rest.

Before going to Nigeria, I married my second wife Helen. Only this time, the marriage ceremony was very simple and held at the local Registry Office in Conway, North Wales. We then spent a few romantic days in France. A couple of months later Helen flew out to join me. This was the first time in my long career that I was accompanied by a family member, it felt wonderful.

Meanwhile, I travelled to Nigeria with Sir David Checketts. We boarded a British Caledonian DC 10 Flight BR375 to Lagos. ISC company rules gave us the privilege to flying first class which thank the Lord, we were most grateful for.

This saved us from the horrendous conditions which at that time, economy class appeared to suffer from not only having a small seat with poor legroom, but it was also full of extremely noisy Nigerians.

One of the main advantages, they allowed first-class passengers to disembark first. This gave us the opportunity to sprint along the airport concourse, enabling one to reach the immigration desk. By doing so, it allowed us to be in front of the other 300 shouting heaving, mass of passengers entering Nigeria.

Not that any great advantage accrued, as it took approximately two hours for baggage to reach the arrivals hall. Invariably, half of the baggage carousels were not working, and the air conditioning was usually "quenched." (Broken down.) After two hours in a temperature in excess of 30 degrees Celsius, one's suit felt like wet cardboard. With armed police, stationed on the conveyor belts to prevent looting, it really was– Welcome to Nigeria!

The drive into Lagos from the airport was equally horrendous. Headlights and rear lights on all vehicles are optional. Any driving licences on close inspection were usually forged. The highway code is non-existent, and all traffic lights ceased to work soon after the British left. Police roadblocks were plentiful. The standard approach was to offer the guardians of law, bribes. These bribes would be in the shape of small amounts of Naira (the local currency) or cheap pens which had been purchased for that purpose. Failure to oblige meant a full inspection of one's vehicle including the boot, plus the contents of one's luggage being strewn in the mud.

Home for the next three years was to be on Victoria Island. The Island is linked to Lagos and the mainland by a bridge. Most European ex-patriates lived on the island, which was considered the better part of the Capital.

Soon after my arrival, it was decided that the original apartment, together with a rather disreputable suite of offices, should be replaced by a villa. The Villa would then serve as both accommodation and the Ferranti offices. After a tiresome search, a suitable two-storey villa in a small compound was found. The compound had been nearing completion when the building contractor decided to abscond with the money!

For a suitable sum, a new contractor agreed to finish the work. The most essential work required was to the interior, as it still needed to be completed and then painted. I had trouble trying to explain to the painters, that accumulated dust and debris on the woodwork, should first be removed before painting.

The locals it seemed, suffered from some strange neuro-muscular complaint. This complaint ensured that they deface all newly painted surfaces. Hand and finger marks appeared in the most unlikely and inaccessible places on walls and doors. Fingers missed light switches at every attempt. They were also incapable of passing through a doorway, without leaving dirty marks on the door or its surroundings. Could this be the basis for an anthropological research paper?

With construction nearing completion, another one of the sub-contractors disappeared. Annoyingly, he left leaving portions of the patio unfinished. The machine being used to wash and polish the terrazzo tiles was abandoned. The supplier refused us permission to use it, informing us the refugee contractor owed him money. Not happy with the situation, money once again changed hands. As it turned out, it was my money... the work on the patio resumed.

To my relief, the villa was completed on the eve of the wet season. However, when the first tropical storm hit Lagos, the roof leaked and flooded one of the bedrooms. The roofing man claimed it was due to a blocked drain. He had probably forgotten to fit it. I decided the wisest thing to do just in case there were any further mishaps, would be to have the whole roof checked.

The teething problems continued. Just when I thought I had won, the Nigerian factor struck again. Having decided to make a final check of the master en suite bathroom, only to find there was no hot water. The plumber was again summoned. I hoped this time he had fixed the problem, though at the expense of leaving muddy footprints in the bath. After he left there was still no hot water. Despite all of the switches having been turned on. Was the immersion heater actually working? No! The electrician had omitted to complete the wiring. In the end, I gave in and completed the job myself.

The day got progressively worse. At 5 pm our stand-by generator, (an essential item due to the constant power breakdowns), overheated and shut down. In addition to that, the main fuse box began smoking merrily. We summoned an electrician from the Nigerian Electrical Power Authority (NEPA.) This person arrived and effected a temporary repair once again giving us power. He left clutching a handful of Naira. To my amazement, the real NEPA man then arrived! The latter complained bitterly about the bogus electrician, but thankfully I persuaded him to return the following day and replace the fuse box. William, our houseboy, described the original box in a derogatory fashion as being Ibo made. A reference to one of the tribal groups from the province of Biafra in Nigeria. The fact that he was an Ibo did not seem to matter.

I was also informed by NEPA, that the house wiring fitted by the contractor, was not only unsuitable but dangerous… To add insult to injury, it appeared that the standby generator had been positioned in its shelter the wrong way round. The radiator had been placed facing inwards, hence the cause of the overheating. The immediate solution entailed removing part of the shelter's roof. I took solace in a large gin and tonic.

Despite the trauma of finishing the villa, I decided to add a swimming pool. What a mad idea that was to prove, I should have known better. As to be expected the project proved endless. We lived with a large hole in the garden, which apparently defied all attempts to be pumped dry by an antique Nigerian water pump. I cringed daily, as the boys waded about in the water and made constant running repairs to a "live" pump connected to the main electricity supply. Living some 500metres from the beach, and the South Atlantic Ocean, prompted me to jokingly ask the pool contractor if the pool water was coming from the ocean, was he trying to empty the South Atlantic. My British humour fell on stony (wet) ground. After many months of frustration, the pool eventually was completed. I knew what emotions must have been experienced by the builders of the Suez Canal, or the Forth Bridge.

By this time, the contractor got quite carried away and offered to fill the pool. Despite my doubts, an ancient water tanker appeared depositing some brackish water into the pool then quickly departed. The initial consignment covered the deep end to a depth of about one metre, and there the day ended. A week later more tankers appeared, eventually managing to fill the pool to a respectable level. To commemorate the event, I had my photograph taken holding the hosepipe. I dreaded the saga of cleaning, filtration and all the other good things a pool requires.

After another week, the pool pump was actually working, and the water which had resembled green pea soup began clearing. I had to admit that the poolside, and underwater lighting was effective, even most attractive.

However, several days later, the water was still like pea soup. My initial doubts about the pool electrician were confirmed, as I discovered that although the water was circulating, it was not passing through any filter. Opening a couple of valves eventually solved things. As often happens in Nigeria, a friend of one of the staff appeared and claimed the job of the pool boy. I parted with money for cleaning equipment along with other materials and was pleasantly surprised when the pool became useable.

Most expatriates living in various countries overseas, find themselves employing locals as household servants. Helen and I, who had now joined me, were no exception. We found ourselves subsidising the country's economy, by employing several of the locals.

A rather curious phenomenon being, that the longer one stays in a country, the larger the household workforce becomes, most having English names.

Our first and essential acquisition was William. Not only was he our house boy, but he was also our cook. Houseboy being a misnomer, as William was almost 50 years old. He was an Ibo from Rivers State and proved a splendid find. He occupied a bungalow at the rear of the villa, together with several of the nine children he had produced. His wife remained in his home village with the remainder of their family. She would of course come to visit him from time to time. William was an excellent cook, and we fed like fighting cocks. At weekends, despite my protests, he always served an enormous "English" breakfast.

His working uniform was a blue jacket and trousers. He would change into crisp whites to serve our evening meal, always minus shoes. We never managed to get him into footwear even when we had guests.

William was the "boss" servant and ran the household with an iron hand. No tradesman, repairman, or supplier entered the compound without his permission and a monetary reward. He was immensely proud and protective of his position as an employee of ex-patriates. We discovered that he invited contemporaries, all of course in "lesser" positions. He loved to open our wardrobes and show them the range of our clothing, in particular Helen's lingerie! When visitors came for dinner, William would arrange the newly laundered clothing on the balcony so that visitors might admire our "wealth."

He held strong views on most things, including my inability to do the shopping. He would say things like,

"Massa don't know these things!"

One night I saw a mouse and discussed this possible problem with him at breakfast the following day. He was typically adamant informing me,

"No like dem, dey eat furniture."

We were obviously harbouring a rare example of the lesser, long-tailed furniture eating rodent often seen in Lagos. William continued with my interrogation,

"Had I killed it?"

Given that I had failed to take this necessary action, he then asked,

"Had I sprayed the room?"

I explained, with little success, that the local product akin to Flit, was not too effective against mice. I called the local fumigation crew, as I did not trust our staff to operate a conventional mousetrap. Anyway, they all thought that cheese was too valuable to waste on mice.

Apart from William, we also had Michael, who was

our driver. Our maintenance man was a chap called Dennis, and Livarno took care of our garden. We also employed a young lady by the name of Rose Marie, who became our maid. Sadly, we lost Rose Marie who was then replaced by Christina. We employed a chap called Emmanuel; he was our general cleaner along with the pool boy. Lastly, there was Haji, he was the first contact to our residence being the gatekeeper.

Ensuring I returned with presents for each member of the staff, after a short visit on home leave to the UK. Felt like having our own Nigerian family, rather than household servants.

Sadly, in 1989, as I stated, we lost Rose. Feeling ill, she had been persuaded to go to hospital but refused to stay being concerned about her young children. After leaving the hospital, William informed us that Rose had taken some misguided advice, thinking she would take a purge of sorts. This purge was falsely labelled Epsom Salts and had been banned as counterfeit by the authorities. Rose was re-admitted to the hospital but unfortunately died.

Her death in fact was from hepatitis. Her demise brought home to us, that curable diseases in civilised society, can be killers in the Third World; aided and abetted by unscrupulous dealers selling counterfeit medicines.

As was customary, we paid mortuary and hospital fees. We also paid for the transportation of her body to her home village and provided a special coffin suitable for the 500-mile journey. Special clearance was necessary due to her death from a contagious disease.

Due to the possibility of hepatitis, I arranged for all our staff to be screened. They were assembled in the boardroom for vaccinations to be given, along with blood and urine samples to be taken.

Despite recent tragic events, it proved to be an amusing few moments, as most of them had not experienced such tests. The elderly gatekeeper being of the Muslim faith was not keen on urinating in a bottle and donating blood to the 'unfaithful'.

I delivered a simple ultimatum – 'No Pee – No Job'. He was also encouraged by lewd gestures from the non-Muslims on how to use the bottle. It was suggested by some members of staff, that William's veins contained pure alcohol, due to his liking for beer. My beer naturally, and the cause of his expanding stomach.

Dennis, our maintenance man, was not the sharpest tool in the box. I would give him a list of daily tasks, which he faithfully carried out, but only for around three days. He appeared to have some deficiency in his memory retention span, and on the fourth day, it would be necessary to repeat the list of routine tasks. On one occasion, I sent him to the market to purchase electric light bulbs. Before he left, I added the comment that they were normally 10 Naira each. He returned minus bulbs, and when questioned replied,

"No buy Massa, as they were 8 Naira each!" I will admit, I collapsed in laughter after he left the room.

Not long after the completion of the villa, we purchased pot plants for the upper balconies. On returning home after a tropical storm, we found that the pots had overflowed with rainwater producing mud. The mud began running down the newly painted (white) walls. Dennis was instructed to whitewash the affected walls. A week later, again returning home during another heavy downpour, we found Dennis painting the walls – in the rain. No doubt he wished to impress us with this show of forward planning and efficiency. Unfortunately, the whitewash also ran down the wall, making a complete mess of the red brickwork below.

Every morning I had a battle with Emmanuel the cleaner, as he persisted in re-arranging my desk before my arrival at work. The drinks coasters would be placed symmetrically at each corner of my desk, the photographs of Helen placed in-line across the front of the desk, and the desk calendar for reasons best known only to himself, he would arrange it facing the wrong way. In addition, no doubt of proof of his efforts, he would leave the light on in the en suite washroom. In the end, I surrendered and quietly corrected the situation without remonstrating with him... The obsession with symmetry is amusing, given that a Nigerian cannot hang anything on a wall other than 45 degrees to the norm.

Haji, the gatekeeper, was a very religious man. Ensuring he performed his obligatory prayers several times a day. The sight of a bikini-clad Helen sunbathing by the pool, caused him great consternation, to say the least!

Michael, our driver was a tremendous asset and took great care of us. He was both chauffeur and minder on our travels around Lagos, and beyond. The traffic in the capital was horrendous. The Government, in their wisdom, introduced a scheme whereby vehicles were permitted entry to the city, based upon the first number of the car's number plate. Odd numbers on Mondays, even numbers on Tuesdays etc. The ex-patriates, and wealthy Nigerians, rather sabotaged the plan. They purchased two vehicles, both with the appropriate number plates. This did not stop the traffic jams as they merrily continued.

During 1989, the new budget was published, in which

the Nigerian Government increased the price of petrol. Taxi and bus drivers were still allowed to purchase fuel at the original price. Needless to say, the taxi drivers had a flourishing business selling petrol to the less fortunate.

The normal utilities expected in the UK were problematic in Nigeria. At the slightest suspicion of rain, electricity supplies failed. The standby generator often ran for many hours before supplies were restored. The payment for electricity was something of a pantomime. The billing of customers by the Nigerian Electrical Power Authority was non-existent. To preserve a supply, one had to deposit money in advance with NEPA, and then endeavour to remain in credit. Staff would issue receipts, but it was widely known that little of the monies reached NEPA!

Dash, the Nigerian word for bribes, was a necessary way of life. We handed dash over to the local mail deliveryman if we expected to have any letters delivered. We also found ourselves handing money over to the policeman, ensuring he would keep an eye on the property. The telephone network was another total shambles. I frequently found myself dialling for half an hour to obtain a line. The same corruption as in NEPA was evident in NITEL the telephone company. At weekends, technicians could be seen opening distribution boxes and changing lines for Nigerians who were willing to pay for the illicit service. During one period, we received several bills for a number that was not connected to our villa. Investigation revealed that we were being charged for a Nigerian official's "love nest" somewhere in the city.

"Dash" was an art form in Nigeria and the system was practised at every level of society.

Shopping in Lagos was problematic and always an adventure. The main source of food for ex-patriates in the city was the United Trading Company's supermarket (UTC). The drive to it, entailed using part of a flyover which was one of the few remnants of British urban development. The exit ramp to UTC was continually gridlocked, as four lanes of traffic fought to leave the flyover. The local traders used the traffic jam to sell their wares. Frequently risking life and limb, by running up and down, between the lines of stationary vehicles. The range of goods seemed inexhaustible, ranging from digital telephones to car seat covers.

The standard practice was to ignore them and keep one's eyes firmly to the front. The slightest glance at them provoked banging on the windows of the car and then being pursued for the next 200 metres when the traffic moved forward. The traders were all fit and lean from sprinting alongside vehicles and enjoyed either haggling or collecting cash from their captive audience.

The adventure of shopping started of course, with the involvement of parking one's car, then going on to pay the local policeman. By doing so, this ensured he did not go on to clamp the car, and lastly paying a small boy to watch it.

There was the need to select another boy. Only this time, for the boy to push the shopping trolley around the store, then carry the purchases back to the car. Between the car and the supermarket, one was accosted by still more entrepreneurs offering yet more goods.

I must have told one gentleman every week for two years, that I did not smoke and therefore did not require cigarettes. Helen also had problems convincing another trader that she had no use for "superglue" – either for sniffing or otherwise!

Shortages were very common, and Heinz beans or soup would disappear from the shelves for considerable periods of time. The word suddenly would spread within the European community that Heinz tomato soup had arrived, prompting there would be a rush of panic buying for these commodities!

The alternatives to UTC were the local markets. The nearest was Bar Beach Market. As the name suggests, it was adjacent to the sea on Victoria Island and was a maze of wood and bamboo shacks. These shacks, however, housed vast quantities of food, alcohol, and household items. Often when UTC failed to deliver, the item was available at Bar Beach. The source of the goods was questionable with the local police raiding it quite frequently. They made several attempts to close it down without success.

The majority of stallholders were very large ladies in colourful national dress- "Mamas" - extremely jolly, but fearsome in negotiation. On arrival, one had to select from a number of small boys, who were all armed with enormous baskets. The little chaps would trot around the market, and for a handful of Naira, would carry the purchases to the car.

The most interesting market was Alaba Market, in Ojo Town. Situated some ten miles from Lagos, colloquially known as "Thieves Market". The Nigerian Government had banned all imports of luxury goods, all of which were on sale at Alaba!

The latest cameras, television sets and Hi-Fi equipment were available at ridiculous prices. I bought a pair of superb German naval binoculars, that had obviously fallen off the back of a Nigerian Navy lorry. As at Bar Beach, sporadic police raids caused only a minor disruption of trade.

William our houseboy also did some of the shopping. He was very caustic about my shopping ability, dismissing my efforts with statements such as,

"Massa don't know about dese things."

It was also uncanny how the goods he bought, always came to the exact amount he had been given to perform the shopping! His visits to the fish market saw him return with the largest fishes we had ever seen, and he produced magnificent fish and chips. He also organised the delivery of beer and soft drinks to the villa. Sometimes when I look back, I remember with fondness how it became routine, that if I had one glass of beer in the evening, William would then go on to finish the bottle.

Dining out in Lagos was possible and extremely interesting. Establishments that were safe for us to eat in included our favourites, starting with, The Blue Lagoon. This restaurant stood on the creek between Lagos and Victoria. One would describe it as having been built in a tropical modern design.

At night it had superb views across the water to the capital Lagos. One of my favourite starter dishes was a delicious assortment of seafood, served in a large seashell.

Unusually for Nigeria, a strict dress code was in force. This code required one had to wear a tie in the evening. Michael our driver, would convey us to the restaurant, once there, I would hand over the usual ten Naira allowing him to enjoy his own meal elsewhere.

The other eating place we enjoyed, went by the name of the Shangra Lai (sic) in the Holiday Inn Hotel. On one particular evening having fed well, it transpired that the cashier had not reported for work. This made it impossible for us to settle the bill. The management's solution was to lock all doors to prevent the customers from leaving. Despite offers to pay later, the management was adamant, and it was several hours before the cashier appeared allowing us to escape. A German Lufthansa crew in the restaurant even feigned illness, but without success.

I normally used the Holiday Inn restaurant to entertain important military officers and Government officials. They insisted on eating there during daylight hours, as they were not prepared to drive at night in Lagos fearing assassination.

For international travel to and from the United Kingdom, I was fortunate to have the use of British Caledonian (eventually taken over by British Airways.) As mentioned previously, I had been given the privilege to travel first class, making the six-hour journey bearable. The only alternative was Nigerian Airways which was not really viable. The national carrier had a fleet of four European Airbus aircraft, of these, one had been impounded at London Heathrow, due to the non-payment of landing fees. Two were unserviceable and were rapidly being cannibalised for spares. Due unfortunately to the collapse of a maintenance agreement with the Irish airline, Aer Lingus. The fourth was still in service between Lagos and London.

Travel to Lagos airport did not inspire confidence. The airfield lighting did not meet the minimum standards required by ICAO, and its communication equipment was limited in terms of range. The calibre of air traffic controllers was also questionable. On one occasion, having landed from London, our DC 10 was directed off the main runway onto a taxiway. The problem being, the captain found it blocked by cement-filled oil drums. Aircraft are not fitted with a reverse gear, and it took considerable time for the airport authorities to find a serviceable tractor to tow the aircraft off the blocked taxiway, enabling the passengers then to be deposited at the Arrivals terminal. The collection of rusting aircraft alongside runways and taxiways, did little to reassure nervous passengers.

KABO and Gas Air are domestic Nigerian Airlines, while TAROM Air is a joint venture with the Romanian National Airline. All three provided air travel within Nigeria and used less than modern aircraft. Lack of spares and aviation fuel shortages caused constant disruption to services.

With the company having both villas and offices in Lagos, and Kaduna in the north, I had to frequently undertake travel within Nigeria itself. To say that this was stressful would be an understatement. Advertised schedules did not exist, and a telephone call to the city office of a domestic airline carrier would elicit the response, "....it was hoped to fly tomorrow".

The only solution was to arrive at the Lagos domestic air terminal, hoping that a flight would eventually be available. Chalk messages left on blackboards suggested provisional times and destinations. Annoyingly, it was then necessary to join the scrum around small ticket office windows to obtain one's ticket. Touts would also be offering tickets at inflated prices. The ticket merely guaranteed entrance to a hot and overcrowded departure lounge, where ceiling fans had long since given up the ghost. There were no desks giving out flight information, and tannoy announcements were not considered a necessity, even if the equipment had been serviceable.

The arrival of an aircraft would provoke a frantic rush of would-be passengers to the parked aircraft. They would run across the tarmac in the hope that the aircraft was destined for their desired destination. Invariably, with no control of bookings, there were many ugly scenes on the steps of the aircraft itself. Fortunately, most journeys were under two hours in duration. Refreshments were limited and usually consisted of a glass of water, or a brown liquid resembling tea.

The quality of aircraft maintenance was also suspect. On one occasion, having managed to obtain a seat and awaiting departure, I observed the ground crew examining one of the aircraft's tyres. Having decided the tyre required further inflation; they departed to find a vehicle with an air compressor. The vehicle refused to start, leaving the ground crew to promptly ignore the problem. I hoped that the tyre would survive the next landing.

Given the state of Nigerian roads, plus the horrendous state of vehicles, and the Nigerian standard of driving, road travel was equally as interesting as air travel, and certainly more dangerous. Rear lights, sidelights and traffic indicators were not considered essential. Tyres were used until devoid of tread with the canvas showing through the rubber. There existed a thriving trade in used tyres imported from Europe.

Accidents were frequent, albeit at low speeds, in the cities due to traffic congestion. Outside the towns and cities, it was a different story. Their accidents were horrendous, the roadsides strewn with the wreckage of vehicles. The majority being huge trucks, due to the driver having fallen asleep after excessive hours at the wheel. At the time, there was no legislation on this matter in Nigeria. Newspapers reported one such incident where a petrol tanker had overturned, spilling a large amount of fuel on the road. An unfortunate motorcyclist skidded on the pool of petrol; the resulting sparks produced a lake of fire. A minibus overloaded with passengers and fifteen Nigerians, plus the motorcyclist, perished, engulfed in the flames. The tanker driver ran away and was never found.

By the law of averages, we were destined to have an accident, despite using Michael as our driver. The inevitable happened as we were returning from a holiday weekend in Abuja. The newly designated capital was being built to the north of Lagos. The journey involved the use of a partly constructed motorway, some 100Km from Lagos. Unfortunately, some sections were incomplete. This meant that traffic had to divert from the southbound lanes to the northbound lanes without any warnings. There had been no attempt to separate traffic moving from a one-way to a two-way system.

Michael found himself travelling head-on towards a very large truck coming from the opposite direction. Michael had little option other than to swerve out of its path, and we were struck from behind by a passenger car travelling in the same direction as ourselves. Badly shaken, we came to a halt with the rear of the car severely damaged.

An extremely agitated Nigerian, who was the driver of the vehicle that had hit us, rushed up and dragged Michael from our car. He then drew a pistol and threatened to shoot him! It turned out that the said Nigerian was a Superintendent in the Nigerian Police Force, and obviously quite drunk. Fortunately, Michael and I, apart from bruising, were unhurt though badly shaken. Had we been injured, it was extremely doubtful that any of us would have survived as we were miles from civilisation, or any sort of medical attention available.

Natives appeared out of the jungle from a nearby village and initially were quite hostile until they realised that the drunken Nigerian was a member of the Police. With this knowledge, their attitudes changed significantly.

By this time, I had managed to quieten the drunken policemen; informing him that not only was I working for the State Security Services, but I was a friend of the Inspector General of the NPF.

Eventually, two rather disreputable policemen arrived on the scene from the village police station. The pair of them appeared quite bewildered, and unaware of what to do. We reached an amicable solution. The solution being, as usual, whereby I agreed to a certain amount of compensation for the Superintendent on our return to Lagos. I would also accompany them to their police post and make a statement. The two guardians of the law, appeared quite relieved as I calmly accompanied them to the police post, situated about half a mile down the road. On arriving there, it was without mains electricity or water, the hovel did not inspire confidence. Furthermore, I had to provide the pencil and paper so that I could make a statement.

The law being satisfied, and the inebriated policeman having left the scene, we turned our attention to our damaged vehicle. The locals produced crowbars and managed to prise the coachwork away from the rear wheels, enabling us to resume the journey to Lagos. With profound relief, we limped away at 20mph to cover the 100Km drive back to civilisation.

After several hours of driving, we arrived back at home around midnight, we found the ever-faithful William asleep under the dining table, having prepared our evening meal.

Surviving a road accident in Nigeria remains an indelible event in my memories of Africa. One was advised never to stop at the scene of an accident. Particularly where dead bodies were involved, as involvement invariably meant demands for compensation from relatives bona fide or otherwise

Needless to report, the inebriated Superintendent duly presented himself at my Lagos office the following morning. He collected the sum of money, which I had promised the previous evening at the scene of the skirmish.

On one occasion, when a company vehicle hit a lamp standard outside our villa, I had to organise taxis to take my injured staff to hospital, then of course pay substantial medical fees. My assistance also strangely extended to lending the policemen a tape measure to collect evidence at the accident site. Our driver, who had not revealed being involved in similar accidents; made off, never to be seen again in our employment.

Before the issue of our permanent Residence Permits for Nigeria, it was necessary to leave and re-enter the country with a new transit visa. We took the opportunity on one such occasion to drive to the neighbouring Republic of Benin. Formerly part of French West Africa, Benin gained full independence in 1960 as the Republic of Dahomey, it was renamed Benin in 1975. During the 19th Century, the territory had been a major centre for the Atlantic slave trade.

After a noisy and squalid Lagos, we drove to

Cotonou. There we booked into the beautiful luxury Sheraton Beach Hotel, to enjoy the French ambience and comforts they provided. Spending several days there. Our room had wonderful views of the vast beach, with its white sand and the very pale blue waters of the Gulf of Benin. One gastronomic highlight of our stay was the "Pacific Express" night. After dark, a model train complete with open trucks was driven around the hotel pool. Each truck representing a Pacific Island, carrying a full load of its local food. Under the tropical night sky, a jazz band played, ensuring the evening was a wonderful extravaganza of food and music.

Not far from Cotonou, is Lake Genvai (Nokoué). The lake is a huge expanse of water, which houses a unique village settlement in its centre. The inhabitants built and took refuge in the village to avoid deportation as slaves in the 19th Century. The thatched dwellings are built on stilts, and the whole community is not visible from the shore. The only access is by rather ancient, motorised boats.

Fish farming supports the village; the makeshift wicker pens can be seen on the way across the lake. The only concession to modern life was the vintage telephone kiosk mounted on one of the many gangways connecting the huts. No doubt the children learn to swim at an early age!

Voodoo is still practised in Benin. Walking around the market stalls, you will find all the ingredients for voodoo activities such as dead cats, the heads and anatomical parts of various animals and other equally disgusting items.

Obtaining a re-entry visa for Lagos required us to visit the Nigerian Consulate. There we spent (as expected) several hours on two consecutive days. Eventually, we met the Nigerian authorised to issue the visas. True to form he suggested to me that the normal charge was 1500 francs, but as a special concession, he would stamp the passports for 1000 francs; providing we did not insist on a receipt. As the custodian of rubber stamps, he obviously had a lucrative business.

During our initial journey into Benin, driving along a jungle road. I had spotted a woodcarver and his wares on the roadside. Providing I was able to find him once again, I had resolved to make a purchase on the return journey to the border. Luckily, I found the clearing in the jungle, and after having fun haggling with him. I bought a magnificent wooden, voodoo figure. The head and shoulders were that of a female and the lower body of a snake. Instantly christened "Rachael". She was placed in the vehicle, and we headed for the frontier with Nigeria.

Waiting in the queue for Customs, we were approached by a group of locals who suggested that we might have problems taking the artefact out of Benin. They also offered, for a sum of money, to transport "Rachael" across the border for us, at some unsupervised point. They informed me; they would then meet us further down the road in Nigeria. Taking on board their advice, reluctantly, I handed over fifty African francs, firmly believing we had seen the last of our prize. Their information on the attitude of Benin Customs Officers was most accurate.

The officials subjected us to a thorough and unpleasant search. One officious female officer, who insisted on emptying my wife's clothing onto the ground. After a considerable time, we were allowed across the frontier back into Nigeria. Further down the road and to my surprise and delight, we met our locals and "Rachael." Two hours later, we were back on Victoria Island, having enjoyed an interesting visit to The People's Socialist Republic of Benin.

Newspapers in Nigeria can sometimes be as highly amusing as any in England. No surprise though, that the newspapers in Nigeria, although under strict political censorship. Are not regulated in terms of the advertising standards commonplace in England and Europe.

I enclose a few "gems" from Lagos newspapers – written as printed! #

"STOP AMPUTATION OF LEGS AND HANDS"

Traditional Hospital – Ondo State Pride

We specialise in the treatments of all ailments but place emphasis on:

Bone fracture.

Stroke and paralysis.

Pregnancy & definite personal problems

Contact us at 11 Ajibawo Street, Off Agbado Road, Oke-Ayo Bus Stop, Agege, Lagos.

Note: Those who have written us earlier should come in person for bone fide reply

Chief Owonifari Antanlogun (Director)

"LEOPARDS HELD TO GOALLESS DRAW"

Kenya's AFC Leopards and Inter FC of Burundi.

Battled to a goalless draw on Saturday in a scrappy first round, first leg Africa Champions Cup

Inter's strikers destroyed their makeshit(!) midfield game, but their scoring efforts were foiled by the Rock steady defence.

GONORRHOEA – SYPHILIS – WEAK ORGAN

Special medicine to wash away diseases like soap, pulse gono, pinching gono, weak organ gono, early morning gono, watery sperm gono, stomachnoise gono, yellowish gono, bloodish gono, black menstruation gono, cut-cut gono, barreness gono, pains gono.

Also, scratching syphilis, boils syphilis, cuts syphilis, and weak or dead organ.

Founded by top African researchers) Head Office: 25 Elutu Odibo Street Abule Ijesha Yaba 3rd Floor

Consultation Fee 10 Naira

HEALTH TIPS

"HOW TO SET A BROKEN BONE"

Pull the hand forcefully and steadily for 5-10 minutes to separate the broken bones, with one person still pulling the hand, have another gently line up and straighten the bones.

Warning: It is possible to do a lot of damage while trying to set a bone. Ideally, it should be done with the help of someone with experience. Do not force.

As I mentioned earlier, my prime interest over many years. I suppose one could say my hobby, had been amateur radio. Luckily, I was able to continue enjoying this pleasure in Nigeria. The villa on Victoria Island proved an ideal location as it was close to the Atlantic Ocean. The locals with their native ingenuity and self-taught skills, built and erected a magnificent 90-foot tower. The tower supported a large rotating antenna. I had won several awards in Morocco, Malaysia, and Pakistan. Now Nigeria provided me with further several contest wins. In one of them, managing in fact, to set up an African points record. Kamaran Island, as I mentioned, was the first of two unique events. Nigeria was to provide the second.

Radio communication at VHF [Very High Frequency] is normally limited to several miles or Line of Sight. Under certain conditions, radio signals may become trapped in the atmosphere's Tropospheric layer, which is the nearest to Earth. Thus, enabling signals to travel vast distances. During the summer of 1989, experts predicted that this anomaly was due to happen. Excited at the prospect of this occurring, I purchased radio equipment from the UK, including a new antenna for the newly constructed tower.

For several frustrating weeks, I listened on the 6 metre VHF band without hearing any signals. Then one late afternoon out of the blue, several stations appeared. I was delighted to establish contact. Later I learned I had set a new world record. Involving the first inter-continental communication at VHF, between Africa, Europe, and the United States of America.

THE ISC-FERRANTI SCANDAL

Soon after my arrival in Nigeria, I took up my position as Managing Director for the Nigerian operations of ISC.

Ferranti, which at that time was a British company, took over ISC at an agreed price of £421 million. Ferranti hoped that the deal would bring in orders from America, where ISC had close ties with the Pentagon. Ferranti also hoped it would increase its sales to ISC clients, in the Far East, Middle East and Africa.

Five percent of the company shares were still owned by the Ferranti family and were naturally opposed to the bid. They had hoped for a merger with the UK company, STC, or any other company they thought suitable. As ISC was quoted on the London Stock Market, it was able to retain work for the Pentagon without being labelled a foreign company, and also avoided disclosing the identity of its foreign customers.

During the month of October, an audit by an eminent firm of British accountants caused a major scandal in the financial world. The auditors found a black hole in the accounts. This unfortunately revealed irregularities within ISC and questioned the purchase price of £421 million paid by Ferranti.

Whether actual fraud had been committed, was not clear. However, it did emerge that certain large contracts, including one with Pakistan, did not exist. Except on paper. The assassination of General Zia, who at that time was the President of Pakistan, effectively destroyed any progress in that country. Also, it emerged that ISC had been supplying arms to South Africa from the USA. South Africa at that time, was under an embargo for such sales. How this situation was missed during several audits, and at the merger stage? One can only describe the situation as incredible, to say the least.

I was particularly apprehensive at the repeated mention of South Africa, in the international press. This did not auger well, for our operation in Nigeria. Apartheid being an extremely sensitive issue at the time. Relations between Nigeria and South Africa in 1987, were somewhat strained! Fortunately, as far as I was concerned, we weathered the storm in Lagos. The Founder of ISC, a man by the name of James Guerin, went to prison in the United States for 15 years. Ferranti UK suffered a severe decline in the long term.

ISC, and eventually Ferranti (Nig) Ltd, became a joint venture. The new company had offices in Lagos, as well as Kaduna in the north of the country. The company in its wisdom had chosen a government organisation as its partner in this venture. In hindsight, this was a mistake, given the lack of commercial acumen one would expect from people in the public sector. The partner chosen was the State Security Services (SSS) – known by most in Nigeria, as the Secret Service. The hope was, that we would gain entry to major public sector contracts in the security and communication fields. This did not happen, and the only contract actually signed, was one to provide security systems for the new Presidential palace in Abuja (the new federal capital).

The contract was badly stalled, the cash flow was non-existent. A contract with the Nigerian Police Force was promised but did not materialise.

Frequent sessions with Brigadier General Aliyu Mohammed, the Financial Controller of SSS. Produced promises, but no cash. Our special advisor, a retired General Washishi in Kaduna. As was expected of him, he appeared incapable of applying pressure in high places. He had become a chicken farmer with 3000 acres, producing seven million chicks a year, he was a man obviously too busy!

I struggled with this situation for some time. Managing to maintain operations along with staff and facilities, on irregular payments of cash that I received from headquarters in London. By late 1989 things were desperate, and it was decided by then to close the Nigerian operation. Ferranti International (Nig) Ltd, was sold to its

Nigerian partner for 1 Naira (ten pence).

How little time changes men who run big businesses, as the same behaviour has once again applied. Only this time, it was Sir Philip Green that repeated history, by selling a hugely profitable business for a pound.

After more than two years in Lagos, we said goodbye to all the "family" of servants and departed for England.

One final memory I have happened on the way to the airport. Michael my driver informed me that riots were in progress in Lagos. To ensure our safe passage through the roadblocks, Michael suggested we place palm fronds on the front of the vehicle.

To this day, I have no idea why, or how this information was relevant in regard to our safety. Needless to say, we accepted his advice, arriving safely at the airport.

On our return, my wife suggested we buy a house in North Wales, this giving me reasonable access to Manchester airport. Not knowing when my next contract might be, or if my wife would be allowed to accompany me. We decided that a small business would perhaps be suitable for her to spend time while I was away. As it turned out, it was suitable for two reasons. One, it kept me amused while not working, the other and more important reason, I had to undergo major surgery to remove gall stones. Needing to rest and recuperate, I must admit, I was pleased that a new contract did not come in at that time.

Chapter 30

Nigeria the Second Time

Having fully rested from my operation, and at last, raring to go, to my surprise and delight, I received a telephone call from a representative of Ericsson in Italy. The caller inquired if I would be interested in a position in Nigeria. After my last experience in that country, I was somewhat taken aback, if not quite shocked. Weighing up the thought of returning for a moment or two. I decided to consider the offer, depending of course what was on the table. After giving me a basic outline, he then asked would I care to fly to Rome to discuss the matter further.

Still not a hundred percent sure, I left England a few days later, bearing in mind the trials and tribulations of my previous contract in Nigeria. Arriving in Rome, I asked a waiting taxi driver to take me directly to the Ericsson offices, situated on the outskirts of the city. Ericsson had thoughtfully booked me into a nearby hotel, allowing me the opportunity to rest in between several days of discussions.

After various discussions explaining what I required, they agreed to my conditions. I then accepted the position of the new Executive Project Manager for Ericsson in Nigeria. Little did I know what lay ahead.

The contract happened to be with Shell Oil Nigeria. This required the installation and maintenance, of a data transmission system for 400 vehicles, using a new mobile telephone network. Along with the upgrade of an existing microwave link between Port Harcourt, and Lagos. The microwave link consisted of parabolic dishes and antennae, on 300-foot-high towers. These towers had been installed in

1967 by Balfour Beatty, which was another British company.

The initial plan was for me to oversee the planning stage in Rome for approximately six months, then take up my position in Port Harcourt for the implementation phase. I flew back to England, then decided with Helen, to make the drive back to Italy by road rather than fly. We proceeded to load the Volvo estate car I had at that time and departed from North Wales once again. On my arrival back in Italy, I hoped the promised apartment, which had been offered to me, would be both available and naturally suitable.

On the long drive through France, I decided to make my first stop of the journey in Lyon. A city I found not only attractive but one full of history. After a refreshing night's sleep, and an excellent breakfast which only the French can cook, I drove on to Italy. As it was spring, and the weather glorious, I made Rimini situated on the Italian Rivera, my next port of call. The following morning, I headed for Rome. Taking the Autostrada del Sol, while still savouring the most wonderful meal, served to us in the seaside restaurant we had visited the previous evening.

Having survived the notorious ring road, along with the antics of Italian drivers. I managed to locate the Via Anonina, the road where my new home was situated. The apartment thankfully was quite close to the Ericsson facility, and a few miles outside the city.

I found to my relief, that my new colleagues and staff turned out to be not only just friendly, also very agreeable, although sadly totally work shy. When a public holiday fell on a Tuesday, I would be lucky to see them by Thursday. At which time, they would be planning an early escape to enjoy their weekend.

On one of my several visits to Nigeria, I had identified two villas, both of which were available for rental. One for staff accommodation, and one for the project offices. To furnish these required a trip back to Stockholm in Sweden. There I was let loose in IKEA, the famous Swedish department store where I spent an entire and thoroughly enjoyable day. Having an open budget, choosing the furnishing which we required for both villas, I managed to spend £40,000. Probably the ultimate retail therapy, and then needing to take forty trolleys through the checkout. A most unusual event I should think for any department store.

Sadly, as events transpired, I never saw the items arrive in Port Harcourt.

After six months, and still in Rome, Shell Oil was anxious to see me on site. The Company was agitated and anxious I should be in Port Harcourt. To do so, meant me travelling back to the United Kingdom. Once there, it allowed me to dispose of the Volvo, and obtain the necessary visa required. Thus, allowing me to enter and work in Nigeria.

At this stage, my problems commenced. The procedure, in theory, should have been quite simple. I was required to visit the Nigerian High Commission in London, to obtain the necessary visa. After visiting the Consular Section of the Commission, one could only state that chaos reigned in that department. You could only describe the scene as being totally chaotic. To my utter dismay, I found four lines of people who were also trying to obtain visas, most of them being excitable Nigerians. Once having reached the counter, I found myself confronted by officious surly Nigerians. Ericsson supposedly had faxed my name to Lagos, ensuring that permission had been given to issue a visa which should have been awaiting me in the High Commission.

Not a hope... my file could not be found. Having already spent several boring hours trying to reach the counter in an overheated, unpleasant, body-odour filled room, I called it a day. The next three days continued to produce an identical result. No fax, no visa. Several unfortunates, who had patiently queued, and by some miracle had actually reached the counter, were then told to join another queue, thus enabling them to pay for their visa. On arriving at the head of that queue, once again they were informed that only cash would be accepted. After four days of observing such stupidity, I decided my time was too precious and called it a day, leaving me without the required visa.

Ericsson by now aware of Shell's impatience to have me on site and decided that I should travel without the said visa. They assured me that everything would be taken care of in Lagos. Despite the serious misgivings I felt, I had no option. Travelling by air from London Gatwick, courtesy of British Caledonian, enjoying the first-class seat provided and all that went with it. I must admit, I was deeply surprised that the airline had insisted that I sign a waiver, absolving them of any penalty for not having that damned visa.

Arriving in Lagos held no surprises for me. Having had of course the experience of the frenetic behaviour at the immigration department on a previous visit. However, not having the obligatory damn visa. As expected, I was arrested and carted off to a small room. Without my knowledge, certain enquiries were made which in turn, allowed me to be eventually released. I can only think, presumably, money had been exchanged by Ericsson. On leaving the arrivals hall, I was mugged, and my passport was stolen. Fortunately, the Ericsson staff who met me caught the offender and returned my precious passport to me. I thought, welcome back to Nigeria.

After a brief stay in Lagos, during which time I purchased several vehicles for the project, Helen and I then travelled on to Port Harcourt. This city was the centre of the Nigerian oil industry and had a real live Wild West feel about it. The oil obtained is not from normal offshore deposits. Instead, the oil field is located in the river delta around Port Harcourt.

The drilling rigs are situated in the swamps, the oil from them is pumped to huge tankers moored offshore.

Some of the drilling rigs were inaccessible other than by boat or helicopter. My staff had to produce a swimming proficiency certificate, before being allowed to work on the rigs. Certainly not the usual requirement for a telecommunications project. Logically speaking. I doubt very much anyone could possibly have survived while swimming in those swamps, regardless had they been a good swimmer or not.

The new furniture I had purchased with such pleasure, was still on route coming from Sweden to Nigeria via sea. Therefore, we were accommodated by the Swedish Telephone Company, SWEDTEL. We were pleased to accept their hospitality. Unfortunately, the bungalow we were offered, like all the bungalows in their compound, suffered from neglect and was sadly very run down.

One of the ways of life I was not impressed about,

were the stories of the wildlife. A neighbour had informed me about a snake that had taken up residence in her bathroom. The snake it seems had entered the bungalow via the overhanging branches of a nearby tree and had entered her baby son's bedroom.

I remember on one particular night, my air conditioning vent in the bungalow, disgorged a huge swarm of large ants. I remember spending a frantic few minutes stamping on and killing these beasties, or at least trying to. I retired exhausted, intending to clear up the mess in the morning. Waking the following day, going to get rid of my most unwelcome visitors. Not a single carcass was to be found on the floor. I could only assume that a snake or lizard had enjoyed a jolly good meal without my knowledge during the night. A thought that does not bear thinking about.

On another night. I had to flee from my bathroom while being pursued by the largest horned black beetle I had ever seen. Life in the tropics…

After a couple of weeks in this idyllic setting, a bombshell was dropped. I received a telephone call to inform me that Helen and I should return to Lagos immediately.

I have no idea who was responsible, but on my arrival, I discovered that the Nigerian authorities had become aware of our illegal status. Such information may have jeopardised the Ericsson contract with Shell.

I was also informed, that I could not rely on either the Swedish or British governments for assistance. Helen and I were therefore hidden in a company apartment in Lagos, to await a midnight flight back to London.

Once at the airport, we were instructed to wait,

ensuring the necessary bribes were in place at each checkpoint for, Customs, Immigration and Security. Adding to my fractured nerves, I was told it would be impossible to bribe personnel at the departure gate, and we should try to attempt to look inconspicuous. Somewhat difficult, being one of only two white passengers on that flight. I was further told by Ericsson, once having set foot on British Airways, we should refuse to disembark from the aircraft. One could certainly describe that part of my life, as nerve-wracking, and never to be repeated.

At the departure gate, there had been a person ahead of us with a problem. Perfect, as this gave us the opportunity to slip through during the confusion. I have often wondered had I been removed by force from the aircraft, and what may have happened to my wife. As it is I was able to breathe a sigh of relief, as the aircraft lifted off from Lagos. Now being persona non grata in Nigeria, also jobless. The time had come for me to visit Stockholm and allow the International Assignments Department to find me a new contract.

Having travelled extensively in Africa, I came to realise just how cheap life is in the Third World, particularly on that Continent. Two remain vivid in my memory.

The first occurred when staying at the Norfolk Hotel in Nairobi, on witnessing a thief being chased and beaten to death in the main street.

The second incident also happened to another thief. This took place, on Victoria Island in Nigeria.

A crowd having caught a thief in Bar Beach market, firstly beat him unconscious, then placing him in a "necklace" which is a column of several car tyres. The crowd then set fire to them, burning him to death.

The sight and smell of that incident will remain with me forever.

Chapter 31

The People's Republic of China

Having been a pilot, I loved the thought of flying home first class. At this time of my life, I also hated the thought of being unemployed. Once leaving Nigeria, Helen and I stopped off in Sweden, hoping with luck to explore alternative employment opportunities with Ericsson before continuing our journey home. The Swedish system was to contact the International Assignments Division (IA) and visit the numerous offices responsible for recruitment worldwide.

On arriving in Stockholm, I met with a representative from IA, who suggested that I might be interested in China and consider it for my next contract.

The Ericsson presence in that country during 1993 was relatively small, although it was forecasted to have a massive expansion. With China desperate for mobile telephone technology and having a population of 1.2 billion, plus the fact there were few conventional telephones in the cities, and even less in rural areas, this seemed a good opportunity for Ericsson to consider the investment.

To my delight, the same thing happened as in Australia. I was handed money, an air ticket, and asked to visit the PRC as soon as possible. My wife and I returned briefly to England. After settling Helen into a hotel, as our house had been rented out, I then made my way back to London to pick up a flight to China.

After an interminable 10-hour flight, British Airways deposited me in Peking (Beijing as it is called today). The Chinese airport was a disappointment. No loudspeakers blaring out martial music, or large red banners with Communist slogans. All seemed very normal, complete with surly customs officials in crumpled uniforms. The type that one encounters all over the Third World. Not that China was in that category.

I was met by a very polite Chinese chauffeur driving a Volvo saloon. He drove me to the magnificent China World Hotel. This Sino-Malaysian joint venture was indeed most impressive. There were two hotels, multi-storey apartment blocks, offices, and a shopping mall. My preconceived ideas about China were changing rapidly.

The following morning, I met Jean le Grand, who despite the name was very Swedish and the current Operations Director. Jean was a very laid-back type of man, almost comatose and extremely vague. I was expecting a normal job interview, instead, I was offered the position of Deputy Operations Director on the spot.

I flew back to England, then drove to Wales to join my wife at her hotel in Llandudno and remained in Wales for a further week. Until, at last, it was time for me to fly back to China, taking Helen with me.

We took a short and welcome break in Bangkok enjoying all it had to offer, before flying on to Beijing. Once again, we were met and driven by another chauffeur back to the China World hotel. Only this time, we were given an apartment that was to become our home for the following three years. The apartment was situated on the twenty-third floor, giving us a bird's eye view of the city. One which I found very interesting. The Ericsson offices were also in the same complex, thus enabling me to walk to work.

Quickly, it became obvious that living in Beijing was not necessarily going to be a major problem, but I do feel my apartment was possibly bugged.

One morning we had a plumbing problem, I told Helen I would report this as soon as possible. I never got the chance to do so, as within seconds there came a knock on the door. On opening it, there stood a plumber. My paranoia that the apartment was already bugged appeared to be true.

China was emerging rapidly from the post-Mao era and enjoying the fruits of its new Capitalist-Communism. The signs in the capital were obvious. There was a proliferation of newly built skyscrapers and western-style shopping malls complete with department stores full of designer goods from the West.

One of the biggest surprises was the number of Mercedes, and a great number of Rolls Royce automobiles on the streets. The young Chinese had quickly adopted western fashions, including the opening of several McDonald's restaurants, and many other fast-food outlets across the city. All well frequented in such a short space of time since the Red Revolution. Mao Zedong must have been revolving in his mausoleum in Tiananmen Square, given the speed of such change.

One major problem, unfortunately, was the horrendous pollution. With the infinite coal reserves China had, they had built the majority of her factories as coal burning, along with her power stations. All cities suffered under a cloud of filth, and sadly still do today.

Ericsson, therefore, provided all of its employees with free dry-cleaning services.

The Chinese Government under international pressure was aware of the situation but had neither the knowledge nor technology to remedy the problem.

Given the minimal penetration of conventional telephone (wire) systems in China, it was obvious to me that the current Ericsson operation was on the brink of an explosive expansion. However, it was obvious the company at that time, was totally under-resourced in labour and everything else.

As the first task in my new role, Jean le Grand had asked me to prepare a report on the number and progress of existing Ericsson contracts. As normal in his vague manner, he thought that we had probably 20 to 30 signed contracts. I found a total of 132. From that point, Ericsson never caught up. The company only survived by virtue of Chinese patience, and their desperate need for telephones.

Not long after my arrival, I was promoted to the position of Director of Marketing Northern China. I was made responsible for the sales and marketing of mobile telephone systems in the northern part of the country. A colleague based in Shanghai was responsible for the southern half, with both of us reporting to the Ericsson office in Hong Kong. The task gave me an enormous territory, covering a huge geographical area. The size of China is almost incomprehensible. I could fly for six hours from Beijing, and still be in China. The same flight from London would see me in Nigeria, or Saudi Arabia. At the end of my tour in China, I had travelled untold thousands of miles both by air and road.

One of the first tasks I needed to do was to set up the new sales and marketing department. I had three expatriate members of staff; I was also required to recruit local Chinese personnel to join the company. This of course was not a problem. We were spoilt for choice, as there was an abundance of many well-qualified applications from

Chinese graduates. All were fluent in English and were desperate to work for a western organization. By doing so, in turn, it would bring them prestige and money. Most of them had First, or Masters Degrees in various subjects. Within China, the competition for a place at university was highly competitive. Their children were coached from the age of eleven in preparation for the multitude of State examinations. Today they start their education a great deal younger. Their performance in these examinations, determined which university they would attend; and which subjects they will study. This direction may be frowned upon in our society, but it ensured that the country was never short of doctors, engineers, and other professionals.

Fluency in English from my staff was essential. Even the top officials in the provincial administrations rarely spoke other than Chinese. For me to learn spoken Mandarin, let alone the written form would have been an almost impossible task in the time available.

The language problem made sales negotiations somewhat tedious and very time-consuming. Given the Chinese trait of avoiding impolite conversation, I was never sure that I was provided with a fully accurate translation. Sometimes, I felt that I was being provided with the answer they thought I preferred. Otherwise, I could not have had a more hard-working or loyal staff.

One of my most difficult tasks in their initial induction and training was to overcome the cultural attitude in the workplace. They had all been exposed to the Leader principle, where they expected total direction with all decisions to be made by their boss.

I recall my first staff meeting, with each member sitting around the table armed with pencils and paper. As I looked around, they sat patiently waiting for me to issue detailed instructions. When I asked for suggestions on a particular topic, there was a deathly silence. Fortunately, that attitude changed with time, and I managed to cultivate a modicum of "free-thinking".

During 1993, Ericsson enjoyed 45% of the world market for mobile telephone systems. Motorola (USA) was our main competitor, with Nokia, (Finland) and NORTEL, (Canada) close behind. Provincial Chinese Administrations were insatiable, and in my second year, we had no problems in achieving a sales forecast of $1 billion, USD…

Despite the difference in cultures, including the language problem, it was not a difficult marketplace in which to operate. Only 7% of the population in the towns and cities had conventional (wire) telephones; with 3% in rural areas. With the investment required, plus the obvious civil engineering problems. Mobile radiotelephones were the way ahead as well as being cost-effective.

After being summoned to a Provincial Telecommunications Administration meeting, held in the city of Harbin in northern China. I must tell you before I go any further. The city of Harbin, incidentally, was and still is famous in winter for its International Ice Festival. Sculptors from around the world would produce and still do, the most amazing array of ice exhibits.

Harbin is one of a number of northern termini for the Chinese State Railway System. As I am a bit of a railway enthusiast even today, for the old steam engines. I decided to visit the rail yards there. With luck, I hoped it would have enabled me to obtain photographs of the steam locomotives which I had never seen before. Unfortunately, I was ordered to leave immediately by the security personnel on duty, minus the long wished for photographs.

On my arrival at the meeting in Harbin, the Chief Engineer politely said to me,

"We need a system." Before having the opportunity to answer him, he continued to say,

"When can Ericsson provide it?" I replied in the affirmative,

"Yes, but we have some problems with the delivery of our equipment, which unfortunately may delay implementation."

The cost was a secondary issue, although many organizations were actually learning the word profit; a word rarely used in the old Communist State. The State paid people to go to work but seemed not to care if they actually worked. I saw workers sleeping at their desks in many of the provincial administrations.

Senior officials were always the most polite and friendly. Once I had established a rapport with individuals, they became loyal customers. Despite my frequent apologies for poor delivery problems from Sweden, they also became good friends.

However, one had to work to maintain the relationship. A request for a meeting meant immediately, even if this involved an air journey of 3-6 hours.

I recall meeting the Chief Engineer of Heilongjiang Province for lunch in Beijing. He appeared to enjoy my strange British sense of humour. The following week hearing of the new business, I returned to Harbin to see him. On my arrival at his outer office, a lesser official politely informed me that his Chief Engineer was in discussion with NORTEL (this being our Canadian competitor) and was unable to see me. At the thought of being in danger of losing a large contract, I therefore instantly asked the minor official, if he would be so kind as to remind the Chief Engineer of my name, and our recent meeting in Beijing. I felt delighted and relieved when the door to the inner office opened, and I was welcomed with open arms. Needless to say, NORTEL left without the new contract.

With translations being necessary, contract negotiations were often long and tedious. They were held in offices without central heating in the winter, with temperatures dropping below freezing. During the summer months, particularly in July and August, the temperatures would frequently climb rapidly, reaching 100 degrees Fahrenheit.

The Director or Chief engineer would make the process significantly longer insisting that all their staff attended the meeting. 20 to 30 Chinese would often face three of us across the table. Everyone had his or her say, ensuring that the final decision (if wrong) was not solely attributed to the "Boss".

We also drank interminable cups of green tea with leaves floating on the surface and praying one would not end up with a mouthful of leaves. The trick was to blow gently, to move them to one side. I acquired this technique, but I could never come to terms with the metal spittoons in corridors and offices. Spitting had been almost eradicated in Beijing but remained a disgusting habit elsewhere.

The Chinese loved the signing of any contract. They really went to town in terms of the actual ceremony. After speeches from both parties, we would then sign the documents. After the signing had been completed, they would proceed by cutting an enormous red ribbon held by several young girls dressed in traditional Chinese costumes. Copious amounts of champagne were then consumed, before proceeding to the usual banquet. On one occasion for the signing of a successful $40 million contract, I decided to purchase several expensive gold fountain pens. After the signing ceremony had come to an end, the pens disappeared like lightning into some Chinese pockets. I managed to retrieve one as a souvenir, which I felt having worked reasonably hard, I had earned it.

Like the Arabs, the Chinese were hospitable hosts. During the course of my visits to customers, I would attend innumerable banquets. I learned very quickly the Chinese enjoyed any excuse for a celebration, which in turn triggered a banquet of gargantuan proportions. Multiple courses were the order of the day, with much food unconsumed. The leftovers confirmed that the host had met his guest's expectations. No one must leave hungry, ensuring that our host would not be considered a poor man. I had to learn the use of chopsticks since western cutlery was rarely provided outside of Beijing. The test for us expatriates was to master the ability to pick up two peanuts! A feat always applauded by the Chinese.

There is a saying,

"If it walks, swims or flies," the Chinese will eat it. This fact led to some interesting offerings; in the North (unlike in the South) we were spared snake.

Unlike the Koreans, the Chinese rarely eat cats and dogs. I did draw the line at bird's feet and fried scorpions on a bed of rice. Neither could I manage the glasses of red and green liquid, which contained turtle's blood and bear bile, respectively.

The consumption of alcohol at banquets was

frightening. A potent rice-based wine is served in vast quantities. I found it almost impossible to restrict one's intake of this firewater, especially when never-ending toasts are the ritual. Invariably, as a guest of honour, I would be seated on the top table. Between each course, one or other of the senior officials would jump to their feet, then shout a toast to someone or something. The response demanded that the rest of us had to drain his or her glass.

To make matters worse, lesser officials from other tables would wander up to the top table, they would then proceed to repeat the process ad nauseum. There was no way of avoiding this intake of wine. Eventually, by some strange coincidence, my system did manage to cope with this well-meaning pantomime.

The Chinese smoked incessantly during the meal, to the extent that not only did I fear chronic alcoholism, I also totally feared liver failure or death from lung problems or such. As a finale, after numerous courses, the host would serve bowls of rice to ensure no one was still hungry!

When travelling around Northern China, depending on the season, I frequently encountered temperatures ranging from 40C in summer, to many degrees below freezing in winter. Thus, making my journeys interesting, with most travel being by air. Only Beijing, and one other Provincial Administration, was close enough to permit road travel. The Highway Code, as we know it, had not yet reached China. This ensured road trips were quite hair raising and I would not allow my staff to travel at night under any circumstances. Expatriate staff were not allowed to own vehicles or drive themselves. All the Chinese staff adopted a western name, which was probably just as well. Had they not done so, we would have had problems with the pronunciation of their given names. A young man who we called John, became my personal driver.

In 1993, Air China was operating aircraft leased from the USSR. We, therefore, travelled nervously, given the safety record of Russian airlines. Particularly flying in aircraft such as the Ilyushin 86, and various Tupolev variants. Fortunately, by 1995. Boeing, and European Airbus, had sold China modern aircraft. Schedules were well maintained until the weather or unserviceability upset things. These events seemed to take the airlines by surprise, and it would take the best part of a week to return to normal. I can remember once being stranded for twelve hours in a snowstorm in Harbin. As compensation, we were offered a polystyrene container of sticky rice and gristly meat. Needless to say, I went hungry.

Travelling by air, sometimes bordered on the farcical. On one occasion, the air conditioning failed in a YAK 40 aircraft as we waited for take-off. With cabin temperatures reaching above 40C, the cabin attendants very kindly issued us all with hand fans. Novel to say the least.

As we took off, a piece of the overhead luggage rack fell off. This incident did not enhance my view of Russian aircraft or Chinese maintenance. At one check-in desk in Shenyang, I was asked if my suitcase was locked. I had to admit it was not, the official reply was,

"You no lock-you no travel."

The situation looked disastrous until the Air China employee rummaged in his desk and produced a small lock and key. Relieved naturally of 10 YUAN ($2) I was then able to board the aircraft, impressed with the entrepreneur behind the desk.

I reproduce here, (no not another offspring) but the

text of a leaflet, issued by Air China to international travellers. Note, that at the time it did not mention weapons! I quote,

"Any passenger suffering from, aids, venereal disease, leprosy, psychiatric disorder, or open (sic) pulmonary TB, shall truthfully declare his or her condition.

"It should be declared truthfully of such products as food, microbes, biological products, human tissues, blood and blood products, used articles as well as animals likely to transmit human disease." Unquote.

Initially, the headquarters for the Ericsson operation in China was based in Hong Kong. This fact required me to travel frequently to what is now our ex-colony. Spending a few days in Hong Kong was quite therapeutic. My wife and I enjoyed the opportunity to do some fantastic shopping, along with the comfort of the five-star New World Harbour Hotel.

We were always met at the airport by a Mercedes saloon. On entering the car, we were handed cold moist napkins which we found most welcoming, making our drive to the hotel very comfortable.

After using the New World Hotel several times, each time Helen and I arrived, we found we had to wait in reception for the duty manager to appear. He would then welcome us formally by shaking our hands.

The hotel was situated on Victoria Island and around twenty stories high. This allowed each of its bedrooms a wonderful view of Hong Kong harbour, and across to the mainland. The harbour it seemed had everything sailing on it, from Chinese junks to modern-day cruise liners. I feel it must be one of the busiest waterways in the world.

As our stay drew to a close, we were usually pleased

to return to Beijing, enabling us to escape from the frenetic pace and claustrophobic atmosphere of Hong Kong.

I can remember on one occasion, writing the following while waiting for my flight from China to Hong Kong,

I was contemplating the expenditure of 40 Yuan ($5) on a Chinese fountain pen in the departure lounge of Beijing Airport when my thoughts were interrupted by the boarding call for the Air China Flight CA101 to Hong Kong. The Boeing 747 "Megatop" swallowed me and the other Chinese passengers like a giant whale feeding on plankton.

The aircraft departed precisely at 7.50 am, lifting effortlessly into the crisp December sunshine. Air China seems to either get its schedules exactly right or horrendously wrong. Winter fog in Northern China often plays havoc with winter timetables. Should an aircraft be grounded at the wrong airport, the problem would then result in chaos, taking days to resolve.

When one experiences a flight cancellation in Beijing, it is almost impossible to obtain any information of a possible transfer or even information on anything.

Two or three harassed employees at the information desk, surrounded by dozens of angry and noisy Chinese passengers, are quite incapable of providing useful information, even if they had any to hand. The only solution is to remain philosophical and accept the standard offering of glutinous rice and indescribable meat, in the ubiquitous polystyrene box.

Any deficiencies in the culinary standard of the breakfast onboard the flight were amply compensated by the attentive and polite Chinese cabin crew. Chopsticks no longer presented me with problems, having very quickly mastered their use; or starve. Travelling by air in this day and age, requires one to have a degree in food packaging, ensuring one is capable of coping with the unwrapping of airline food. I remember struggling with a wax carton of milk until one of the cabin crew produced a penknife. He then thankfully went on to remove a corner of the stubborn item. These triangular missiles have exploded on me in the past, covering the adjacent passengers and myself with its contents.

The flight south was smooth and soporific in the monster Boeing 747. Fuel consumption at the normal cruising altitude is approximately 12 tonnes per hour, representing about 3,000 gallons. This useless statistic surfaced from some remote data cell in my brain. The video monitor above my head also displayed incomprehensible information:

'Height 12,090 metres.' My non-metric British brain failed; is a metre 39 inches?

Outside temperature – minus 65 degrees – true ground speed 825 Km/hour and the time in Sydney was apparently 1335 hours, all most useless stuff.

As the ancient Chinese proverb says, "You can always fool a foreigner."

Why does flying at 550 Knots at 40,000 feet over Shanghai seem incongruous with Confucius, bound feet and concubines?

I managed to doze off, only to be rudely awakened by the captain's announcement,

"We have commenced our descent into Kai Tak airport."

The aircraft descended between green hills, smoothly side-slipping between high-rise apartment blocks, and skimmed across the harbour to flop onto the narrow finger of reclaimed land which serves as Kai Tak's only runway.

A morbid thought instantly crossed my mind, in the event of pilot error, one could either drown or burn to death.

Typical English weather greeted me, as it was raining in Hong Kong. The aircraft parked at the ramp alongside a shiny new Boeing 747 of Singapore Airways. The logo on the side which had been painted in bright blue, read,

'The 1,000th 747'.

I wondered if it was a mere chance that Singapore Airlines, had managed to buy that particular aircraft?

My mental arithmetic calculating the cost of 1,000 Boeing 747's was interrupted by the usual stampede of Chinese passengers disembarking. The lines in the immaculate Immigration Hall were choc-a-bloc.

Amongst the cosmopolitan throng was a party of Tibetan monks, dressed as normal in saffron robes and complete with shaven heads and opened toe leather sandals. Must be a Harry Krishna convention or maybe a package tour for the lads from Lhasa, to sample the naughties in Wan Chai.

Why, in all my travels did I manage to choose the wrong line? Invariably, my line stalled with a problem passenger. Usually, a non-English speaking person with two wives, six children and no visa.

After immigration, I hurried to the men's room to release a copious quantity of jasmine tea, which I had consumed during the last three hours.

I pretended not to look at the monks who were ahead of me. Would they pull up their frocks, or did the designed robe provide a suitable aperture? Their secret even today is safe with me.

After 25 minutes, at last, I was outside the terminal in the warm rain. Such timing compares very favourably with most international airports, apart from Saudi Arabia, and Nigeria. At those, one can wait hours for the luggage, or in the case of Lagos, no luggage.

My luck I am afraid to say did not hold. I managed to find the only non-English speaking taxi driver in the entire Crown Colony. Repeated utterances of New World Harbour View Hotel. Only produced a torrent of Cantonese and much arm-waving.

My first solution was to repeat the words with ever-increasing volume. My father-in-law, after having served overseas, insisted that if one spoke very loudly, the native would come to understand. This time, unfortunately, the trick failed miserably. Eventually, technology came to my rescue, as I was handed a microphone to speak to a disembodied voice somewhere in Hong Kong. The voice then instructed the driver where to go. Thankfully, we quickly set off from Kowloon to Hong Kong Island.

My luck unfortunately again did not hold. As inexplicably the voice failed, and we became inextricably lost and confused in the Wan Chai area. This area had been the notorious "Red Light' district. Today it is more of a pink hue with numerous bars and restaurants. The last busy period having been during the Vietnam War when used for Rest & Recuperation by US forces. I could see myself spending my entire visit inside a taxicab. In the end, we found the hotel and I escaped into the opulent calm of one of the best hotels in town.

Hong Kong is frenetic with wall-to-wall people. The huge number of skyscrapers that have been built, reminds one of New York, all accompanied by its flyovers. Since building on this small piece of land can only be upwards, due naturally to the lack of space. Therefore, one only catches glimpses of the sky. The noisy trams now reaching a hundred years old, and the constant squeal of mobile telephones. I must admit that after several days in this claustrophobic, noisy, humid environment, which you come to realise is Hong Kong, and despite the luxury of the air-conditioning in a magnificent hotel, including its view. I was glad to return to the relatively open spaces of Beijing.

I remember the huge digital clock which had been erected in Tiannamen Square, counting down to mid-1997, when Hong Kong would revert to mainland China. As things have now turned out, not a good decision perhaps after all. My taxi driver may not have to learn English, but I suggested he make an effort to master Mandarin.

Travel around Beijing was normally by company car. On weekends I found myself at the mercy of Chinese taxi drivers. There were hundreds of small yellow Suzuki vans operating as taxis. Expatriates referred to them as "bread vans" There were several problems with this form of transportation. Starting with the language.

This meant prior to any journey, one had to have written down (in Chinese) both the destination and one's apartment or hotel for the return journey. Street names were almost non-existent. Not that it mattered, as most taxi drivers, simply did not know the location of places. This was a particularly annoying problem at weekends. Peasants from the rural areas outside Beijing replaced regular drivers. Taxi rides were indeed an adventure!

There were, of course, millions of bicycles in the city. They ranged from traditional western models to three-wheeled rickshaws, which carried enormous loads. The female cyclists were the most immodest lot. They tended to ride with skirts tied to the handlebars, in some cases, not a pretty sight.

One of the fringe benefits of working in China was the fantastic availability open to me of sightseeing some of the world's most incredible monuments.

Starting with Beijing; there you would find a multitude of sites to see, including the Forbidden City. The city of course had been forbidden not just to the outside world, but to the Chinese people themselves. The site is incredibly huge, I found it to be truly awe-inspiring.

Another wonderful place I visited was the Summer Palace.

The origin of the Summer Palace, we are led to believe, dates back to 1153. The construction is built around lakes and beautifully set out gardens. The design of the palace was based on a legend in Chinese mythology. The decline of this amazing place started in 1820 until eventually, the structure became too dangerous, and an order went out to dismantle it.

The French and English looted the palace at the end of the Opium War. The British went on to burn the palace down, the order given by Lord Elgin (of Elgin Marbles Fame) who was the British High Commissioner at that time. He did this as an act of revenge after two British envoys had been captured and murdered.

The palace was rebuilt, thanks to Empress Dowager Cixi, to celebrate her 60th birthday. She paid 22 million silver taels, money originally that should have gone to pay the Qing navy.

I continued my sightseeing by taking a look at The

Tombs of the Ming Dynasty, many of which are still unopened. Beihai Park, being another site and one to behold. The numerous lakes, full of beautiful, coloured water lilies. All connected by a series of exquisitely designed and built bridges.

Then of course you have the renowned Tiananmen Square (including Mao's Mausoleum).

Back then, all foreigners, especially those with blond hair, were objects of curiosity. The Chinese people would stop you, and politely request to take your photo, some even wishing to demonstrate their mastery of the English language. I dare say, my likeness appears on many mantelpieces in Chinese homes.

The Great Wall of China was only two hours by road. Once we arrived there, we had an exhausting climb enabling us to walk on the section that was still fully intact. So much has been written about this amazing feat of man.

The American illustrator Robert Ripley made a fortune with his famous cartoon. Believe it or not. He told the world, it was the only structure that could be seen by the naked eye, from the moon.

Until man was able to travel into space, everyone believed this theory. Strangely enough, it was the Chinese astronaut Yang Liwei, who making the first Chinese space flight, said he was unable to see any part of the wall.

Perhaps the most interesting visit that I had was the privilege of seeing the city of Xian, in Shangxi Province. Having firstly to take a two-hour flight from Beijing, would ensure you reached the home of the fascinating bing ma yong or "Terracotta Army".

We were fortunate to have visited this unique site along with nearly 2, 000,000 other tourists who visit annually. Local farmers discovered the terracotta figures in March 1974. Construction of the mausoleum began in 246 BC and is believed to have taken 700,000 workers and craftsmen 38 years to complete. Qin Shi Huang, the first Emperor of the Qin Dynasty was interred in the complex in 210 BC.

Archaeological excavations still continue over 30 years after its discovery. This is largely due to the fragile nature of the material and its difficult preservation. After firing, each figure was coated with a coloured lacquer finish to improve durability. Some figures still retain traces of this material.

8,000 figures have been unearthed to date; no two facial features are the same. These figures include infantry, archers and officers in a crouching or standing pose. Each figure was given a real weapon, such as a bronze spear, or a hallbard, crossbow or sword. Along with the soldiers, chariots made with great detail and precision were also included as part of Qin Shi Huang's army.

To date, the terracotta figures have been found in four separate pits. The largest pit so far excavated. Holds over 6,000 figures, with horses and chariots, and covers an area of 172,000 square feet. A second pit contains 1,400 figures and is thought to represent a military guard since it is much smaller – measuring 64,500 square feet. A third pit contains the Command Unit. This comprises of high-ranking officers, and war chariots drawn by four horses and is the smallest of the pits, containing 68 figures within a 5,000 square foot area.

Evidence suggests that excavations are far from

complete and there are many years of work ahead for the Chinese. I regarded it as a privilege to have seen such a magnificent site.

Another of the fascinating diversions particularly at weekends was visiting the markets in Beijing. There are literally hundreds of outdoor, indoor, and street markets around the city. There is a market for every imaginable item. These included tropical fish, pet birds, coins, stamps, silk, clothing, CD's (illegal) and antiques. The list was endless.

Haggling with the traders enhanced the pleasure of this type of shopping. I particularly enjoyed the practice having honed the requisite skills, in places such as Nigeria and the Far East. One of the particular pleasures I enjoyed, having been a collector of watches. I loved adding to my collection by haggling, then obtaining, though illegal, excellent copies of world-famous timepieces, such as Rolex, Omega and Breitling. I also amassed a large collection of Mao Zhedong brooches, and badges, dating of course from the Cultural Revolution era. Overcoming the language problems, the Chinese trader would produce a calculator. This would then be passed between buyer and seller. The price and offers in turn would then be displayed until an agreement was reached and sealed with a handshake.

The Chinese love their music, unfortunately, it tends to be somewhat loud and strident, and quite painful to Western ears.

One of the hotels I used in Harbin, had an evening with both male and female singers performing traditional songs often from the Cultural Revolution era. Invariably at these evenings, several attractive ladies were present and more than eager to dispense their services. Unfortunately, any involvement could result in the inevitable arrest by Chinese police, followed by possible deportation or even sanctions being applied to one's company.

The Chinese are obsessed with karaoke. After the many banquets I attended, I had to sit through interminable sessions of this torture. Chinese's guests, having seized a microphone, then attempted their rendition of pop music.

Someone once described the importation of karaoke into China, as Japan's revenge for that country's historical defeat by the Chinese in Manchuria. My liking for karaoke I left in China and have no wish to resurrect it.

The export of antiquities is expressly forbidden from the Republic. When I finally left, the Department of Antiquities had to vet my possessions and provide the required permission I needed enabling me to pack, and remove certain objects.

One inducement available to me to assist in the process of selling mobile telephony systems to the Chinese, was to include management training as part of a possible contract.

'Management Training' was a euphemism for an overseas trip for senior officials, in other words; overseas travel, with all expenses paid.

Thanks to this idea, I escorted several groups from Provincial Administrations to the United States. These trips usually involved flying via Shanghai to the west coast of America. Taking in visits to Los Angeles, San Francisco, and Las Vegas. Then north onto New York and Washington before returning to China, via I am pleased to say, Hawaii. Not having been there before, I was most curious to see it. We then continued our journey back to China via Hong Kong. A strenuous trip in approximately 14 days.

Apart from paying all expenses, Ericsson provided each person in the group with an allowance of $50 per day. A sizable sum of money given the usual wages in China. Even after each person had been given this amount, I found myself in the position of paying for drinks and snacks, at airports or at various tourist sites, until we reached Hong Kong. On reaching Hong Kong, and to my amazement, each member of the group then bought gold items.

Many of the group had never travelled by air and certainly had never stayed in a western hotel. Leaving the hotel after our first night stop, I naturally went to settle the bill. Only to find that one of the group had managed to run up a telephone bill of $1,200! Apparently, he was homesick and had spent the night on the telephone to China. From then on during our stay in whatever hotel we were in, I had all telephones blocked, except one in the Leader's room.

During the limited time available, we visited most of the usual tourist attractions. Disneyland in Los Angeles was of course a firm favourite. At most sites, I bought the group a souvenir. At Disney, I ushered them all into the Warner Brothers store and suggested they choose their own item. Twenty minutes later, they had still not emerged from the store. I decided it was time I went in, only to find that nothing had been purchased. Reminding them of the timetable, I suggested that they get a move on. The group emerged a few minutes later all carrying the same t-shirt, identical to the one which their leader had bought. Some Chinese habits do not change.

At each destination, the obligatory photographs had to be taken. The individual would stand, usually with his or her arms folded, and refused to smile while the moment was recorded for posterity. I felt that the requirement for photographs appeared to take priority over the actual tourist attraction itself.

By the time we reached San Francisco, I was looking forward to visiting the notorious prison of Alcatraz. Situated as we know, in San Francisco Bay. The group trooped off the required ferry, then lined up for the regulation photos. To my astonishment, they turned to re-embark on the boat. I had to remind them that I, for one, actually wanted to tour the prison. I found Alcatraz fascinating and enjoyed seeing that part of American history.

During the return to our hotel, we drove via the "gay" district of 'Frisco. The group was open-mouthed at the sights of gay couples, both male and female, as some had no protective clothing covering their arses. Such goings-on were almost a capital offence in China, and I believe still is today.

They all enjoyed Las Vegas. In particular, the casinos and the slot machines. I handed out a few extra dollars for them to gamble. One gentleman won a jackpot of $200, proceeding quickly to pocket the lot.

Arriving in New York, once again the usual photos were taken, particularly at the Statue of Liberty and the UN Building. At the top of the World Trade Centre, hamburgers and Coke were consumed, again at my expense. I find it such a tragedy that the Twin Towers are no longer there, having had a unique experience when visiting them.

The loss of life even to this day is incomprehensible.

Our next stop of course, was Washington, and the White House. The group were deeply impressed with what little they could see of the building. They were, though, very amazed by the various protestors permanently camped outside the gates. This behaviour most certainly would not have been tolerated in China.

On reaching Hong Kong, and for the first time, I was deeply surprised to see the daily allowances being spent on gold items. I was informed this was mainly jewellery for future investment. We then continued our journey back to Beijing. Well photographed, with a pocket full of dollars and with unbelievable stories to tell their friends, I hoped my efforts would be rewarded in terms of future contracts, which of course they were.

After almost three years, my stay in China came to an end. It was not as I had planned, but I felt that given certain attitudes in Sweden, it was time to move on.

By mid-1995, Eriksson had obtained fantastic business in the Northern provinces. Over the past two years, I had achieved the required sales budget which amounted to $2 billion dollars.

Most of the north of China had at last been supplied with Ericsson mobile telephone systems. One remaining province sandwiched between two of its larger neighbours, was in negotiation regarding the purchase of Ericsson equipment.

Such a purchase would have completed the jigsaw and total domination of the Northern Provinces. Given the long-term value of such a situation, I negotiated a very favourable price with the Jilin Provincial Administration. I reasoned that a short-term "loss" would clinch the deal, and then ensure long-term rewards.

Unfortunately, the corporate powers many miles away in Sweden did not share or even fully understand the logic of the offer. They placed outright profit before a considered strategy for the future. They refused to approve the contract price, which placed me in a difficult position with a loss of credibility and destroyed a customer relationship I had worked so very hard to establish.

After some thought, I decided it was time to move on and tendered my resignation.

Under the terms of my contract, I was required to serve a six months' notice period, which I duly did. I spent some of the period identifying other positions within the Ericsson Empire.

After a visit to India, I was offered the position of Deputy Operations Director in New Delhi. I decided the working conditions in India, and a much-reduced salary did not appeal. I also visited Ericsson UK in Guildford, Surrey but again the financial rewards were not acceptable.

During my stay in China, I had visited Malaysia while on holiday. I had also attended a marketing course (as a lecturer) at the Ericsson Academy in Shah Alam near Kuala Lumpur. To cut a long story short, I was offered the position of Deputy Principal at the Academy and moved to Malaysia in January 1996.

As the name suggests, the Academy was an academic institution, set up to train both customers and Ericsson staff in the Far East and the Pacific Rim countries.

Malaysia was a most pleasant place. It was very green, had a relaxed attitude to most things, and everyone spoke English. By this time Helen had returned to Wales, and although now on my own, I was provided with a villa in one of the many housing golf course complexes, which at that time were being built around Kuala Lumpur.

My staff were a mixture of Malay, Chinese and Indians. The Malays were laid back, one could say even lazy, whereas the Chinese and Indians were keen and industrious. Unfortunately, the latter races suffered quite outrageous discrimination in terms of education and jobs etc.

The Academy, of which I became Deputy Principal, was formally opened during a state visit to Malaysia, by the King and Queen of Sweden.

While King Carl Gustaf and Queen Silvia, accompanied by various dignitaries from both Malaysia and Ericsson toured the complex, it gave me the opportunity to meet their Majesties, and to explain my role within the Academy.

During my stay, I had the opportunity to make a number of interesting trips. One memorable trip was driving down the coast to Malacca. The home of exquisite Malaccan furniture, which Malaysia exports across the world. I must confess, I came away with a couple of wonderful pieces.

Another small trip was a brief holiday to Penang Island. Not having been there before, I decided to stay in a hotel on the beach. My decision to do so paid off handsomely. The hotel was adjacent to a palm-fringed beach of dazzling white sand. Not only was the hotel and surrounds amazing, but they also certainly earned the five stars that had been given. From the moment one required food, starting at the beginning of the day. The hotel provided the finest, most comprehensive, breakfast buffet I have ever experienced anywhere in the world.

Another interesting trip was to the USA. This was to attend a Training Management Convention, organized by Ericsson, in Richardson, in Texas. The Americans work extremely hard, leaving one very little opportunity to explore. My week in Texas ended with me having met some interesting people and enjoying a useful exercise. Saying all that, I was ready to return to Malaysia, happy to rest during the long flight back

As in most developing countries, the localization of senior positions is the ultimate aim. After 18 months, a suitable candidate was identified to assume my post of Deputy Principal, and it was now time for me to return home to the UK.

My journey home, as usual, was not without incident. I flew down to Singapore, then boarded a KLM flight to Amsterdam. After flying many thousands of miles both in the RAF, and my civilian career, it was ironic that the KLM flight was the nearest thing to disaster I was about to experience.

An hour out of Singapore and over the South China Sea, one of the Boeing 747's engines gave up the ghost. The loud bang did not seem to disturb other passengers – excluding me!

The captain duly announced that we have to return to Singapore while trying to reassure all on board that the B747 could cope well on three engines.

I shudder to think of what might have been, and how we could all have ended up in the South China Sea. Perhaps it was a message that the time had come for me to stop flying.

Safely back in Singapore, we were informed that it would take five days to obtain the replacement engine. I decided otherwise and organized myself onto an Air France flight to Paris and home to North Wales...

At the age of 67, I decided to retire, or so I thought at the time.

Chapter 32

Fate Plays her Hand

After a most interesting civilian career, and now officially retired, taking a few days of rest and relaxation, I made an attempt to clear the guttering at the side of the bungalow. I wish I had not bothered as I celebrated my efforts by falling off the damn ladder. Good job my pleas of just a sprained ankle were disregarded, as annoyingly the following morning I found myself being carted off to the hospital. My leg was massively swollen, and the injury I had sustained, was a fracture to my lower tibia. The thought crossed my mind, what a damn good job I no longer played a serious game of football or cricket.

The plaster was to remain a part of me for a further six weeks. Though I was still able to drive the car, two things were now encroaching on my emotions. One being the immobility to do as I wished, due of course to the heavy plaster which I found terribly restrictive. More importantly, the feeling of extreme boredom began to take hold.

Having the enforced time to give the situation a great deal of thought, I concluded that a form of part-time employment would perhaps solve my need to once again join the world of work.

Once the plaster had been removed, I secured a position as the Administrator for the Annual Llandudno Festival of Music and Arts, a position I held for a number of years. The position involved me organizing the publicity for the festival, along with the printing and distribution of programs. In addition to all that, I had the task of deciding the choice of various venues, along with the use of accommodation, and any travel arrangements needed for the artists taking part, which, incidentally, all had been chosen by the Festival's Director.

This being my first exposure to people in the music and arts profession, I became aware of the somewhat lackadaisical attitude to their work. The Festival Director was a Professor from the Royal College of Music in London, having the same approach to detail as the others.

At one of the events at this particular festival, he had chosen a recital for the harpsichord, which was to be played by a German female. True to form, he had promised to provide the so-called harpsichord for her. Apparently, this important requirement had obviously slipped his mind. On the Friday evening prior to her performance, I received a phone call from a somewhat arrogant German woman, who went on to ask me for the technical details of the harpsichord.

Apart from knowing absolutely nothing about harpsichords and the like, I was now panicking, as we did not have one.

Where on earth in North Wales, at that time of night, would I be likely to find such an instrument?

After spending a great deal of time researching, I finally managed to locate a gentleman who lived somewhere in Lancashire. This gentleman thank goodness, had a business restoring harpsichords.

Apologizing for disturbing him at such a late hour, I proceeded to explain my need for doing so. This very obliging man, not only offered to lend us one of his precious instruments, but he also went on to say he would deliver it first thing in the morning. Not a moment too soon…

After the festival, and with my knowledge of

harpsichords complete. I decided my liking for the world of entertainment after a number of years, had also now come to an end.

From the world of entertainment, my next job was a little more to my liking.

Glancing through one of the daily papers, I found and answered an advertisement for the position of a Marketing Manager. This job was to be for a newly formed Robotic Engineering Company.

A gentleman who had recently retired from the well-known company, Hotpoint., had set up a small business to design and manufacture mechanical robots for various applications.

Unfortunately, his financial acumen did not match his engineering knowledge, and sad though it was, he rapidly went into bankruptcy.

Even at this juncture of my life, I still felt the need to work. Walking home one afternoon, I glanced as one does when passing shop windows. Just as I was about to pass the local estate agents, I caught sight of an advert they were literally just placing in the window. The advert was offering a position for someone to escort prospective clients to view certain types of properties, in and around the local area.

Strangely, I found myself intrigued. The thought of having the opportunity of going into various homes ranging from Grand Georgian Mansions to luxury town apartments which under normal circumstances, I would never have the opportunity to do so. The thought of also being paid for the privilege of doing this seemed perfect.

My liking for being with people, I certainly missed. The more I thought about this job, the more appealing it became.

On the spur of the moment, though not suitably dressed for an interview, I walked into the agency.

Introducing myself, I immediately applied for the job. After some discussion and their request for my CV, which I took in the following day, the job was mine.

Looking back, I will admit I was ridiculously nervous, as I thought after they had read my CV, they would feel I was seriously overqualified.

Spending a year with the company, and now approaching my 78th birthday, I made the decision it was now time to fully retire.

Never say never! A motto I believed in. The year was now 2007. Fate played her hand as I cast my mind back to my young days. I decided I would very much like to perhaps enjoy my final years on the beautiful Mediterranean Island of Malta.

After much research about the Island, all appeared to be perfect. There were of course no language problems, constant sunshine. No income tax for me to be concerned about, acceptable medical facilities available as Malta was now part of the EU. All in all, a perfect Island for an Englishman.

Making my final judgement, Helen agreed with me, and we sold the apartment in Llandudno for a good-sized profit and departed from Manchester on a cold spring day to head for the warmth of sunny Malta.

On landing at Luqa airport, I remembered with fondness, could it really have been over 54 years since I landed in the Vickers Wellington aircraft.

Taking a taxi to the hotel in Sliema, little seemed to have changed. I did wonder if the Egyptian Queen in Straight Street still did business, and what had become of

Pee Bucket Annie?

After ten days having visited a number of estate agents, we eventually obtained a luxury apartment. For such a small island, it amazed me how many there actually were.

The apartment block belonged to a Mylene and Adrian Meli, as landlords, they proved to be great people who remained friends for many years.

For anyone who has lived in Malta, they, like me, would tell you; life was far from difficult. With many wonderful restaurants to choose from, adequate supermarkets together with a tremendous number of small shops of interest to browse through.

Most importantly, there was a fine modern hospital which was just a few blocks away, named St James'. I know from personal experience just how good it was. Day trips and cruises were available around the islands that make up Malta, or Italy if a change of scene was required.

Unfortunately, after the first 12 months of living on the island, my wife's health began to deteriorate. Despite the excellent hospital facilities, and to our dismay, a change in legislation by the EU, meant that the Maltese consultants were no longer in a position to prescribe, and administer the medication my wife required.

Reluctantly, a move had now become necessary. Wishing to remain living in the sun, it was time to decide just where. Firstly, I thought about France. I had always considered France, a country that was truly beautiful and one I had loved living in. Annoyingly though, France has punitive inheritance tax laws. With this knowledge, it was out of the question instantly. Next came Spain. The bureaucracy and horrendous crime rate, particularly along

Spain's eastern coast, made living there out of the question. A number of other countries came to mind, each having many things to offer in their own right, but none, it seemed, suited my needs. After making further inquiries, fate stepped in yet again, as I settled for Cyprus.

By June the following year, my wife and I sadly left Malta and travelled, courtesy of Emirates Airlines, to Cyprus. Tired, and still feeling sad at the life we had just left behind, we arrived at Larnaca airport. We stayed overnight in the airport hotel, and like all tourists, we had pre-booked both a holiday flat and a hire car.

After an initial stay of a week in Pissouri, I was fortunate enough to find a large penthouse apartment in Upper Paphos.

My first choice had been for an apartment in the port/beach area, but as most people know, that area in summer is full of tourists. Usually, noisy, boozy Brits on their vacation.

The suburb of Upper Paphos was perfect. Once again life returned to being quite pleasant, despite the severe water rationing that was in place during that time, due to the island having no rainfall for five years.

What shocked me, and most certainly I did not find so pleasant, was the sewage situation.

Having travelled across the world, and experiencing many primitive toilet facilities, this to me was beyond any of them. The fact when going to relieve one's bowels was not a problem. However, the toilet paper was banned from the porcelain throne. The soiled paper had instead to be placed in the bag provided. UGH!

Our apartment was above the Savas' family home. We were very lucky to have such landlords, as they were extremely hospitable to us. Each Sunday, they would invite us to have lunch with them, which turned out to be a multi-course gastronomic event indeed. Their garden housed a typical bread oven, which enabled us to sample delicious freshly made Cypriot bread.

Unusual for a family home of just two floors, the Savas' home had a lift. I will never forget the time I found myself trapped in it. The temperature gradually rising to over 100 degrees. Annoyingly the emergency telephone did not work, and I remained trapped in the damn thing until Mr Savas returned home after work. I emerged soaking wet and desperate for a shower.

Medical facilities, as expected, were also adequate for our needs.

After one year, it was necessary for us to apply for residency permits. After waiting for several hours in a stuffy crowded uncomfortable hot office, we were informed in contravention of EU regulations, the Cypriot government insisted that expatriates now required health insurance.

Due to my now advancing years, and my wife's pre-existing medical condition. I felt it would be unlikely we would be in the position of being able to obtain the required insurance, should something untoward have happened. For example, the need for hospital treatment. This fact alone meant we could not obtain a residency permit, and although we could have stayed illegally, sadly we felt we could no longer stay in Cyprus.

I needed to decide what was now the best option. After giving it a great deal of thought, and with a heavy heart, I knew we would have to return to the UK. Before doing so, I decided to take a holiday break in Southern

Ireland.

We departed Cyprus on a wonderful October day in the afternoon, and arrived at Heathrow to a typical cold autumnal evening, as one expects in London.

Having pre-booked a hotel room at one of Heathrow's many airport hotels, I felt a little down. Not as down as I would feel the following morning when I stepped back out of my shower, executing a perfect swallow dive.

Landing with some force on the bathroom floor, ensuring there was obvious damage to my rib cage with the amount of pain I was in. The hotel provided me with a car and driver, who took me directly to the nearby Hillingdon hospital.

The Indian doctor who attended to me diagnosed severe bruising. Adding the comment, we do not do investigative X-Rays or provide pain relief. Welcome to the NHS.

With the severe pain I was in, my day just got worse. I managed to join the midday flight leaving Heathrow via Aer Lingus into Cork.

On the approach into Cork, a severe crosswind produced a rather violent landing. Conditions were so bad, with torrential rain and high winds, that we were the last flight into Cork that day. Taking a look at the weather and being in severe pain, made me feel very sorry for myself. What a way to start a holiday.

I thought nothing further could go wrong. The gods had other plans. Being unable at that time to lift anything, a very kind passenger helped me to collect my baggage.

Next, I needed to collect the car I had booked. On arriving at the car hire desk, the agent responsible categorically refused to hand over the keys to me. He stated that the reason being for his intolerable behaviour, was my age.

I informed him in no uncertain terms, that I had checked most scrupulously the company's terms and conditions on their website before booking. The idiot refused to budge.

Fortunately, a rival company, employing someone with intelligence, offered a hire car for the onward journey I wished to make.

The gale and torrential rain continued. Until in the end, we were the last vehicle to pass through one particular section of road, before the river eventually burst its banks.

My destination was to be Killarney, where I had hired an apartment for Helen and I. Annoyingly, I was to see very little of Killarney, spending most of the time in bed. The one trip we did take, after suffering a full week in pain, was in an ambulance which drove me to a hospital 40 miles away in Tralee. The latter was a run-down affair, and literally, flea-ridden. At least I was duly given an X-RAY, then thankfully informed there were no fractures.

Once the week ended, we decided to return to the UK to visit friends and family. We managed to find a direct flight from Waterford to Manchester.

A taxi drove us from the airport direct to a hotel in Llandudno, a place we thought 18 months earlier we would not see again.

The plan was for me to convalesce, and to rest as much as possible, giving my bruised ribs time to heal. However once again fate intervened.

My wife fell and suffered a crush fracture of one of her spinal vertebrae. I knew then any hope of returning to

Cyprus was out of the question. I immediately commenced a search for an apartment in Llandudno. Being a seaside town, apartments for long term rental were not plentiful, at least not the type I wanted.

From my previous employment as Administrator for the Llandudno Music Festival, one of my contacts just happened to be the General Manager of Mostyn Estates. I was so lucky, as he produced a beautiful newly refurbished apartment in the town centre.

I contacted Mr Savas, sending him a fairly long e-mail. Firstly, explaining all that had occurred, then sadly asked him to cancel our tenancy. I told him I would arrange for our personal effects to be shipped home and thanked him for all he and his family had done to ensure our sojourn in Cyprus had been perfect.

Given the state of our health, moving into our new apartment was a bit of a problem, only eventually to get worse. Little did I realise just how my present life would end there.

My wife's health deteriorated due to the rapid onset of chronic osteoporosis. Several treatments, some revolutionary suggested by various consultants over a period of years, were unsuccessful. Additional medical problems Helen had endured due to her travels with me were Typhoid and Malaria. On top of those illnesses, Helen also suffered from glomerulonephritis, an acute problem with her kidneys, brought on due to a damaged immune system. Sadly, my wife also suffered from a gluten intolerance. These problems combined, meant that she was eventually confined to a wheelchair. Eventually unable to sleep in her own bed at night during the last two years of her life.

Her health continued to spiral downwards. During this time, Social Services refused to provide the sort of care I felt she should have had. They informed me they did not have the financial rescores to do so. Having been a taxpayer since my early years in the RAF, I found this a disgusting statement. Leaving me to wonder what my country had come to. Maybe we are also heading into becoming a third world country, as help was not on offer. At the age of 78, I became her carer.

During 2018, my wife suffered three further falls. Unfortunately, the last one caused a fracture of the femur. After being rushed into Glan Clwyd hospital, the orthopaedic consultant there informed us he was unable to perform a hip transplant, due to the now advanced osteoporosis. Sadly, for Helen, the nursing care at the hospital was abysmal - no... Worse than abysmal, it was disgraceful. They refused to take Helen to the bathroom when she tried to retain her dignity, instead, they left her to relieve herself in her wheelchair. One of the nursing staff observing this kind of behaviour, quietly took me to one side advising me to report the inhumanity doled out to Helen. I gave his words a great deal of thought. Maybe due to my advancing years, I did not have the fight in me to take on board the NHS. After a few days, I brought Helen home.

As I sat in my armchair watching her sleep, my thoughts slipped back to the beautiful vibrant woman I met through a friend. He ran a dating agency, and while I was not short of a date, I had nothing planned that particular weekend. My friend gave me Helen's phone number and we arranged for me to meet at her home. I remember the first time I saw her. Her blond hair was shaped into a bob, her eyes were brown and twinkling, and she had a trim figure. The first night we met she was wearing black slacks with an alluring backless white silk blouse.

The rest is history. A few days later Helen passed peacefully away in her sleep.

Her passing for her was a great relief. She had been in excruciating pain for many months, even the pain killers the hospital recommended to help her, she had barely been able to take. Tragically, close to the end, something as simple as taking pills became an impossible task.

We had been married for nearly thirty years, and as stated, Helen joined me as often as she could. Naturally, there were certain places I could not take her. Now it was my turn to be left at home, and on my own.

For the first few months, I needed time and space to grieve. Not particularly thinking, and certainly not knowing which direction my life would strangely take.

Our beautiful home, now empty of the woman who made it all so perfect. Looking after a very sick wife, watching the constant pain that wracked her delicate body, had been exceptionally hard both mentally as well as physically, especially for a man of my age. Now I felt there was nothing left for me. No wife, no job.

Summer turned to winter, my loneliness knew no bounds and grew interminably. I lost my appetite, not too bothered what I ate, which had anyway by now become quite infrequent. Quite frankly, I cared little what became of me. The weight rapidly began to drop off, and my clothes hung on, what was now no more than a deathly looking skeleton.

During my years in the RAF, or on various missions, I had been alone many times during the Christmas holidays. I had accepted that was part of the life I had chosen in the service of my country. After losing Helen, that Christmas was the loneliest of them all. I had never felt as isolated in my entire life. Not one person to talk to or wish a Happy Christmas. Had I been flying crossing the Sahara Desert or some far off jungle, I could not have felt more as if I were the only man left alive. Life held no interest, and I was pleased to see the back of the holidays.

They say time heals, and strange though it may seem, I did begin to find the memories of Helen and my marriage though comforting. My pain indeed gradually began to subside.

Seven months had by this time passed by, the emptiness and loneliness though continued to grow. During that time, I realised I no longer wished to stay in the apartment. All but a few very personal possessions were removed by my stepson. I now had so little to show for my life except my computer, a number of photos and my precious RAF log and file books, which told the story of my life.

Then out of the blue, my Guardian Angel, as I most certainly do believe I have one, having asked for help more than once during some of my more dangerous missions. I also believe in Mother Nature, who in some respects helps a man to heal quicker perhaps than a woman. Certainly, in my case I felt were now working overtime on my behalf.

I had heard of a very lovely lady author, who though dyslexic, had written books to raise money for the Christies and Oswestry hospitals. I am convinced to this day that my Guardian Angel guided me towards her.

I managed through a friend to find her phone number, and then made that vital first call which I will never regret. After that I wrote to her frequently, exchanging a great number of e-mails, until at last, she consented to meet me. From that moment I knew I was about to start a new chapter in my life. Her untold kindness, limitless patience, and love, as well as that of her family, know no bounds. Not easy for her, when dealing with a man my age.

I made the decision to move, only instead of moving into some tiny flat alone in Llandudno, I moved closer to this wonderful lady. With her help, I found a beautiful apartment in Wigan, which is situated in the Greater Manchester area.

Fate indeed played her hand and completed the circle. I have been treated with the utmost respect by everyone I have so far come into contact with. The hospital services are second to none, already having used them. My new doctors are first class in every respect. What amazes me, is how incredibly friendly and helpful everyone is. Nothing is too much trouble, and I have been shown every kindness to ensure I have everything I need. Something I have never come across in my long and travelled life.

With the good Lord's blessing and to my utter amazement, not only did this very special lady help in every way she could to bring happiness once more back into my life. Christmas was wonderful, having spent it with her and her family, so completely different from the many sad Christmas's of the past. With the good LORDS blessing, I am now looking forward to 2020, and all the magic it may bring.

This wonderful lady also decided, the world should know a little about my unprecedented life. It is thanks to her; you are now reading part of my story.

Postscript

Escape from the Island of Death

During duties on the Island of Cyprus, I have many memories, some good and sadly some very tragic. As I had previously mentioned, I had been stationed at RAF Nicosia, and would often fly into RAF Akrotiri. During that time, the island was undergoing change; the people of Cyprus decided they wanted independence from the United Kingdom. Civil disobedience erupted, with hundreds of young men joining a terrorist organisation that became known around the world as EOKA. They were ruthless and showed no mercy, killing hundreds of United Kingdom military personnel, as well as many civilian Cypriots. The Turkish Government eventually invaded the island so many years later, wanting Cyprus as her market garden.

After Turkey invaded in 1974, the United Nations intervened, and Cyprus was partitioned. The border between North and South Cyprus is famously known as the Green Line.

When living in Cyprus, I did not take the opportunity even though I could have done so, to cross the Green Line and visit the territory now occupied by Turkey.

After completing my autobiography, and a third book which Denise is hoping to publish in the summer of this year, I asked her if she would join me on a holiday to Cyprus, allowing me to reminisce.

I wanted to show her where I had been stationed, and where I had lived during my retirement, also introduce her to the friends she has written about.

Denise is a lover of Greek Mythology and had written about Aphrodite in her first novel. Joining me would give her the opportunity to see the goddess's legendary birthplace.

So, on January 22nd, 2020, we flew to Cyprus hoping to see all the things we wished to, and with luck enjoy some winter sun.

Our holiday started wonderfully well. On our first trip out, the sun shone in a clear blue sky, the waters surrounding the legendary rocks of Aphrodite's birthplace, were calm leaving Denise to feel delighted.

A couple of days later we set out for Famagusta, enabling me at last to cross the Legendry Green Line. Leaving the rest of our party to visit some interesting sites, Denise and I went for lunch in a marvellous restaurant, then did a little window shopping before joining the others. Another excellent day out.

We were looking forward to our next trip to the Troodos mountains. As usual, we had been allowed to sit behind the driver, due to there being extra legroom. The driver that day, unfortunately, was in a poor state of health. He literally coughed and sneezed all over us, never once using a handkerchief, or covering his mouth with his hand. He admitted he was feeling really ill but had to work. How he managed to drive up the twisty narrow roads and not have an accident, one could only say was a miracle.

Annoyingly, the following day, Denise and I felt extremely ill. Denise went to a chemist to buy some medication, which did nothing to help.

After two days and experiencing a great deal of stress after we had been taken to a private hospital. The hospital's Irish administrator demanded we pay 20,000 euros (which was scandalous). She informed us we would not be allowed to leave, basically kidnaping us.

We in turn asked for help from the British High Commission, who was amazing and immediately got in touch with the F.O. We found ourselves within the hour rushed to the St Georges Blue Cross Hospital, fighting for our lives in the hospital's Intensive Care Unit, suffering we were told from Influenza A, and in my case, also Bronchitis.

Thanks to the good LORD, and the magnificent care of Doctor Andreas G. Demetriou and his staff, who literally fought day and night to save our lives, that we are alive today.

While in the hospital, we met Allan Hodgson. Allan is the Royal British Legion's Padre for Cyprus. A truly wonderful man, who gave us his help, support, and comfort, in some of the darkest hours of our illness. Allan and his lovely wife Ellao have now become the most welcome friends who enrich our lives.

As to Andreas, his care did not end at the hospital doors, far from it. Once back in our hotel, he visited on various days to ensure we were still making good progress until eventually, he was happy about allowing us to be repatriated home.

Back home in England, and after many weeks of loving care from Denise's family, we are now very well.

I would just like to take this opportunity to also thank Avanti Insurance Company, who helped tremendously, giving every support they could, during what were some very worrying days. They are an excellent insurance company and one I highly recommend.

Sadly, I never managed to return to Nicosia or see my friend. Under the circumstances I am not sure I will ever return to Cyprus, though with my Guardian Angels help, still hoping to do so.

After experiencing, and seeing for myself, as well as researching that sadly over 27,000 people have died on the island since 2017, suffering from various viruses and in particular Influenza A, which could now very well be the Coronavirus.

Having served in Korea, Iraq, Ireland, and other theatres of war as well as Cyprus, I count myself incredibly lucky, that it was not a bullet that nearly killed me, but a very nasty virus. Denise and I were indeed lucky to escape from the Island of Death.